Visual Basic® 2008

FOR

DUMMIES®

Visual Basic® 2008

FOR

DUMMIES®

by Bill Sempf

Wiley Publishing, Inc.

Visual Basic® 2008 For Dummies®

Published by
Wiley Publishing, Inc.
111 River Street
Hoboken, NJ 07030-5774

www.wiley.com

WILEY

About the Author

I am **Bill Sempf,** and you'll notice that I don't write in third person. I have spent an inordinate amount of time in the last several years writing about, thinking about, and coding in VB.NET. I am a coauthor of *Professional Visual Studio.NET*, *Effective Visual Studio.NET*, *Professional ASP.NET Web Services* and *Professional VB.NET* (among others), and a frequent contributor to the Microsoft Developer Network, Builder.com, Hardcore Web Services, Inside Web Development Journal, and Intranet Journal. I have recently been an invited speaker for DevEssentials, the International XML Web Services Expo, and the Association of Information Technology Professionals. As a graduate of Ohio State University with a Bachelor of Science in Business Administration, Microsoft Certified Professional, Certified Internet Business Strategist, and Certified Internet Webmaster, I have developed over one hundred Web applications for startups and Fortune 500 companies alike.

I began my career in 1985 by helping my father (also named Bill) manage Apple IIe systems for the local library. Since then, I have built applications for the likes of Lucent Technologies, Bank One, the State of Ohio, Nationwide Insurance, and Sears, Roebuck and Co. I specialized in data-driven Web applications of all types, both public and private. Currently, I am the Senior Technology Consultant at Products of Innovative New Technology in Grove City, Ohio, a Microsoft Certified Partner, working on a Learning Management System for OmniPath, inc. (www.omnipath.com). I can be reached at bill@pointweb.net.

Dedication

This edition of the book was heavily influenced by the thousands of readers all over the world who took the time to e-mail with thoughts, questions, complaints, criticism, praise and ideas. To be honest, they are why I write. The majority of my good projects have come from people who read my books and call to collaborate.

This book is dedicated to those readers. If you have taken the time to e-mail me or review the book or contact Wiley — good or bad — about this book series, thank you. Even if you are peeved because of a problem or error, you are helping make this a better product and that helps everyone.

Despite what people often think, even with the best of editing and authoring, these books aren't perfect — they are a community effort. Without that community, the books wouldn't be good or necessary. It's a self-replicating cycle, and I love it.

Author's Acknowledgments

I cannot begin to thank the amazing team at Wiley who led me ever so carefully through the process of updating this book. Katie Feltman kept on me to revise the ideas I presented, and Mark Enochs saw to it that I stuck to schedule. The entire Wiley team, in fact, is the best an author could ever hope to have. I have gotten to know them well over the last several years, and I love them all.

A project at Wendy's International led me to ask the most detail-oriented person I have ever met — Mike Spivey — to review the technical details of this edition. Jeff Simmons reviewed the original code, and did a good job, but this book is all the better for multiple sets of eyes.

My army of peer reviewers from the original edition was fantastic: Theresa Alexander, Jim Andrews, David Deloveh, Rex Mahel, Greg McNamara, Rob Morgan, Blake Sparkes, and Gary Spencer. Here's a special note about my father, William E. Sempf, whose education background was of inestimable help in reviewing the early concepts for the book. Then, he let me use him as a guinea pig for Part I! What a trooper!

Finally, a shout to the many Microsoft people who gave me a hand with specific questions about VB, Visual Studio, and the framework in general: Jan Shanahan and Susann Ragsdale in the Author Support Group, and Brad McCabe, Daniel Roth, Jay Roxe, and Steve Lasker, among many others, on the development teams.

Publisher's Acknowledgments

We're proud of this book; please send us your comments through our online registration form located at www.dummies.com/register/.

Some of the people who helped bring this book to market include the following:

Acquisitions, Editorial, and Media Development

Senior Project Editor: Mark Enochs

Senior Acquisitions Editor: Katie Feltman

Copy Editor: John Edwards

Technical Editor: Mike Spivey

Editorial Manager: Leah Cameron

Media Development Project Manager: Laura Atkinson

Editorial Assistant: Amanda Foxworth

Sr. Editorial Assistant: Cherie Case

Cartoons: Rich Tennant (www.the5thwave.com)

Composition Services

Project Coordinator: Kristie Rees

Layout and Graphics: Alissa D. Ellet, Shane Johnson, Christine Williams, Erin Zeltner

Proofreaders: John Greenough, Caitie Kelly

Indexer: Potomac Indexing, LLC

Publishing and Editorial for Technology Dummies

    Richard Swadley, Vice President and Executive Group Publisher

    Andy Cummings, Vice President and Publisher

    Mary Bednarek, Executive Acquisitions Director

    Mary C. Corder, Editorial Director

Publishing for Consumer Dummies

    Diane Graves Steele, Vice President and Publisher

    Joyce Pepple, Acquisitions Director

Composition Services

    Gerry Fahey, Vice President of Production Services

    Debbie Stailey, Director of Composition Services

Contents at a Glance

Table of Contents

About This Book

No matter who you are or what your background is, you are not a dummy if you're reading this book. You might, however, be a dummy about what Visual Basic is, how to use it, or why it can help you do your job better.

This book is expressly designed to make you a good Visual Basic programmer. As such, I don't spend every page talking about the features of the language, how to use Visual Studio, or how to connect to a database. I spend a fair amount of time talking about how to make good decisions, build the right software for the problem you need to solve, and not make common mistakes.

Visual Basic — despite all appearances — is really very easy to use. Much of the complexity of the language is hidden in tools provided to you by Microsoft. Many of these tools are not expressly for Visual Basic, but they will become very important to your success as a programmer. This book is also about those tools, because they make writing good, working programs faster and easier.

This book is also about you, the programmer. I'm a programmer like you. I have been writing in BASIC since 1981, and I've lived through all the ups and downs. For about 15 years, Visual Basic was a program, not a language, and I lived through that. Now the tables have turned — Visual Basic is again a language (Visual Studio is the program). In this book, I help you become a good Visual Basic programmer.

Conventions Used in This Book

I have written this book to be easy to read while you are programming. As such, I use certain conventions to make for easier reading:

  - ✔ Words that I want to emphasize or that I'm defining are placed in *italics*.
  - ✔ Terms that are used in Visual Basic code are in `monotype` font.
  - ✔ Menu selections look like this: File⇨New. This is shorthand for "From the File menu, select New."

I use numbered lists to guide you through a sequential process such as building a Windows Forms application. The **bold** part of the step is a technical description of the action you are to perform, and the normal (not bold) text that follows provides further explanation or describes how I implemented the step in my examples.

Introduction

* *

*W*elcome to the new version of Visual Basic for 2008. As its name implies, Visual Basic is a *visual* way to create new programs for the Microsoft Windows family of operating systems.

And though it is *basic* in many ways, the Visual Basic language is also very powerful. You can create new class libraries and XML Web services, as well as programs that you can use on your PC or your Web browser, or even your phone or PDA. Anything that can be done in Windows can be done in Visual Basic.

Programming in Visual Basic is easier than you might think, thanks to the visual tools supplied by Visual Studio. You don't have to type line after line of code to create a working program — Visual Studio automatically generates some code for you when you drag and drop components with the visual tools. Of course, being able to read and write code is important, too, and this book provides plenty of code samples so that you can understand the inner workings of your programs.

This book also shows you some best practices to keep in mind as you get further along in your programming. Your first programs may be very simple, but when you start getting into more complicated applications, you really need plan out your program before you start writing the code.

Previous versions of Visual Basic were complete development environme The latest version of Visual Basic is really only one part of a three-part p gramming strategy:

- ✔ **A language:** For this book, it is Visual Basic 2008. Other popular la include C#, J#, Perl, and 24 others.

- ✔ **An Integrated Development Environment (IDE):** For this book Visual Studio 2008. Other IDEs include Borland, Adobe, and se other tools.

- ✔ **A project:** In this book, I cover four types of projects: Windo Web Forms, class libraries, and XML Web services. You can to build Windows services, console applications, Smart De tions, Mobile Web Forms, and many other project types.

Bulleted lists are used to create memorable lists. For me, one of the toughest things about programming is remembering key points, like features or best practices. I use the bulleted lists to help with those kinds of things.

Code examples are broken out from the rest of the paragraph, as follows:

```
If DateNumber.Text.Length > 0 Then
    DateInterval = CInt(DateNumber.Text)
End If
NextWeek.Text = DateChooser.Value.Add(TimeSpan.FromDays(7)).ToString()
```

The code blocks are usually written in such a way that you can copy them right into your program. They will be in monotype font, and sometimes will have *linefeeds* (the space and underscore character at the end of the line) in inappropriate places because the printed page is only so wide. Remember that when you're writing out the code and you're looking at it on-screen, you won't need to use so many linefeeds. If you have a question about where a break should be, check out the sample code, which you can find on this book's companion Web site, www.vbfordummies.net.

What You Don't Have to Read

If you're not working with graphics right now, you can skip the chapter on graphics. If you don't use a database, you can skip the database chapter. See where I am going? If you don't use Web services, you don't have to read about them.

Effectively, this is a modular book. Aside from Part I, which everyone needs to read, there are no requirements to read anything in any particular order. Read what you need, and ignore the rest until someone comes into your office and needs something done on that topic. Then you can pull the book out again and read that chapter.

If you have a copy of *Visual Basic 2005 For Dummies,* you will find many similarities to this book There were not too many changes between VB 2005 and VB 2008, fortunately. I will strive to document the differences between this book and the 2005 book and post them on www.vbfordummies.net.

Foolish Assumptions

I assume that by buying this book and reading it, you are interested in finding out how to program in Visual Basic. Beyond that, I also assume that you have the following:

- A PC running some flavor of Windows (Windows Vista or XP, most likely)
- A copy of Visual Studio 2008 Professional installed on your PC
- Access to the Internet, for downloading code samples and further reading

How This Book Is Organized

This book is meant to be read as a series of articles, but it can easily be used as a reference or read straight through. I recommend reading it at your computer, with Visual Studio running.

Each part is designed to teach you something that you need to know. The only part that I strongly suggest you read, however, is Part I, "Getting to Know .NET Using Visual Basic." After that, you can read whatever you need to get the job done, or read the whole book all the way through — it is up to you.

Part 1: Getting to Know .NET Using Visual Basic

After a quick jump start, I discuss the tools and concepts in this part. Chapter 1 is a *Hello World* introduction to the language, which experienced VB programmers will find useful and new programmers will find vital. Chapter 2 is a tour of the development tool you will be using, Visual Studio 2008.

Chapter 3 is arguably the most important chapter in the book. It is about designing good software with Visual Basic. You may want to read that one twice. I wanted to print it twice, but the publisher wouldn't let me.

Part II: Building Applications with VB 2008

This part gets you started programming. You find one chapter here for each of the four most-used project types (Windows and Web Forms, DLL files, and XML Web services) and then a chapter discussing how to debug all of them.

Part III: Making Your Programs Work

This part is actually about Visual Basic the language. You see, the projects discussed in Part II are actually available to lots of languages. You can write a Windows Forms project in Java (Microsoft calls it J#) if you want to. The actual VB language doesn't kick in until you write a program that needs more than the visual design.

Part IV: Digging into the Framework

Finally, in Part IV, you look at the last part of the puzzle — what the .NET Framework can do for you. Tons of tools that are built right into the framework are available to all languages but have a special twist when used with Visual Basic.

I begin with the important stuff, specifically security. Then I cover data, files, networks, and drawing. Throughout all these chapters, I provide code examples that can help you through the tougher problems that you may encounter in your VB career.

Part V: The Part of Tens

Some things fit nowhere. That's what the Part of Tens is for. In this part, I collected the most useful tips that didn't fit elsewhere and made them into top-ten lists. For more of these kinds of lists, check out this book's companion Web site at www.vbfordummies.net.

Icons Used in This Book

One of the things I like best about the *For Dummies* series of books is the ease of reading. Important facts are easily distinguishable from tips or technical details by this cool series of icons in the margins. I hope you find them as useful as I do.

This is the icon I use most often. It highlights a best practice, a common usage, or just something that I think you will find good to know about a feature or tool.

I use this icon to point out something that you want to, well, remember. The famous *gotchas* that all programmers are so familiar with get this icon. Some usages aren't always obvious. I hope to help you help yourself by pointing them out.

This icon points out something you do *not* want to do unless you're willing to suffer the consequences. Read the paragraphs next to the Warning icon so that you'll know how to avoid the pitfall, trap, or mistake.

These icons are pointers to places where the My object, new to Visual Basic 2008, can be useful.

Sometimes, I give you more information that you really need. When I do that, I try to use the Technical Stuff icon. You will find things you never wanted to know about the inner workings of the .NET Framework, design ideas, and other geeky stuff alongside this icon.

I use this icon to highlight a new feature in Visual Basic 2008.

Where to Go from Here

If you're completely new to Visual Basic and Visual Studio, start out by flipping the page and reading Chapter 1. If you're interested in looking up a particular topic, skim through the Table of Contents or the Index and turn to the indicated page.

When you're feeling more familiar with the language, tool, and project type, branch out by checking out the list of tips in the Part of Tens to take your next programming step.

You can, of course, read the book all the way through. Another great way to figure out how Visual Basic works is to follow a project path all the way through. For example, start with a Windows Forms project with `System.Drawing` elements, and go through the examples in the chapters that discuss those topics (Chapters 4 and 18, in this case).

Be sure to use the code samples for this book, provided at `www.vbfordummies.net`. They will give you a broad starting point for a lot of other, larger programs that you might want to write.

You also might be in the position where you have to quickly learn how to use this language for your job, and there might be special libraries and standards that you have to work with there. I recommend that you take the book home, where you can work undistracted, and give yourself a good foundation in the language. Then you can take the book back to work and use it as a reference for your future programming efforts.

Things change in the software world, and Microsoft software is especially prone to change. Things have probably changed since I wrote this book. If the software changes, I can't update the books that have already been printed. However, I can (and do) list any errata and updates on this book's companion Web site, `www.vbfordummies.net`. Check it out often.

Part I

Getting to Know .NET Using Visual Basic

The 5th Wave   By Rich Tennant

©RICHTENNANT

Gee, Richard, you'll have to tell me where on the toolbar you found an icon labeled "Overkill."

In this part . . .

Everyone must start somewhere, and I start at the beginning in this part. You write your first Visual Basic program, and, in doing so, you discover some of the ideas behind the .NET Framework (the backbone of this version of the language). You then get to do the only required reading in this entire book. First, you go over the use of the tool, Visual Studio. Second, you design the example application that you write in the next part.

Chapter 1

Wading into Visual Basic

In This Chapter

▶ Seeing where Visual Basic fits in with .NET

▶ Writing your first Visual Basic 2008 program

▶ Exploiting the newfound power of Visual Basic

*T*o get started with Visual Basic 2008, I recommend that you jump right in and write software! And to help you with such an assertive approach, this chapter gives you just what you need to test the waters of the Visual Basic pool and get comfortable with its place in the larger Visual Studio environment.

Then you can really get your feet wet as you build *Hello World* — your first VB 2008 Windows Forms application — right here in the first few pages! You find out how to launch Visual Studio 2008 (the development tool for your VB applications), how to start a new project, and how to build a form visually and make it work with code.

Also in this chapter, I give you a glimpse into the deeper power of Visual Basic. Specifically, I introduce how VB 2008 integrates with the Microsoft .NET Framework and offer insight into what that means to you as a programmer.

Visual Basic's Role in the Framework

Microsoft created the .NET Framework to make development for the various Windows operating systems easier. But because of the differences between Visual Basic 6.0 and Visual Basic 7.0 (the first .NET version), most VB developers found development much harder. For example, VB 7.0 made all variables into objects, which removed the programmer's ability to define a variable type on the fly.

But developing applications in .NET doesn't have to be harder than it was in VB 6.0. The .NET Framework and Visual Basic 2008 can be powerful tools, and the trick is discovering how they work together through the Visual Studio Integrated Development Environment (IDE).

Part of the difficulty that many programmers face when moving to the .NET Framework is the terminology, which can get confusing. I'd like to put the problem with terminology to bed right now, so check out this list of the potentially confusing terms used in .NET development:

- ✔ **Visual Basic 2008:** The programming language described throughout this whole book. No longer can you run or load Visual Basic as a separate entity. It is simply one programming language that speaks to the Microsoft .NET Framework, which is the next term in the list.

- ✔ **.NET Framework:** The layer that sits between the language (in this case, Visual Basic) and the operating system, which can be Windows 98, Windows Me, Windows 2000, Windows XP, Windows Server 2003, or any of the subversions of those (such as the Tablet PC edition). The .NET Framework layer serves to provide functionality based on the operation of the Windows system on which it resides, as well as to provide libraries for other functionality (such as math computations and database access). Figure 1-1 is a visual representation of the relationship of all the layers in the framework.

- ✔ **Visual Studio 2008:** The tool that you use to create any kind of application using any compatible programming language. Visual Studio replaces the Visual Basic 6.0 program that was formerly part of the Visual Studio suite (all individual suite components were labeled Version 6.0). When you go to write a new program in the .NET environment, you run Visual Studio 2008 and select the kind of program you want to write in the programming language you want to use. For example, you may choose to create a Windows Forms program using the Visual Basic language, just like the old days. Or you might want to write an application for a smart device using C#. You can also mix languages, for example, writing the forms in VB and the classes in C#. In this book, I will be using VB for everything — because it is a book about VB!

.NET Framework 3.5

| LINQ | ASP.NET 3.5 | CLR Add-in Framework | Additional Enhancements |

.NET Framework 3.0 + SP1

Figure 1-1: The .NET Framework hierarchy.

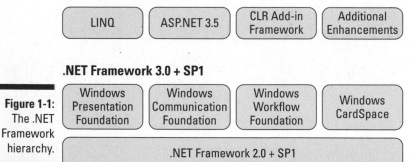

| Windows Presentation Foundation | Windows Communication Foundation | Windows Workflow Foundation | Windows CardSpace |

| .NET Framework 2.0 + SP1 |

- ✔ **Windows Forms:** The new term for an old-fashioned Visual Basic application. This term refers to an application that is written using the .NET Framework and has a Windows user interface.

- ✔ **Web Forms:** The term for an application with a Web page interface written using the .NET Framework. Creating a Web Forms application is very similar to writing a Windows Forms application.

- ✔ **Web services:** The class libraries that are written using a standard defined by the same people who defined standards for the World Wide Web. Web services are used for interaction between divergent systems.

The .NET Framework is what you may already know as the Win32 layer in the old Windows DNA system. Like the new .NET Framework, the Win32 layer gave you the ability to get to the functions of the operating system when developing for a Windows platform. Also, the .NET Framework includes a lot of adjunct functionality, such as math and data libraries, that makes programming a more cohesive experience.

Basically, everything that Windows does is exposed by the .NET Framework. Specifically, the .NET Framework gives a programmatic name to nearly every object and event that Windows can control. A programmer can use that name to refer to anything existing in the operating system. Do you need to tell the printer to make two copies of your document? Try referring to `My.Computer.Printers.DefaultPrinter.PrinterSettings.Copies = 2`. Do you need to paint some item on the screen blue? Try referring to `System.Drawing.Brushes.Blue`.

In this .NET world, the programming language becomes just a way to interact with the framework and, therefore, with the Windows operating system. All programs need a set of established rules to handle the flow (decisions, loops, and so on) within programs. Visual Basic provides one such set of rules, and the framework provides the objects and events to interact with.

Saying Hello to VB 2008!

In the following sections, I get you started with the classic Hello World program. Although this isn't the single most exciting application you can build, it helps to make sure that your development environment is set up the best way possible.

How VB 2008 differs from VB 6

Visual Basic 6 was a stand-alone program, and Visual Basic 2008 is one language in a larger development system. To go back to VB's roots, Basic was a programming language used 20 years ago as part of MS-DOS. In 1985, Basic became Visual Basic and was made into a part of the Windows application-building tool. You find a lot more to the Visual Basic 6 program than just the language — its form-building software, for example, is called *Ruby*.

Visual Basic has gone through a few revisions since VB 6. VB 2002 (a.k.a. VB 7), VB 2003 (VB 7.1), and VB 2005 (VB 8) are all just revisions of the language as it uses the .NET Framework. VB 2002 brought on board a whole new way to think about building applications in Windows, and VB 2005 brought back a lot of the features that VB 6 programmers depended on — like ease of use.

In Visual Basic 2008, you have a new way to build user experiences and, with it, a new way to interact with the Windows operating system. The real reason to understand the extent of this larger development system — and the complexity of the .NET Framework that surrounds VB 2008 — is so that reading related books and documentation is easier.

Installing Visual Studio

To follow this example, you need to start by running Visual Studio 2008, which is the development environment used throughout this book to build applications in Visual Basic. Before you can run Visual Studio, you need to install it!

Visual Studio comes in a number of editions:

- ✔ **Team System:** Designed for full programming staffs in large corporations, this edition includes large-scale application system design tools such as test-driven development and Team Foundation Server.

- ✔ **Professional Edition:** Designed for the developers working with users in a stand-alone setting. The Professional Edition is more common for the solo developer or for mid-sized application development. This is the edition I use in this book.

- ✔ **Standard Edition:** Designed for building smaller, stand-alone applications, this version is perfectly functional for 80 percent of applications built. But if you plan to build large systems that need to be enterprise quality and may have many users, go for the Professional Edition.

- ✔ **Express Edition:** Designed for students and hobbyists. This version lacks a lot of the project types that the other versions have. If you are running Express, some of the examples in this book won't work for you. On this book's Web site (www.vbfordummies.net), I have posted a few Express articles and some projects that I have altered to work in Express edition.

If you don't have access to the MSDN Library (Microsoft's handy technical archive), I highly recommend getting it. You can load up a machine with your choice of sample code, documentation, and other reference material on Visual Studio editions, operating systems, and server software. You can find out about the library at `http://msdn.microsoft.com`, and you can buy subscriptions from several resellers, including your favorite software dealer.

Installing Visual Studio can be rough, so I recommend going with the defaults for your first time. The installation process takes quite a while, too. Even if you are using the DVD, expect to spend two hours installing the program. If you are working from the CDs, expect to spend four hours.

After installing Visual Studio, you can run it by choosing Start⇨All Programs⇨ Microsoft Visual Studio 2008⇨Microsoft Visual Studio 2008. The environment loads, and you can get started on a program by choosing File⇨New⇨Project. Next, you need to make choices about your project type and language, as described in the next section.

Starting a Windows Forms project

After you choose File⇨New⇨Project in Visual Studio, the New Project dialog box appears, as shown in Figure 1-2. In the Project Types pane, you find a folder structure that lists the languages loaded with your installation and the project types available for those languages. I suggest beginning with a plain old Windows Forms Application — which is the Visual Basic 2008 answer to the traditional (and perhaps familiar) VB 6.0 application.

Figure 1-2:
The New
Project
dialog box.

Project types:	Templates:	.NET Framework 3.5
⊟ Visual Basic	**Visual Studio installed templates**	
— Windows	Windows Forms Application	Class Library
⊞ Office	WPF Application	WPF Browser Application
— Smart Device	Console Application	Crystal Reports Application
— Database	Empty Project	Windows Service
— Test	WPF Custom Control Library	WPF User Control Library
— WCF	Windows Forms Control Library	Reports Application
— Web		
— Workflow	**My Templates**	
⊞ Visual C#	Search Online Templates...	
⊞ Other Project Types		
⊞ Test Projects		

A project for creating an application with a Windows user interface (.NET Framework 3.5)

Name: Hello World

Location: C:\Documents and Settings\sempf\My Documents\Visual Studio 2008\Projects\VBFD   Browse...

Solution: Create new Solution   ☑ Create directory for solution

Solution Name: Chapter 1

OK   Cancel

To get started building your Hello World application, follow these steps:

1. **Select the project type from the Templates pane in the New Project dialog box.**

   For this example, select Windows Forms Application. Also, make sure that Visual Basic is the language selected in the Project Types pane. If you loaded other languages during installation, you may have other choices.

2. **Type the name you want to give your project to replace the default name in the Name text box.**

   In this example, I type **Hello World** in the text box.

3. **Click the OK button.**

   Visual Basic loads the default form (called Form1) and presents it to you in the Design View. The default form comes complete with a workspace, the title bar, and familiar Windows elements like the Resize buttons and the Close button. You do most of the work to customize your form using this visual view.

4. **Click the word Toolbox on the left side of the screen and open the Common Controls tree.**

   The Toolbox appears, with Windows Forms controls loaded, as shown in Figure 1-3.

5. **Double-click the Button control.**

   Visual Studio loads a button onto the default form in Design View.

6. **On the default Form1, click the Button control and drag it to reposition it on the form.**

   Figure 1-4 shows the result of dragging the button to the middle of the Form1 window.

This step list gives you the beginnings of the Windows Forms application, which you see as Form1 in the Design View. But to see where Visual Basic comes in, you have to find the code behind the form. Visual Studio offers you (surprise!) the Code View when you're ready to use Visual Basic to add functionality to your form.

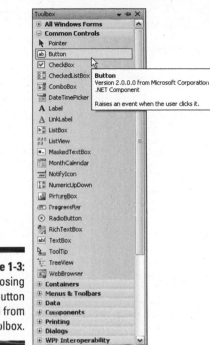

Figure 1-3:
Choosing
the Button
control from
the Toolbox.

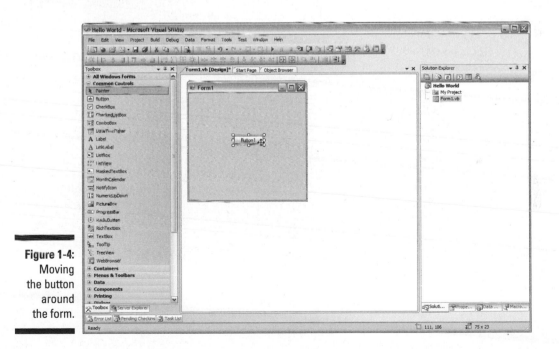

Figure 1-4:
Moving
the button
around
the form.

Adding functionality to the form with VB code

To add a little functionality to the Windows form you build in the preceding section, follow these steps:

1. **Double-click the Button control to enter Code View.**

   In the Code View window, you see basic button-click code that looks like the following:

   ```
   Public Class Form1

       Private Sub Button1_Click(ByVal sender As _
           System.Object, ByVal e As System.EventArgs) _
           Handles Button1.Click

       End Sub
   End Class
   ```

   This code is a template that wraps the code that will be run when you click the button. Visual Studio does the hard part for you, making sure that the formatting of the Sub is correct!

2. **In the Code View window, type a line of code to change the text that appears on the Button control to *Hello World*.**

   Specifically, type the following code on the line preceding the End Sub line:

   ```
   Button1.Text = "Hello World"
   ```

   Your button's code now looks like the following:

   ```
   Public Class Form1
   Private Sub Button1_Click(ByVal sender As _
           System.Object, ByVal e As System.EventArgs)
           _
           Handles Button1.Click

    Button1.Text = "Hello World"

    End Sub
   End Class
   ```

Running and operating your Windows form

So this experience is pretty cool, right? Programming with Visual Basic is so easy that, here in Chapter 1, you can already write a Windows Forms application. But what can you do with it? Check out the following:

- **Run your Windows Forms application within the Visual Studio environment.** Press F5, and Visual Studio opens your active project as a Windows program. It appears on your taskbar and everything. Click the button on your form, and the button text changes to "Hello World" (or whatever text you specified in the code). Pretty neat, huh? Your Windows form should look something like the image in Figure 1-5.

- **Run your application outside of the Visual Studio environment.** If you are still in Debug mode, you will need to stop your program first by using the Stop button on the toolbar or by closing the form window. Then you can save and move on.

The very simple way to run an application outside of Visual Studio is as follows:

1. **Choose File⇨Save All.**

   Visual Studio will save your project using the defaults you supplied in the Add New Project dialog box.

2. **Choose Build⇨Build Program Name.**

   In this example, choose Build⇨Build Solution, and Visual Studio compiles your application into a usable Windows program (with the file extension .exe) and stores it in the default folder.

3. **Navigate to the default folder containing your new Windows application.**

   For my application, the path is C:\Documents and Settings\ sempf\My Documents\Visual Studio 2008\Projects\ VBFD\Chapter1\Hello World\bin\Debug.

Figure 1-5:
Your Hello
World
application.

If your local configuration for the project happens to be set to Release mode (not recommended for this book), you might find it in `C:\Documents and Settings\sempf\My Documents\Visual Studio 2008\Projects\ VBFD\Chapter1\Hello World\bin\Release`.

> **4. Double-click the filename for the compiled program to run it.**
>
> You may see a lot of files in the default folder, but in the example, `Hello World.exe` is the file you're looking for.

There is a more complex method for running your VB programs outside the Visual Studio environment. You use a Setup Project, which is a very cool tool but beyond the scope of this book. Research the term *Setup Project* in the MDSN Library when you're ready to find out more about this device, which helps you distribute your application to other users.

Finding More Power in Visual Studio

Earlier in this chapter, I showed you the Windows Forms application development environment and a little of the new Visual Basic 2008 code. If you are familiar with VB 6.0, the form and the code look pretty familiar at this point. In fact, the major Windows development tools for any programming language work pretty much this way.

But when you look beyond the Windows form and the code structure, a few more details become evident. For instance, Visual Studio takes your VB code beyond the Windows form. The following sections give you an overview of the development power that you find in Visual Studio.

Visual Studio doesn't just do Windows!

The first evident change that sets Visual Studio apart as a development tool is this: You can use Visual Studio to write programs that run on the World Wide Web as well as on Windows computers. When you click the File menu to add a new project, notice the second option in the menu. As shown in Figure 1-6, the second project option is a new Web site.

Choose this option to create a Web application, which incorporates a whole host of technologies — the .NET Framework, ASP.NET, Visual Basic, and HTML — that each have essential roles for enabling an application to run online.

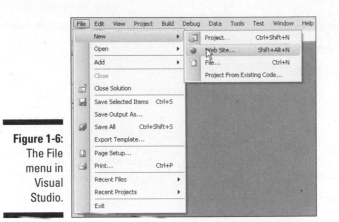

Figure 1-6:
The File
menu in
Visual
Studio.

Visual Basic goes mobile

Mobile computing made its appearance in Visual Basic 2005 and really shines now in Visual Studio 2008. If you follow development for mobile devices, you may have noticed the plethora of releases from the Mobile team over the past few years. They are all baked right into Visual Studio 2008. Pocket PC 2003, Mobile 5.0, and Mobile 6.0 all make their appearance in Visual Studio 2008, and can be programmed in VB 2008 — just like every other type of project.

I don't give examples of these specific project types in this book because you can create a mobile device application in the same manner that you create a Windows Forms application (like the Hello World program discussed earlier in the chapter). You should know that getting familiar with the Visual Basic language as presented in this book puts you on the right track for creating applications for a Pocket PC. Mobile computing applications require some special programming practices, so make sure to grab some device-specific information when you work on those project types.

Writing routines to use with other software is easier with Visual Basic 2008. You can write add-ins for Microsoft Office apps, including Excel and Word templates with VB code running behind them. These routines don't use the VBScript that you may have seen before; a completely new part of Office 2007 allows you to write templates with special, built-in functionality. For example, I've built a Word template that automates a reporting process by asking the user for a report number, checking that number against a database of all the reports filed, and filling out part of the document-in-process with the relevant information from the database. You can also customize the ribbon bar and create and deploy add-ins easily.

VB as your one-stop development shop

Generally, Visual Studio and the .NET Framework are designed to be the one-stop shop for any kind of development on Windows machines. But in this version, Visual Basic 2008 can also do it all. The language can now touch all the parts of the .NET Framework that any of the other languages can get to, without resorting to the cryptic function calls necessary in prior versions of VB.

The new features covered in this book include the following:

- ✔ **The Windows Presentation Foundation:** Microsoft has updated the formula to design new user experiences again with even more power.

- ✔ **The Windows Communication Foundation:** Making interconnected applications even more powerful, the WCF is an advanced step that I'll touch on later in the book.

- ✔ **Language Integrated Query:** LINQ brings data constructs right into your code with new query mechanisms for collections of objects.

- ✔ **System.XML:** If you are working with Extensible Markup Language, VB 2008 brings new meaning to the word *simple*.

Chapter 2

Using Visual Studio 2008

*B*efore you can effectively work with Visual Basic, you must know its tools inside and out. For the purpose of this chapter and this book, I will focus on just one — Visual Studio 2008. Visual Studio gives you access to the drag-and-drop controls that were introduced in earlier versions of Visual Basic.

Although I don't cover the specifics of code in this chapter, I do cover all the code-generating tools that Visual Studio 2008 provides for Visual Basic. For example, I discuss the new, improved IntelliSense, which can help you remember the 288,000 methods, properties, and events in the .NET Framework, but I don't cover the framework itself.

Understanding Visual Studio Tools

Part of the joy of programming in Visual Basic 2008 is using the tools that are provided by Visual Studio. Rapid Application Development (RAD) is a buzzword now, but when Visual Basic was first developed, it described (among other things) the ability to code faster by reusing bits of code built into the development tools.

This ability has never been more apparent than it is with Visual Basic 2008. Even though Visual Basic is a language, and it depends on Visual Studio for its environment, many tools make RAD real. In the following sections, I cover these tools. These tools are language independent, project independent, and indispensable.

Keep in mind that Visual Studio isn't necessary to make Visual Basic programs. You can, in fact, make complete applications in the old-school style by using a command-line compiler.

Additionally, much of the documentation provided by the Microsoft Developer Network (MSDN) Library assumes an understanding of the tools. The documentation refers to the tools by name and often doesn't clearly describe them. You must know where you are working before you can work, so the following sections take you on a tour of the Visual Studio tools.

When you installed Visual Studio, you were probably asked to install the MSDN Library. You will find it an indispensable tool (it's what you get when you go to the Help menu, in fact). Additionally, you can find the library online at http://msdn.microsoft.com/library.

Touring the Design View

When you launch Visual Studio (usually by selecting its icon on your Start menu) and begin any visual project, you see the Design View. The Design View is where the Graphical User Interface (GUI) work takes place. Generally speaking, anytime you are working with pictures of forms, not code, you are working with the Design View. When I use the term *designer window,* I am referring to the actual place you do the work. The term *Design View* refers to the state the application is in.

In the Design View, you can accomplish the following:

✔ Manufacture windows, Web, and smart device forms by dragging controls directly to the form in a What-You-See-Is-What-You-Get (WYSIWYG)–type environment

✔ Work with databases and XML files visually

✔ Create software components by visually managing the parts

In general, Design View is the core part of Visual Studio. Many of the other tools in Visual Studio depend on the Design View, in fact, and are disabled when you use another view, such as Code View, to work on your project.

Using the Design View tabs

The designer tabs have the word [Design] in the tab name, as shown in Figure 2-1, to indicate that you are using the Design View. Tabs are used in the Design and Code Views. The gray tab represents files that are open but not active. An asterisk (*) next to the filename means that you've made changes, but not yet saved the file.

The white tab is active and contains the editable form. When you have more than one document open, you can edit only the active form. You can drag the tabs to the left and right to change their order. Right-clicking a tab gives you a menu from which you can choose several screen management options, as shown in Figure 2-2.

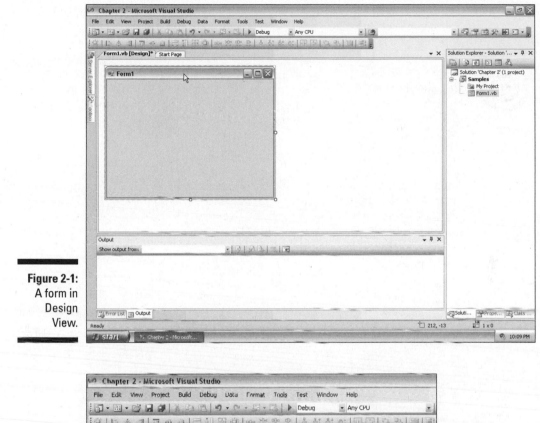

Figure 2-1: A form in Design View.

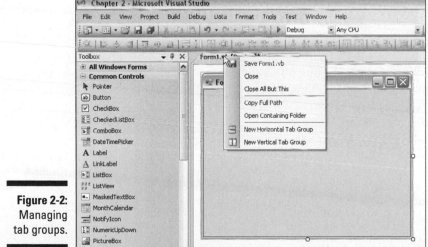

Figure 2-2: Managing tab groups.

Understanding tab groups

Tab groups make it easier to copy information out of one form and into another. For example, you can have one set of pages on the top half of the screen and another on the bottom half, and copy from one and paste into the other without changing screens. You can also save and close from this menu, or get information, such as the current path or the containing folder.

Accessing controls with the Toolbox

To add form components, such as buttons and text, to the form in the Designer window, you simply drag them from the Toolbox. The Toolbox, usually seen on the left side of the Visual Studio environment and to the left of the Designer window, is where the RAD components of various project types are held for use until you need them. The Toolbox is shown in Figure 2-3.

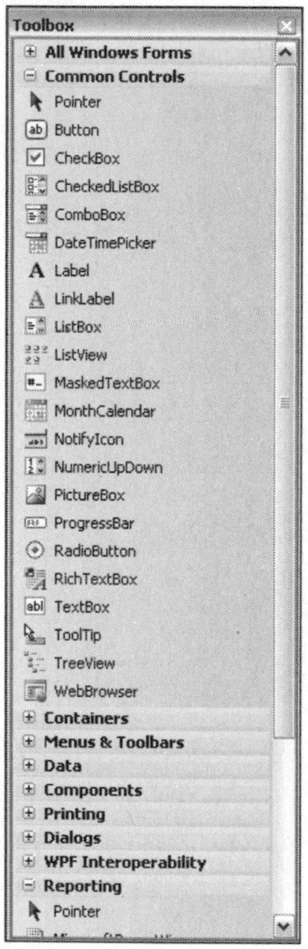

Figure 2-3:
The Toolbox.

The Toolbox is *project-sensitive,* meaning that controls for Web pages and smart devices don't show up when you are writing a Windows Forms project. Because those controls can't be used in those project types, the Toolbox doesn't even let you see them.

You can access the controls in the following ways:

- ✔ Click a control and drag it to a form, dropping it exactly where you want it.
- ✔ Double-click the control, and it appears in the upper-left corner of the active form.

If you lose the Toolbox, or if it isn't showing on your screen, you can open it by choosing View➪Toolbox or by pressing Ctrl+Alt+X. Right-clicking the Toolbox gives you layout options, including ordering and movement. One of the options is Reset Toolbox, which puts it back the way Microsoft had it — a great feature.

The gray dividers, labeled Data or Windows Forms among other things, divide the tools in the Toolbox by category. To open a closed category, click the divider.

Visual Studio is extendable because of the Toolbox. You can use third-party components with your programs. For example, a clock control that enables the user to set the time would show up in the Toolbox. You can also use the Toolbox to store often-used pieces of text, such as comment blocks.

You can actually drag a little block of code onto the Toolbox for reuse, such as a common comment block or a sample. I use this all the time when I am presenting. I just make a new section by right-clicking the Toolbox and selecting Add Tab. Then I can just select code in the Code View (which I cover in a few pages) and drag it right under the new section header.

Changing details with the Properties window

After you drop the controls on the form designer, you will need to edit their properties. Size, name, activity, color . . . these are the kinds of things you find in the Properties window. The Properties window, shown in Figure 2-4, is usually on the right side of the screen. It contains all the editable values associated with a control.

If the Properties window isn't on the right side of the screen, you can find it by choosing View➪Properties Window, or you can press F4.

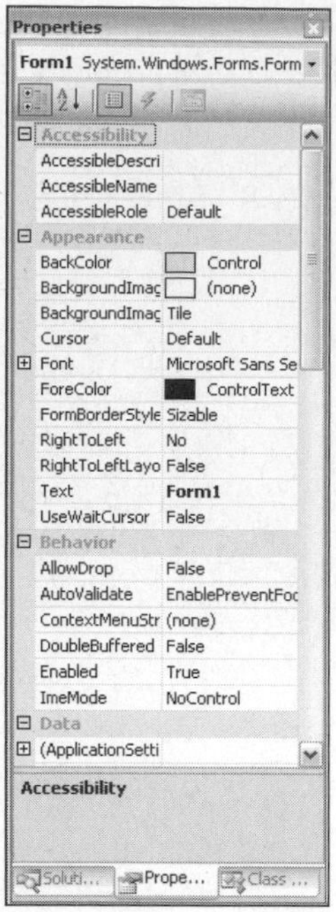

Figure 2-4:
The
Properties
window.

At the top of the Properties window, you see the form element whose properties are being viewed. You can select a different control by clicking it in the Designer window or by selecting a new control from the drop-down list. In Figure 2-4, the form itself is selected.

Beneath the selected control, you find a few buttons that resort the list or filter by category. Of special interest is the lightning-bolt button, which allows you to define what the control does under certain circumstances — a pattern called *events*. I cover events in depth throughout Part II.

The table that takes up the majority of the Properties window contains the properties of the control. This is a simple hash table format — the properties are on the left, and the possible values are on the right. To change a value, you can usually type in the cell and press Enter. Some properties have an ellipsis button (...) that opens a form to simplify adding complex details, and I cover those as I discuss them in other chapters.

The grouping buttons at the top of the Properties window are a useful feature. The Category button is great when you are just starting out, because you can find the properties based on what you need. The A-Z list is better later on, when you know exactly what property you are looking for.

The bottom of the Properties window has a brief description of the property that is being edited. This information is right out of the documentation and is a very handy feature.

Organizing your project with the Solution Explorer

Solutions and projects hold forms and components like files in folders. In fact, solutions and projects are represented by folders in the Visual Studio Projects directory of your My Documents folder. The Solution Explorer is Visual Studio's tool that allows you to manage the files that make up your project.

If you envision your projects like folders, you can imagine that you would group like folders together in a folder one level up, right? That's what solutions do. They are both physically and logically exactly that — folders full of projects.

In Figure 2-5, you see the important files in your project, and a whole bunch of buttons above to help manage them.

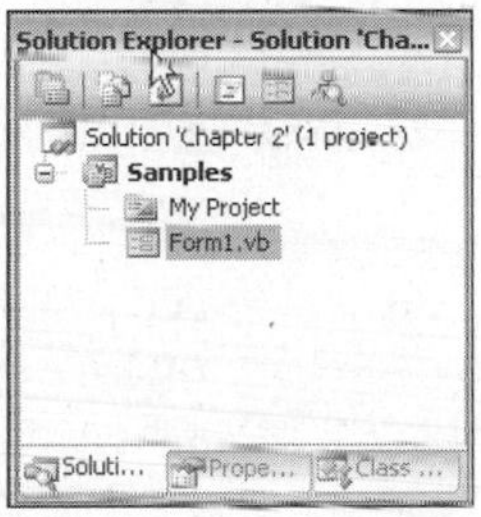

Figure 2-5:
The Solution Explorer.

To open a file, double-click the file's icon or name. To rename, copy, or delete a file, right-click the file and choose the desired action from the context-sensitive menu that appears. In the Solution Explorer, you can also make new folders and move files into them, or right-click the project to make a new form or support file.

The buttons above the files themselves are the most significant part of the Solution Explorer. They are as follows, from left to right:

- ✓ **Properties:** Opens the Properties window.
- ✓ **Show All Files:** Shows hidden files. This is more significant in VB 2008 than before. Even more files are hidden from normal view.

- ✔ **Refresh:** Checks the solution folder for new files that may have been added by another tool. This button is very handy when you're using third-party tools.

- ✔ **View Code:** Opens the selected file in Code View.

- ✔ **View Designer:** Opens the selected file in Design View.

- ✔ **View Class Diagram:** Opens the selected file in Diagram View.

Visual Studio stores a lot of files that keep metadata about the project in the My Project folder in Solution Explorer. Metadata is information about data — in this case, extra information about your project. If you click the Show All Files button in Solution Explorer and expand My Project, you will see no less than seven files with information about your project. You won't need to edit these files often, but if you just can't find something, you might want to check them out.

Accessing outside resources with the Server Explorer

Going outside of your project to access needed resources is one of the most common features that *isn't* supported by most development environments. That all changed with Visual Studio 2002 and has gotten better ever since with the addition of the Server Explorer, shown in Figure 2-6. You can open Server Explorer by pressing Ctrl+Alt+S or by selecting it on the View menu. Now getting to the servers that provide your necessary services is easier than ever.

The Server Explorer is one of the more dynamic tools in the Visual Studio environment. In Figure 2-6, I am using my virtual development machine, XP. What you see in the Server Explorer depends on your local configuration.

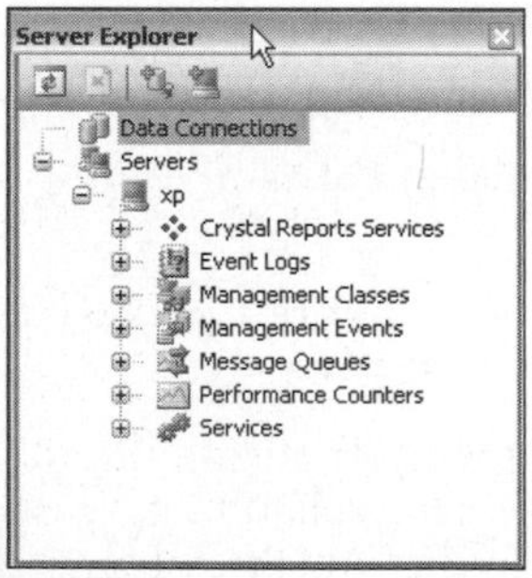

Figure 2-6: The Server Explorer.

The Servers node in this explorer shows up in some editions of Visual Studio. At press time, the Professional edition was one of them. Also, the Team System edition certainly has it, and you can get that edition from the Microsoft Web site in a trial version.

Server Explorer gives you access to remote (or local) resources from a management and a code perspective. The tree view inside the Server Explorer can show many servers, and beneath each server are the functional bits that you have access to.

Most developers are looking for a one-stop shop for development; most often, that includes needing the ability to manage development server(s) and look at databases. The Server Explorer handles both of these, but the new Data Sources window is even better, and I cover it in the following section.

The services available to you in your Server Explorer depend on your environment, but here is a brief description of some of the services that are common:

- **Crystal Reports Services:** Crystal is a third-party reporting tool that is included with Visual Studio. The services include Crystal Enterprise, Report Application Server, and Web Services.

- **Event Logs:** This represents the normal old Windows NT–style event logs that you can access from the Control Panel. Logs are available both programmatically in .NET and for management from the Server Explorer.

- **Management Classes:** Management Classes represent Windows Management Instrumentation (WMI) classes such as Network Adapters, Printers, and Services, all of which you can touch programmatically on remote machines.

- **Management Events:** They allow you to register for WMI events, like network changes and hardware warnings.

- **Message Queues:** Message Queues are a way to help manage the number of requests to a very large application. The individual queues are made available here.

- **Performance Counters:** This is access to PerfMon from the Windows operating system. Each counter is available both for viewing and programming.

- **Services:** The services from the Control Panel are available here. You can stop and start the Web services, for example.

- **Data Connections:** This is a special category that isn't directly related to the servers shown. The Data Connections relate to connections you have set up over time on your instance of Visual Studio, and are remembered for your convenience.

In Design View, you can actually drag an Event Log or Performance Counter into the form to write code to adjust its properties. Aside from these programmatic capabilities, the Server Explorer does provide that one-stop management shop.

The Data Connections node allows you to connect your application to a data source. Right-click the Data Connections node and choose Add Connection to add a new connection. After selecting a Data Provider (I picked SQL Server), the Add Connection dialog box appears, as shown in Figure 2-7.

Visual Studio installs SQL Server Express as part of the package of programs provided. If you have access to no other databases, you can always use that one. It will appear as Machine/SqlExpress in the Add Connection dialog box.

In Figure 2-7, I selected my local machine (XP), the SQL Express instance, and the Northwind database. You probably don't have the Northwind database installed by default. You can get it from www.microsoft.com/downloads or www.vbfordummies.net.

This selection connects your project with a database, which then allows you to use the Data Sources window, manage the data objects within the database, and edit data directly. When you have finished adding the values to the connection, click the Test Connection button to make sure that your project can get the database you selected.

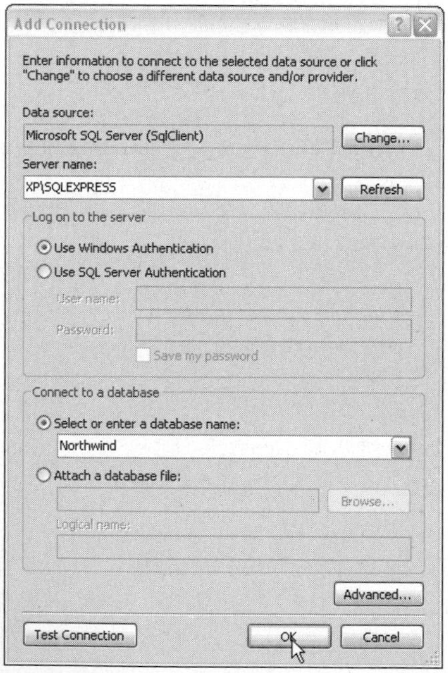

Figure 2-7:
The Add
Connection
dialog box.

Dynamically editing data with the Data Sources window

When you start a new project, the Data Sources window says "Your project currently has no data sources associated with it." (If you can't see the Data Sources window, choose Data⇨Show Data Sources with a project open, or press Shift+Alt+D.) To maintain data in the .NET world, as with any other environment, you must connect your application to a data source. The Data Sources window is the primary way to do that.

To connect to a data source (like a database or XML file), follow these steps:

1. **Click the Add a New Data Source button.**

   Doing so starts the Data Source Configuration Wizard.

2. **Click the Next button.**

   The wizard shows the data source options. You can select the Database option to use an SQL Server or Oracle database, the Service option to connect to an XML Web service, or the Object option to connect to a data access layer.

3. **Select the connection to Northwind that you made in the "Accessing outside resources with the Server Explorer" section, and then click the Next button (shown in Figure 2-8).**

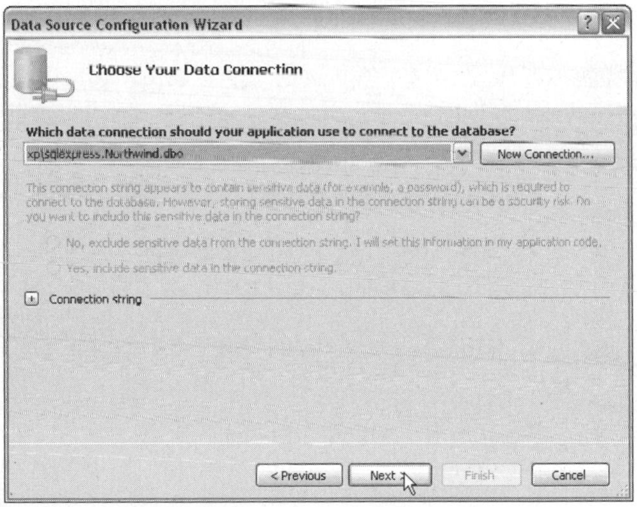

Figure 2-8:
The Data Source Configuration Wizard.

4. Accept the default connection name (probably NorthwindConnection) and click the Next button.

You are given a choice of what objects to include in your dataset. I cover datasets in Chapter 15.

5. For now, select the first view in the Views checklist: Alphabetical List of Products.

6. Click the Finish button.

As shown in Figure 2-9, each of the columns in the view you selected appears as the editable object types that can represent them. You can now drag them to the Design View to create a data-bound control.

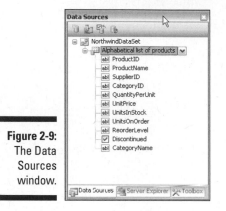

Figure 2-9:
The Data
Sources
window.

Just for fun, drag the QuantityPerUnit field onto the blank form that was created for you when you started the project. Visual Studio will create a bunch of data piping for you and then add the field and a label to the form. Using the Data Sources window like this provides you with fantastic functionality for quickly developing data applications.

In Figure 2-10, I have a picture of my screen as I dragged the field into the form. You can see in the Design View bottom, where the background is gray, that five components have been added to Form1. *Components* are functional items from the Toolbox, not things that are visible on the screen. The Data Sources window makes all those components and adds the control to the page, just based on the field you moved. That is the point of these RAD tools.

Frankly, the Diagram View is a very sophisticated tool, which I don't cover in this book. It allows enterprise architects to build component-based software by taking whole blocks of code and moving them in a graphic environment.

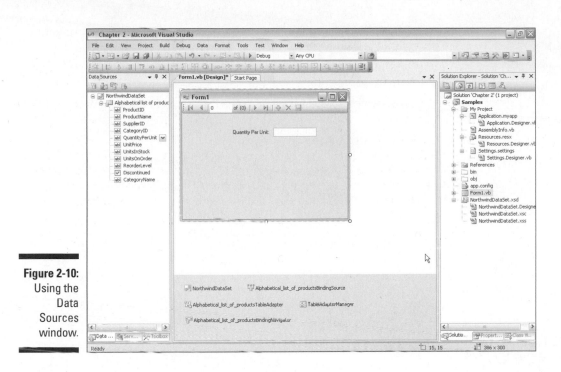

Figure 2-10:
Using the
Data
Sources
window.

Every now and again, when you have written something in Visual Basic, go ahead and load up the Diagram View. You can enter Diagram View by right-clicking a file in the Solution Explorer and selecting View in Designer from the context-sensitive menu. It will create a new file called `Classdiagram1.cd` in your Solution Explorer and show you the piping behind the software you have built. It can be an educational experience — try it!

Moving a Tool Window

You can customize the Visual Studio environment to make it easier for you to work in. All the tools, windows, and views are part of an Integrated Development Environment (IDE) that provides a home location. This makes organization of your personal development space a lot easier.

Most often, you will want to move a tool window around to put it in a more convenient spot. You can display a tool window in the following ways:

✔ **Floating:** A floating window is very mobile — you can drag it around by its handle to place it anywhere you want.

✔ **Dockable:** When you drag a dockable window, though, you are given the option by Visual Studio to dock the window. This is demonstrated in Figure 2-11, where I am dragging the Solution Explorer window around in the Design View.

✔ **Tabbed Document:** You also have the choice to drag the window to the center and have it become a tab at the top of the view window, like the `Form1.vb` and `Start Page` files shown in Figure 2-11.

You have five options to dock the window. If you drag the window over the top, bottom, left, or right arrow, it will dock to that side. When a window is docked, it has a thumbtack that you can pin or unpin. When pinned, it stays on the side, moving the Design View over. When unpinned, it slides out of the way toward the side it is pinned to. It is a brilliant feature.

If you drag the window to the center of the four-pointed star, the window becomes a tab in the other central windows — much easier than the old triple-click that was so hard to use. The triple-click still works, but you don't need it anymore!

Working with Code

Of the programs you create with Visual Studio, most of what you want the user to see are the controls and the forms. But you will be spending most of your time working with code. Fortunately, Visual Studio has a ton of tools to help you write code.

Getting to Code View

Code View, like Design View or Diagram View, is just another way to look at a file in the Solution Explorer. To get to Code View, you have several choices:

✔ You can right-click a form in the Solution Explorer or in Design View and select View Code from the context-sensitive menu.

✔ You can click the View Code button in the Solution Explorer.

✔ You can double-click an object in a form.

When you're working in Code View, most of the tool windows will become inactive. The Toolbox and Properties windows, for instance, have little to nothing available because their features are designed for use with the Design View rather than the Code View. This is by design, to keep the code out of your way when building business logic.

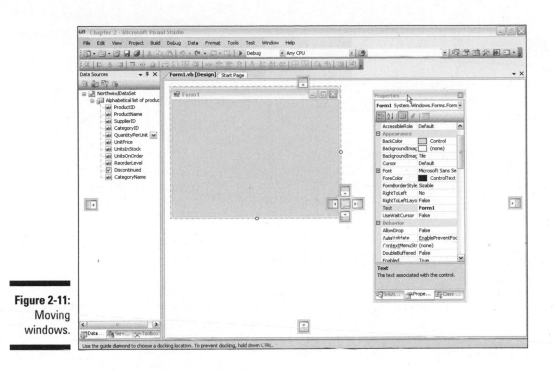

Figure 2-11:
Moving
windows.

Using IntelliSense

The problem with using Code View is that you need to know what to type. Welcome to programming! To help you get started, you can use some very productive code-based tools, such as IntelliSense and Smart Tags.

The remainder of the book is about the language, but I want to give you something to start with so that you can see how great these tools are. When you are working with the code as the primary goal, the tools should be second nature. Get started with these steps:

1. **In the default project, double-click the blank Form1 to move to Code View.**

2. **Start to type** My. **in the** `Form1_Load` **method. (Just press M on the keyboard, and you can see what I mean).**

   A special context-sensitive menu (the IntelliSense menu) appears when you start typing, as shown in Figure 2-12. This menu shows the code that is available to you. It guesses what you need based on what you are doing — in this case, it doesn't have much to work with so it started with the MID method.

Finish typing 'My.' and you will get all the available methods, properties, and events in the My object. It's a great way to remember the best way to get things done.

You can continue to use IntelliSense menus as long as Visual Studio thinks there are more types after the selected object. For instance, double-click Application in the context-sensitive menu and then type **.** (period). You see another IntelliSense menu.

Using this method, you can access everything in the Visual Basic language. Even when you write your own reusable code, IntelliSense will pick it up for this special context-sensitive menu. It makes it much easier to work in the .NET Framework with Visual Basic.

Reading the documentation

Rarely does an author have to write about how to read the documentation, but in the case of Visual Studio, there is so much power in the documentation model that it deserves a little space. The most straightforward use of the documentation requires little more than clicking on or in the object that you have a question about and pressing F1 to launch context-sensitive Help.

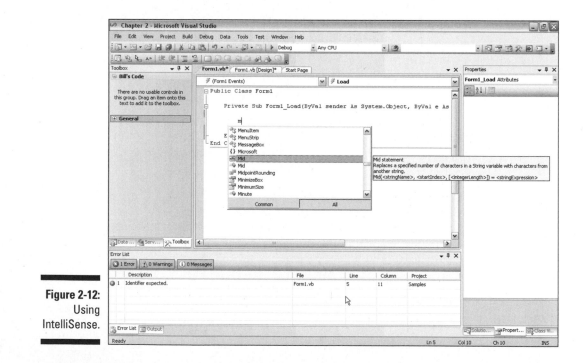

Figure 2-12:
Using
IntelliSense.

For instance, in any application, click somewhere on the form (make sure that you click the form and not an object on the form) and press F1. The Microsoft Document Explorer launches with the Form object documentation loaded.

The Document Explorer has a sophisticated set of tools, mostly represented in the Document Explorer toolbar, shown in Figure 2-13. The tools you find there give you various ways to access the documentation, as follows:

Figure 2-13:
The
Document
Explorer
toolbar.

✔ The toolbar's first section has navigation buttons, a Refresh button, and font size maintenance.

✔ The How Do I button has preset questions that relate to the selected topic, and may help with general queries about certain types of development; if you are stuck, give it a try.

✔ Clicking the Search button allows phrase searching. The Index button and Contents button allow browsing through the index or TOC (table of contents) of the documentation. You can save favorites in the Help Favorites just like you can in Internet Explorer. The double arrow is handy — it synchronizes the Contents panel with the page you are currently viewing.

✔ The Ask a Question button takes you directly to the NNTP newsgroups (using a Web-based viewer) hosted by Microsoft, where you can ask questions and have them answered by Microsoft MVPs, authors, and other experts. If you aren't participating in the user community, please do so — see Part V for more information.

You have all these options, and they're only one part of the documentation in Visual Studio. IntelliSense shows information from the user documentation when you pause the mouse cursor over a piece of code. The Properties window shows the documentation for a property when it is selected. Everywhere you look, Help is there!

And don't overlook the online tools provided by Microsoft. Choose Help➪ Technical Support to access a wealth of information available on the Web, right from inside Visual Studio.

Customizing with Options

The options available in Visual Studio are amazing. For starters, as with many other Windows applications, the toolbars and menus are completely editable. Choose Tools➪Customize to access the Customize dialog box. Click the Commands tab to get lists of all commands available in Visual Studio. To add a button for a command to a toolbar, simply drag a command from the list to the toolbar.

For instance, as shown in Figure 2-14, I dragged the Build icon to a toolbar so that I can access it anytime. It is a fantastic feature for designing your own custom environment.

The other significant customization is available by choosing Tools➪Options. The Options dialog box has many options that are in a tree view on the left side of the dialog box. Well over 100 options screens are available for editing in such categories as Environment, Source Control, Database Tools, and Windows Forms Designer.

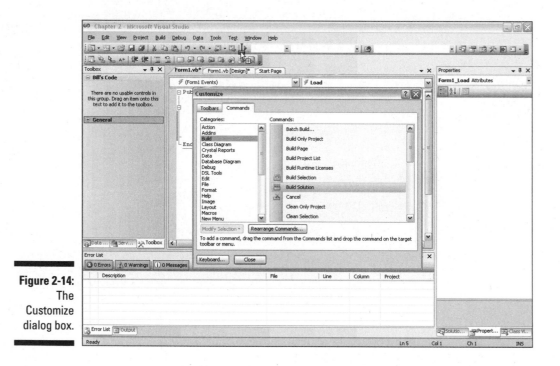

Figure 2-14:
The
Customize
dialog box.

The General Environment variables in the Options dialog box are shown in Figure 2-15. I don't discuss every option available in the Options dialog box because there are bunches of them, but take ten minutes to look at these options and see how they can help you develop programs. You might not see what they all do now, but when you do need them, you will know that they are there.

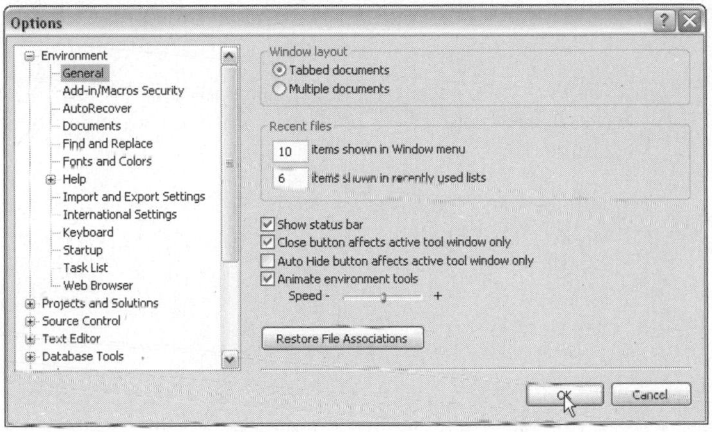

Figure 2-15:
The Options
dialog box.

The Restore File Associations button changes the layout of the windows, tool-boxes, and panels to the Microsoft default for your profile. It's great to use if you changed everything around as described in the earlier section "Moving a Tool Window."

Increasing Efficiency with Third-Party Tools

Visual Studio offers a structure for third-party developers to write piggyback programs called *add-ins*. Add-ins give you, the programmer, more flexibility and functionality in Visual Studio. Most companies actually use Visual Studio to develop these add-ins. I don't cover third-party add-ins in this book, but it makes a great topic for later research.

Microsoft has included a number of add-ins with the Visual Studio 2008 installation. While Microsoft provides a remarkable tool, it doesn't provide everything, and instead leans on partners to provide extra functionality in the way of add-ins.

Take Dotfuscator, for instance. By definition, .NET applications are self-documenting. Anyone can take an application written in .NET and look at the basic structure of the code with little effort. With tools available on the Internet, you can reverse-engineer this code to Visual Basic. (Bet they didn't tell you that in the marketing.) I'm sure you can imagine that this fact upsets a few people.

Enter Dotfuscator. This add-in application, which is completely integrated into Visual Studio, provides the ability to obfuscate compiled .NET applications, making it very difficult to reverse-engineer the code to Visual Basic — thus the product name. To run Dotfuscator, choose Tools⇨Dotfuscator Community Edition and accept the terms. You then see the default Dotfuscator window, as shown in Figure 2-16.

This application allows you to specify a finished project and perform some magic. Dotfuscator speeds execution, shrinks the package size, and protects your intellectual property. In my opinion, Dotfuscator was a good choice for Microsoft to include with Visual Studio, and it shows the power of third-party add-ins.

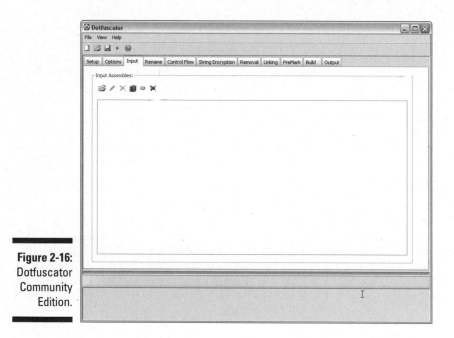

Figure 2-16:
Dotfuscator
Community
Edition.

Chapter 3

Designing Applications in VB 2008

*B*efore you discover the diversity of all the projects you can build, the ease of Visual Basic, and the power of the .NET Framework, you must know how to design software. By *design,* I mean planning your work. The classic comparison is that building software is like building a house. Would you hire a contractor who was going to build your house without blueprints? Of course not. Likewise, you shouldn't expect to be able to write software without designs.

In this one and only design chapter, I show how the .NET Framework makes it easy for you to figure out how to build software right from the start. I also show you the structure of the .NET Framework and describe how it works with Visual Basic and Visual Studio.

Next, you discover the foundation upon which the .NET Framework is built. I explain the abstract concepts that make the .NET Framework so easy to use and some concrete examples of how it is used.

Planning for building software is also covered in this chapter. Believe it or not, accepted, structured ways exist to design software. Following this structure is a great way to get your design plans on paper. In this chapter, I discuss how to design the software that you build in Part II.

Finally, I cover how to describe software from the perspectives of reading and writing the designs. When you finish reading this chapter, you can plan an actual software project.

Making Software Simple Using the .NET Framework

.NET as a concept is a library of connected software developed by Microsoft that connects people and the systems and devices they use with the information that they need. The .NET Framework is the development environment that makes it all happen from the Visual Basic perspective.

Visual Basic is just a piece of the .NET Framework. As shown in Figure 3-1, Visual Basic is only used to write the client, server, and connectivity software that makes it all happen.

Well-designed applications include the following layers:

- ✔ Clients in the .NET world include devices like cell phones and PDAs, PCs running Windows, a Smart Client like Microsoft Office, or a Web browser on any operating system.

- ✔ Servers in .NET usually run Windows Server and SQL Server. The server platform is much less flexible than the client platform in the .NET world. Other options are available, too, such as the Oracle database. Sometimes, servers like BizTalk or SharePoint Services are used. Generally, servers provide services. Makes sense!

- ✔ In the middle are XML Web services or other connectivity. XML Web services represent a cross-platform strategy to get information from servers to clients, clients to other clients, or even among the services themselves.

The developer tools represented in Figure 3-1 are Visual Basic and Visual Studio. Visual Basic is the language, and Visual Studio is the tool. The third piece of the puzzle is the plan — the project type. The plan is the focus of this chapter.

At the top of Figure 3-2, you can see all the structures that make up the developer tools represented in Figure 3-1. The focus of this book, VB (Visual Basic) is way up in the upper-left corner.

How VB interacts with the other parts of the diagram is very important, too — that's what your software does. Your program will use the services provided by the .NET Framework via the tools in the language. This interaction is the key to everything — it is where you need to focus your planning. How do you take advantage of the interaction of the framework's pieces? That's what you design for.

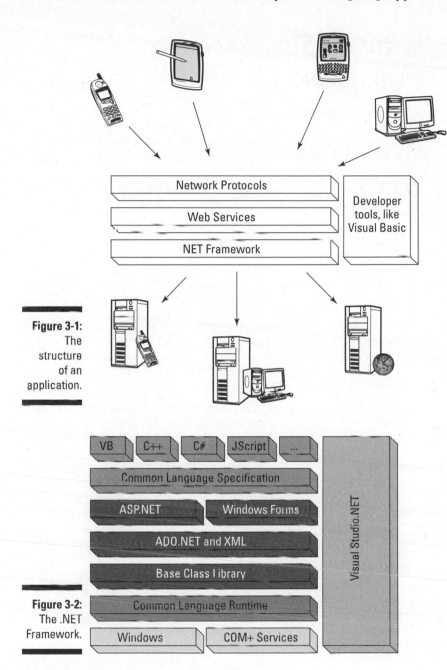

Figure 3-1:
The
structure
of an
application.

Figure 3-2:
The .NET
Framework.

Before you get to the plan, you need to know what the .NET Framework can do for you as a part of Visual Basic. One of the hardest parts of planning software is knowing what your program needs to do, and what is done for you by the services in the .NET Framework. In the next few sections, I explain what the .NET Framework can do for you.

Getting to the operating system

The primary function of the core of the .NET Framework is the Base Class Library (BCL), which provides access to the functions of the operating system and services like graphics and databases. A lot of auxiliary pieces of the framework cover other things, but getting to the operating system is the big sell for Visual Basic. Why? Visual Basic programmers used to have to jump through hoops to get to these services.

The path to the Windows operating system from Visual Basic is long and winding. The My object is the shortcut to that path. It is also a fantastic example of how the .NET Framework can help you, the VB programmer, get the job done.

The My object gives you access to the computer through the eyes of the operating system. The My.Computer object allows your program to easily interact with all the computer parts, such as

- Keyboard and mouse
- Printers
- Audio and video
- Clipboard
- Clock
- File system

Some of the common tasks that can be performed easily with the My object include

- Uploading and downloading a file
- Reading from, writing to, and clearing the Clipboard
- Controlling the computer's connection to the Internet

These tasks are fairly difficult in most business languages, but are made easier in Visual Basic 2008 using the .NET Framework.

Furthermore, you find two more primary objects in the My collection. The My.Application object helps your programs learn about the environment in which they are running. The My.User object helps you gather information about the user who's logged in to the computer, such as his or her name and e-mail address.

Look for the My object icon throughout the book for tips on making your development easier with the My object.

Integrating servers and services

In Figure 3-2, four boxes are in the middle section — two are user-interface oriented and two are service oriented. ASP.NET and Windows Forms are user-interface oriented, and I cover those in the next section. ADO.NET and other components in the BCL are important, in part because they help you to integrate servers like databases and services like BizTalk.

ADO.NET covers the primary server that you will want to integrate — a data server. Databases, like Microsoft SQL Server 2005, represent the most common kind of interaction for Visual Basic programs. Business programs tend to need to get information from user to user, and that information is often stored in databases.

ADO.NET allows you to take data from the database, show it to users, accept their manipulation of that data, and update the database without a lot of wiring code. By that, I mean you can concern yourself with building the business logic of your application, and not with how the database connection itself works. I cover database connections and ADO.NET in Chapter 15.

You find more types of servers than database servers. Enabling you to connect to those servers without writing piping code is part of the job of the Base Class Libraries. Some of the prebuilt plumbing provided by the BCL includes the following:

- ✔ **Enterprise Services:** Tools needed by very large applications, like transactions and activation, provided by the Component Service.

- ✔ **Input Output (IO):** Access to the file system, drives, and storage on servers of various operating systems. I cover IO in Chapter 16.

- ✔ **Messaging:** Use of the Queuing service in Windows. (Not instant messaging, I should add — that is different!) This kind of messaging is used by applications to get messages back and forth about data and user interaction.

- ✔ **Management:** Access to the Windows Management Instrumentation services, which give you an idea of the health of the server.
- ✔ **Net:** The network and Internet. All Web sites and e-mail servers are accessible thanks to the Net collection in the BCL. I cover Net in Chapter 17.
- ✔ **Drawing:** Making decent art is tough, and the BCL gives you that power by simplifying the set of Windows graphics tools known as GDI+. I cover drawing in Chapter 18.

Interacting with the user

The other two boxes in the middle section of Figure 3-2 are ASP.NET and Windows Forms. ASP.NET and Windows Forms help you the most of any of these by enabling interaction with the user.

I mention previously that you find three parts of development with Visual Basic. The first is the language, Visual Basic itself. The second is the tool Visual Studio 2008, which I discuss in Chapter 2.

The third and final piece to this puzzle is the project type or platform, and that is controlled by the ASP.NET or Windows Forms. ASP.NET has all the bits for Web pages, mobile Web, and XML Web services. Windows Forms has all the bits for Windows applications, console applications, and smart device applications.

For more information on interacting with the user, see Chapters 4 and 5.

Comparing Abstract Concepts with the Real World

You spend a tremendous amount of your time reading about abstract and concrete concepts when working in .NET. Though it isn't as common in this book, when you search for articles or documentation on the Web, you'll read a lot about *classes* and *objects*.

Classes

Classes are a philosophical construct. They are vessels that can be filled with things. They are frameworks, skeletons awaiting their flesh. They are a series of pots with dirt, waiting for plants. They are conceptual, not concrete.

A class is a definition of a thing, with a list of what can be done to it, what is known about it, and what it can do. Without being "instantiated" into an "instance of the class," a class is just a series of holding pens for animals that aren't there.

Objects

Objects are concrete items that exist in your application. They are what classes become when they grow up. When you instantiate a class, the class goes and gets dressed, and it becomes an object.

When you define something in an application, you are making a class. "A House has a Color and a FrontDoor" would be an example of a class. It is just the definition. An *instance* of the House class would occur when you instantiate that class and it fills with data, and becomes your house, the MyHouse object. You can build as many houses as you want from the blueprint that is the class, because each one has its own space in memory where it stores its own information, called its *state*.

I cover developing classes in Chapter 6, but classes and objects are discussed throughout the book and throughout the language. Everything in .NET is an object, fleshed out by the existence of the application itself. When Microsoft developed the objects, though, they were just classes!

Planning for a Project Using the Project Lifecycle

Preparation to create a new project consists of two distinct stages, planning and design. *Planning* consists of defining the project and gathering the requirements. *Design* consists of writing down the screens and logic that will fulfill the requirements, and figuring out how to test to see whether they are right.

Rather than just write about how to follow this prescription, I walk you through the planning and design of a project that you build in Part II. The sample project is a program that calculates dates. What the Date Calculator program does and how it works are things that you figure out as part of the project development lifecycle.

The project lifecycle is a process that is best shown on the Gantt Chart in Figure 3-3.

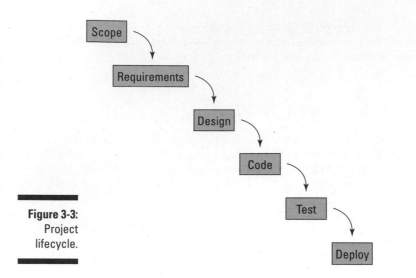

Projects should be completed using this process. If you have been coding in Visual Basic for a while, you might have noticed that a lot of programmers of other languages are sometimes disdainful of Visual Basic. Part of the reason is that it is so very easy to write programs without any planning with Visual Basic. Doing so is not a good thing.

I should tell you that this project lifecycle is just one of many design processes. You may hear a lot of industry terms thrown around, and these terms represent various angles on the same basic paradigm. Just remember that no matter what you call your development process, planning and design are good things.

To write a decent application, you must first have a plan. Even though steps may overlap, each step should be completed. Even in small projects, an hour spent in design is worth the time. The bugs that you discover while planning are about ten times cheaper in terms of time than the bugs you find and squash in development and testing.

As you're going through the steps in the project development lifecycle (refer to Figure 3-3), you'll find that the first three steps raise questions that you need to answer to figure out the requirements of your project. When planning the application that you are creating in Part II, the questions might look something like this:

- ✔ **Scope:** Does the date calculator need any other calculation capabilities? What platform is it for? Does it need to be international?

- ✔ **Requirements:** Exactly what is the program calculating? How will the user enter dates? What results does the user expect?

✔ **Design:** How will the program calculate the dates? What user-interface elements will best show the data? What will trigger the application to calculate? How will the screen look?

Scoping out the system

Scope is the most important part of the design process because it defines exactly what the application will do. If someone asks you what your application does, you should be able to tell him or her while standing on one foot. Maybe more importantly, the scope defines what your application won't do. The term "out of scope" refers to this.

Try writing the definition of the application in 101 words or less. Doing so enables you to keep the scope short because you are thinking about the meaning of every word.

For the Date Calculator, a 101-word scope might be a little much, because the system is fairly simple. Bullet lists are convenient ways to write scopes:

✔ The Date Calculator is an application that finds differences between two U.S. dates.

✔ It runs on a Web page or Windows computer, or as a function in any kind of application.

This scope defines the application. When a user says that he or she expects that the Date Calculator would add two numbers because it is a calculator, you can reply that the feature was out of scope. If this is an expected requirement, the scope must be altered, which takes you back to the drawing board in the planning stages.

Gathering requirements

Requirements are the specific rules that govern the application. Think of requirements as the problems that must be solved in the design step of the project lifecycle. For the Date Calculator, these problems are fairly straightforward:

✔ The Date Calculator accepts a U.S. date startDate and an integer span, and returns the date endDate that is span number of days from startDate.

✔ The Date Calculator also may accept two U.S. dates startDate and endDate and return the number of days between the two dates as an integer span.

✔ The Date Calculator must be able to be implemented as:

- A Windows application, as an executable file

- A Web application, run in a client/server environment

- A reusable component in Windows

- An XML Web service

✔ If possible, the previous five calculations will be stored by the application and saved from use to use.

"If possible" requirements are surprisingly common. Basically, they consist of features that may or may not fit into the budget. Leave those for last.

I have collected all the information that I need to describe the functionality of the application. This information should be placed in a document, appropriately enough called a *requirements document*. This document can be a Word file, a text file, a piece of notebook paper, or a cocktail napkin. Creating and using a requirements document helps ensure that the finished application does what it is supposed to do.

Each of the points of the requirements document must be covered by a point in the next stage, the design document. You may want to number the points in your requirements document and in your design document to ensure that each requirement has a related design.

When the requirements are settled, it is time to describe the software from a technical perspective: the end of the design phase. In the following section, I cover the steps: drawing screens and defining logic.

Designing the Date Calculator

The steps at the bottom of the project development lifecycle chart are more technical topics. The design, code, test, and deploy steps are usually handled by the developers rather than the business analysts in a large development shop. If you are working alone, you get to do it all!

You should describe software carefully and thoroughly so that you could hand the document to an intern to code. For the Date Calculator, you need to look at three primary points. Dividing the effort into these logical sections makes your life easier when building most software:

✔ Design your data.

✔ Draw your user interface.

✔ Diagram the connections between the business layer and the data layer.

Understanding n-tier design

An *n-tier system* is one that has the presentation layer, business logic, and data access physically running on different platforms, with at least one single layer divided among those platforms. Web applications are perfect for n-tier architecture, because the presentation layer is divided between the Web browser and Web server, and the business and data components can be divided — much like a client/server application — among an Object Request Broker and a Database Management System.

When designing a large system, I like to define the database first, known as the Data Layer. Then I usually build the User Interface, or the Presentation Layer. Finally, I tie the two together, using the Business Logic Layer.

The benefit to an n-tier system is twofold. The modularity of a good n-tier design allows the removal or replacement of a particular component without affecting the functionality of the rest of the application. Also, separation of the business logic from the database allows load balancing, security, and general stability in highly available systems. The bottom line is that n-tier transactional systems are replacing the reams of COBOL code that run the world economy. If you want to have an impact, you need to understand n-tier systems.

Storing data

The Date Calculator stores the information that it collects and calculates. If you carefully read the requirements given in the "Gathering requirements" section, earlier in this chapter, you will note that only three values exist:

- ✔ The first date, startDate
- ✔ The second date, endDate
- ✔ The number of days between the startDate and endDate, span

You may also want to consider storing the following data:

- ✔ The date that the calculation was last run
- ✔ The user who last ran the Date Calculator program
- ✔ Some way to refer to the search

You can store these in one data entity, which you can call Calculations. Usually, these are described using a grid that looks like Figure 3-4. This diagram is an Entity Relationship (ER) diagram because, if more than one entity existed, the relationships would appear as lines between the grids. Databases are commonly shown in this way.

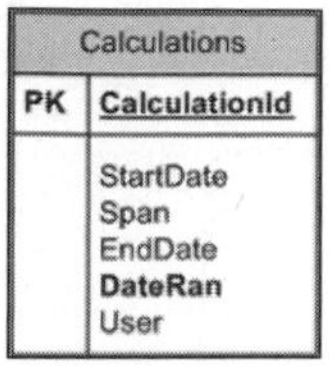

Figure 3-4:
The Entity
Relationship
diagram for
calculations.

Calculations	
PK	**CalculationId**
	StartDate
	Span
	EndDate
	DateRan
	User

By using the ER diagram, you can see the type of information that your application will be handling — a very useful endeavor. Three of these pieces of information, or *fields,* represent user information, and three of them represent system information. In the following section, I show you how to design a screen mockup that uses these fields appropriately.

Designing screens

Referring back to the "Gathering requirements" section, you can see that this application must be a multiplatform application. Of the four platforms that you need to develop, only two of them (Windows and Web Forms) have user interfaces, and they are pretty similar. You should be able to use the same user interface design for both of them.

Based on the requirements and the data design, you need to create three user-identifiable field controls and have some way to submit the information to the system. Then you need to create some type of control to handle the "last five" features.

My recommendation is to start with the field input and output. You will need three implementations of the fields. The simplest way to gather the user's input is to just use three text entry boxes for this, and label each text box appropriately.

This is where the user interaction parts of the Base Class Library come in. If you do a little digging in the documentation, you'll discover that both the ASP.NET and Windows Forms boxes hold a control that allows the user to pick a date from a calendar. This is where knowledge of what the system can do for you comes in handy. Many developers might build their own date chooser, not knowing that one was already available.

So knowing that, you need to use two date choosers, one text input box, and a button the user can click to have the program perform the calculation to determine the number of days between the two dates. The mockup of these components looks something like the window shown in Figure 3-5.

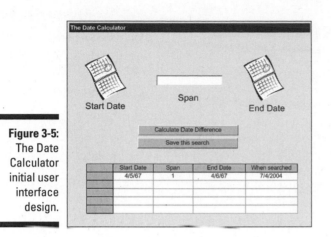

Figure 3-5:
The Date
Calculator
initial user
interface
design.

At this point, you might not know exactly how the calendars will work, so you can't create an accurate picture. But that's okay. You know what the calendars are going to do — let the user pick a date.

User interface design is sometimes a matter of experience. I can see that this design will work in both the Web and Windows worlds. That is not obvious to everyone. If you are not familiar with Web design and have an ASP.NET requirement, get a Web developer to help. Nothing is harder than trying to write a Windows application using the Web as a platform.

The second major requirement is the ability to save the last five searches. For example, you might choose to show this requirement in the design as an expandable grid that appears to show the user what searches had been saved. This breaks into both ADO.NET and the user interface controls. In ADO.NET, you can collect the last five searches for this user by asking the database for them, and both Windows and Web Forms have a Data Grid viewer.

Therefore, you need a grid that will show the user the starting date, ending date, span, and date searched, and that will allow the user to click a saved search and view it. This grid can just be added to the bottom of the screen, as shown in Figure 3-6.

You use software, and you know what interfaces you like and don't like. Strive to design interfaces that you would like to use. Take popular software, such as Windows, Office, Quicken, and so on, and design your own apps that way. Remember, as proven several years ago, you can't patent look and feel!

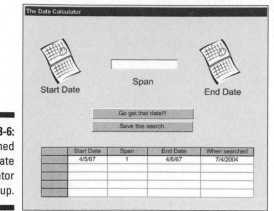

Figure 3-6:
The finished
Date
Calculator
mockup.

Defining logic

So now you know what the software is storing and how it will look to the user. The last step is to connect the user interface and the data. This is usually called the Business Logic Layer, and sometimes it is separated from the rest of the application and put on a totally different machine.

You will find that in the world of Windows development, it is best to just figure out everything that a user can do in the application, and then write pseudocode that describes that functionality.

Pseudocode is language-neutral instructions that describe functionality. Think of it as writing your program's code in English. The goal is to create a line-by-line description of what a given user interaction is supposed to do so that if someone else happens to code it, or figure it out after you are gone, that person can see what you wanted to accomplish. Most methodologies call these *use cases, user stories,* or *scenarios.*

A limited number of user actions are in this application, and the application can do a limited number of things. Here is a breakdown, and what your design would look like:

✔ **Application load:**

• Set the `startDate` and `endDate` equal to the current date and leave `span` empty.

• The assumption is that the user wants to search for the numbers of days between two given dates.

• Load up the Saved Search grid from the data source, listing saved searches in the inverse order of date and time saved.

✔ **When the user clicks the Calculate Date Difference button:**

- If a value is in the `startDate` and `span` fields, add the `span` number of days to the `startDate` and display the calculated date in the `endDate` field.

- If a value is in `startDate` and `endDate`, put the difference in days between the two dates in the `span` field.

- If a value is in all three fields, assume that the user wants to calculate the `span`.

  Assumptions kill software projects. Never make an assumption in the design, like I just did. Always ask the user what he or she wants. I just made this assumption for the sake of simplifying the example.

✔ **Save this search:**

- Add the `startDate`, `endDate`, `span`, current date and time, and current user to the data storage fields.

- Refresh the grid with the new search, keeping the newest search on the top.

✔ **When the user clicks a search in the grid:**

- Load up the `startDate`, `endDate`, and `span` values into the fields.

- Replace the current values in the `startDate`, `endDate`, and `span` fields with the values from the search.

  Everything else remains the same!

That should about cover the functionality that the user expects from the application, and it meets all the requirements. The system is designed!

Writing a test plan

Before you start coding, write a test plan. It is simple and will make sure that you have hit all the important parts of your design. The steps are simple:

1. **Review the requirement that a particular design point supports.**

   For instance, the Date Calculator application has the requirement that the user can enter a starting date, ending date, and a span.

2. **List the design point in question.**

   The Date Calculator interface must have controls that accept data entry from the user.

3. **Describe what will be needed to make sure that the design point works.**

   You make sure that the user enters dates by focusing the entry using a Calendar control. And what about the span? It needs to be an integer!

4. Describe what could happen to make the design point break or cause an error.

One question you need to ask in the test plan is "What happens if the user enters a noninteger in the span field?" Of course, under normal circumstances, such an entry will cause an error of some kind.

You might need to alter your design to make sure that the user can enter only a number. Does a text box allow that? If you do a quick Google search, you find that such a text box exists for Windows, but not for the Web. For more in-depth information about how Visual Basic can help you validate user input, see Chapters 4 and 5.

Just make sure to have a written test plan that you can give to a third party to make sure that your application does what you expect. It is best for you not to test your own application. You should either have another person work through the plan or use an automated test system like NUnit or Microsoft Team System.

Sticking to the plan

Now that you've created the plan, the trick is to follow it. The following pointers may help you stick to the plan:

- **Don't reinvent the wheel.** Look for solutions in similar applications or sample applications before you rewrite something.

- **Research and read the documentation.** Don't be a power user, an "I'll figure it out myself" kind of person. The .NET Framework is just too big. Learn how to use the docs — I discuss them in Chapter 2.

- **Code the way you want to see the application look.** Don't give up. If you think you should be able to do something, keep digging until you see how it is done. If it isn't worth it, you can redesign it.

- **Write less code.** Use the user-interface tools that Visual Studio gives you. Don't give in to the code snobs who think you should hand-code everything.

- **Be consistent.** Use the same names as you did in your design. Decide what to call concepts. Don't use *x* to refer to a number.

Part II
Building Applications with VB 2008

The 5th Wave   By Rich Tennant

"Did you click 'HELP' on the VB.NET menu bar recently? It's Mr. Gates. He wants to know if everything's all right."

In this part . . .

Visual Basic is about writing software, and, in Part II, you write programs for Windows and the Web. You start by creating a traditional Windows application, and you also build class libraries to go with it. Then you build a Web application and XML Web services.

Chapter 4

Building Windows Applications

*B*uilding a Windows Forms project with Visual Basic 2008 is a great way to start working with the language. You are familiar with Windows applications, such as Microsoft Word, which I'm using to write this book. When you are done reading this chapter, you might check your e-mail with Outlook Express or Groupwise. Every program that is used on a Microsoft Windows computer is a Windows application by definition, but they are not all developed by Microsoft. Some are developed by programmers using a tool such as Visual Studio 2008, using a language like Visual Basic 2008.

In this chapter, I take a look back at how the language has changed since Visual Basic 6.0. Then I cover the building blocks of Windows Forms — the collection of Windows Controls provided with the language. You also find out how to build your first application — the Date Calculator you design in Chapter 3. Finally, I go over adding the features your users will expect to find to your Windows Forms applications — features such as text entry, menus, status bars, and ToolTips.

A Quick Look Back at Visual Basic

When you think about Visual Basic, you probably also think about Microsoft Windows applications. For 15 years, developers have used the Visual Basic program's Ruby Forms engine (shown in Figure 4-1) to write common business applications. When a program was defined as a VB program, it was, by default, a Windows application.

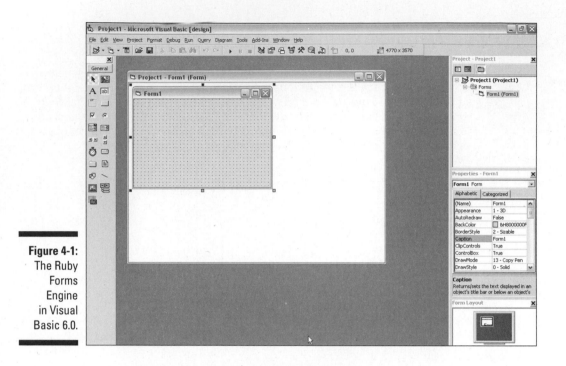

But the scope and versatility of Visual Basic grew with the introduction of Visual Basic.NET. (Refer to Chapter 1 for in-depth information about this transformation.) Visual Basic.NET is a language, just like Java, COBOL, or C++, that you can use to write any kind of application that is supported by an API (Application Programming Interface). Now when a program is defined as a Visual Basic program, you must ask, "What kind of program? Is it a Windows application? A Web site? A Windows service or XML Web Service?"

The Windows application — now called a Windows Forms application — is far from dead. Although Web applications are clearly growing in popularity, the rich environment of a Windows application is not only familiar but also hard to beat for many uses. In this chapter, you discover how to use the still-powerful tool, Visual Studio, to build a Windows Forms application. Specifically, I show you the kinds of elements that Microsoft provides, how to structure a Windows Forms application in VB 2008, and details beneath the surface of Windows Forms.

Windows Forms has many more features than I can cover here in this one chapter. Over 60 Windows Forms controls are built into Visual Studio 2008, and you can also very simply create your own. Visual Basic is a powerful language in its own right, and combining it with the controls you find in Windows Forms brings almost complete control over the user experience.

Discovering Windows Controls

Over the years, a standard way to build Windows applications has developed because users expect applications to work in a certain way. Menus, toolbars, status bars, and cursors have all become standard equipment. As shown in Figure 4-2, the calculator has a title bar, text boxes, and a button, as well as text on the screen. All of these standard Windows interfaces are developed using controls provided to you by the Toolbox in Visual Studio 2008.

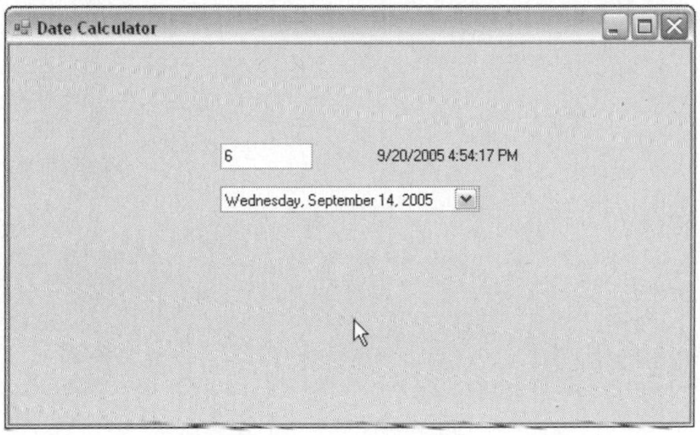

Figure 4-2:
The Date
Calculator
as a
Windows
application.

To make using standard Windows features easier, Visual Studio includes all of them as standard equipment for the developer, too. These pieces of standard equipment are called controls. *Controls* are preprogrammed pieces of user interface code that handle a lot of the plumbing for you, the Visual Basic programmer. You can use them in your Windows Forms application to provide the features your users want.

The word *control* is generic and often overused — even by Microsoft. Generally, though, I use this term to refer to the code that makes a feature you recognize (such as a text box or a button) work the way you expect.

Using controls is easy. In the following sections, you find out how to do the following:

- ✔ **Position a control** by dragging it from the Toolbox onto the form.
- ✔ **Write code for a control** by double-clicking it in the form, which takes you into Code View.
- ✔ **Change the properties of a control** by clicking it and changing values in the Properties window. For more details on changing properties of a control, see the section "Adding Features to Windows Forms," later in this chapter.

The power of using Visual Basic.NET to build Windows Forms is in the controls. Table 4-1 shows you some common form controls and their uses.

Table 4-1	Some Form Controls	
Control	**Toolbox Icon**	**Uses**
Label		Displays text on the screen that isn't editable by the user
TextBox		Accepts basic text input from the user
RichTextBox		Offers word processing types of functionality such as bold and italics
Button		Causes the application to perform a predefined task
DataGridView		Displays an editable table on a form
DateTime Picker		Allows the user to select a date from a calendar
TabControl		Provides user-interface navigation, along with other tools such as buttons and tree views
MenuStrip		Displays a menu bar, as you would find in Word or Outlook
ToolStrip		Offers Office-type toolbar functionality, including open/save and cut/copy/paste
PrintDialog		Gives users easy access to printing
ErrorProvider		Communicates input problems to users
WebBrowser		Includes a browser right in your application
DomainUpDown		Allows users to select from a list

Making a Windows Application

A good place to start building an application is with a user input form (because that's what a VB programmer does most often), and the following steps lead you through that process. The example I use is a Date Calculator that accepts input (a date) from the user and then returns a calculated value (a future date) based on that input. Follow these steps to make a new Windows application:

1. **Open Visual Studio 2008 and click the New Project button to access the New Project dialog box.**

   No matter what kind of VB application you want to make, you begin at the New Project dialog box, shown in Figure 4-3.

2. **Select Windows as the Visual Basic project type and select the Windows Forms Application template.**

3. **Enter an appropriate project name in the Name and Solution Name text boxes, and click the OK button.**

   I named my application DateCalc and then put it in a solution name called Chapter 4, because I build a similar application for Chapters 5, 6, and 7.

   Visual Studio generates a new project for you, including a new form (`Form1.vb`) and the MyProject folder.

   At this point, Visual Studio does a bunch of work for you. Initially, it seems as though a form (`Form1.vb`) and a Project file (`MyProject`) are created, but actually much more is accomplished. Visual Studio creates the following:

- **A References folder** to hold parts of the framework that you will be using for this project.

- **A bin folder** to hold the finished program and any components.

- **An obj folder** to hold any resources specific to the application.

- **The MyProject folder** to hold configuration files. You can edit this folder by double-clicking it in the Solution Explorer. Visual Studio provides you with a tabbed form to use to edit the various configuration details, as shown in Figure 4-4.

4. **Rename the default form (`Form1.vb`) by right-clicking it in the Solution Explorer and choosing Rename from the context menu.**

   I named the form `DateCalc` in the sample application. In your programs, name the forms appropriately so that your projects are somewhat self-documenting. After you rename the file, Visual Studio prompts you to rename all referencing objects. Go ahead and let it.

5. **Resize the default form by clicking the handle in the lower-right corner of the form in the designer and dragging it to a new position.**

   In this step, design starts to become important. If you don't know how many controls are going in the form, you don't know what size to make it. Although you can always resize it later, it is much easier to just know what you plan to put in there! (I cover the design of the Date Calculator in Chapter 3.)

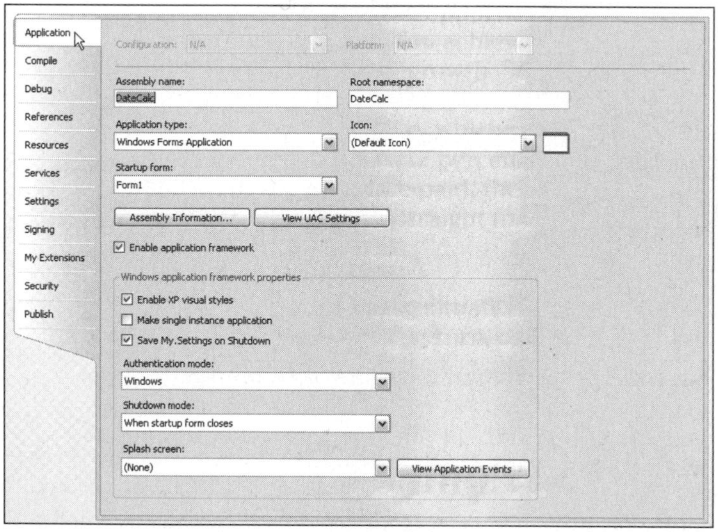

Figure 4-4:
The MyProject configuration form.

6. **Drag controls from the Windows Forms toolbar onto the renamed default form.**

   You can add controls such as the `TextBox` or a `MenuBar` to your forms by simply dragging them from the Windows Forms Toolbox to the form. The type, number, and location of the controls you add to your form define its look and eventual function. When you drag controls to your form, the controls assume the default properties that Visual Studio supplies. Specifically, the name of the instance of your control is set to the name given to that type of control followed by a number. For example, `Label1` is for a `Label` control, or `DateTimePicker1` is for a `DateTimePicker` control.

   I used a `DateTimePicker` control as one of the primary controls on the form. Adding this control enables users to pick the starting date.

   You also need to add a `Label` control to show the results of the operation. A `Label` control can be preset now, at design time, and left static. Or it can be modified by your code, at runtime, to show the results of an operation.

   There are controls, and there are instances of controls. The term *control* applies to a `DateTimePicker`. After you drag a control onto your form, it becomes an instance of the control, referred to by a reference name. Default reference names are the type name followed by a number in sequence.

7. **After all the appropriate controls have been added, right-click each one and press F4 to open the Properties window, where you can change each default name to something memorable.**

   I name my `DateTimePicker` control `DateChooser` and my `Label` control `NextWeek` because that's what it will show when the user selects a date.

   Leaving your controls' properties set to the default values (for Name and Content Text) is a bad idea. If you don't reset the values to something more logical, you probably won't remember what controls you're working with when you see the default values in Code View.

   You can also change the Text value of the form to show something nice in the title bar of the application. I used *Date Calculator.*

8. **Save the project by clicking the Save button.**

At this point, you should have a form that looks about how you want it to look when it runs. The form in my sample application looks like Figure 4-5. Your form might look a little different from mine, and that's okay. Next, you need to add some business logic to the form so that it actually does something.

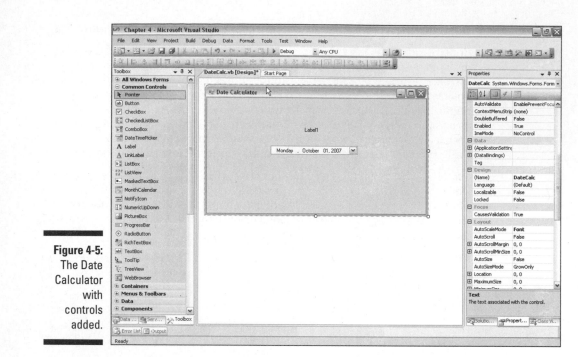

Figure 4-5:
The Date
Calculator
with
controls
added.

Adding Functionality to a Windows Form

As with most other Integrated Development Environments (IDEs), Visual Studio 2008 separates the look of the forms you are creating from the functionality behind them. When you assign the controls a meaningful name, you give yourself a way to refer to those controls from code. Each control has predefined functionality that you can access from the code.

You can add VB 2008 code to controls in Code View. You can get to the Code View window in several ways, but the easiest way is to double-click a control. Doing so generates an event handler for that control's default event and switches the interface to Code View. For example, double-clicking a command button takes you to the button's click event in Code View.

Event handlers are special methods that are run when a particular event occurs, like a button being clicked or a timer reaching its assigned time.

To get started entering the business logic for the controls on your form, follow these steps:

1. **Double-click a control to create its event handler and go to Code View.**

   Controls in a Windows application have to do more than look good; they must also do something in response to a user interaction, or an *event*. Visual Studio helps you easily add functionality to your controls. When you double-click a control, Visual Studio does two things: It creates the definition for the code that runs when the default event occurs — such as a value changing or a button being clicked — and it adds some linking code (which can view in the Windows Forms Designer Generated Code section) that links the event itself with the code that needs to run.

   I started with the `DateTimePicker` that I named `DateChooser`. Double-clicking this control creates a `ValueChanged` event handler. That is, the code in the event handler is run when the value in the control is changed for whatever reason (usually by the user). The subroutine template for the event handler looks like this:

   ```
   Public Class DateCalc

       Private Sub DateChooser_ValueChanged(ByVal sender As System.Object,
               ByVal e As System.EventArgs) Handles DateChooser.ValueChanged

       End Sub

   End Class
   ```

2. **Add code to the event handler to perform appropriate functions.**

   All the magic is based in those few simple words. Aside from the functionality built into the controls themselves, all the functionality of every application that you write will be in one event handler or another.

   For the Date Calculator, you need a piece of code that will fulfill the requirement from Chapter 3 — that is, accept the date, add a value, and then display the result. With the .NET Framework, you can do all of that with one line of code. Between the line beginning with `Private` and the line beginning with `End`, enter the following:

   ```
   NextWeek.Text = DateChooser.Value.AddDays(7)).ToString()
   ```

Here's a breakdown of that line of code:

- ✔ On the left of the equal sign is the `Text` property of the `NextWeek` object, which is a `Label` control. This means that you are setting the text of a label equal to something.

- ✔ On the right side of the equal sign is the `DateChooser` object. You are adding something to its value — which would be the date that the user has set. In this case, you are adding seven days and then converting it to a string.

So the finished code looks something like that shown in Figure 4-6. Visual Studio inserts a lot of code for you, and you add the important functional code that makes everything perform to the functional requirements. Click the Start Debugging button, shown in Figure 4-6, or press F5 to run your new application.

Pick a date, and the label will change from a blank value to display a date that is one week from the date you selected. It's a neat toy, but it doesn't do too much for the user. Next, I show you how to add a few features to the program.

Adding Features to Windows Forms

To meet the functional requirements of your applications, you need features. The more complex the feature request, the more complex the code has to be. Take the current application, the Date Calculator, for example. All inputs have to be variable for the calculations to be truly useful. Currently, only the starting date is variable. You need to change this situation if you want to add functionality and features.

Start Debugging button

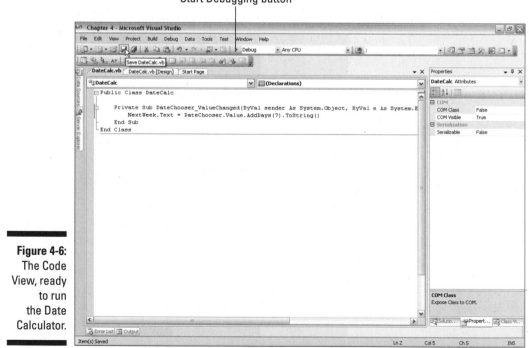

Figure 4-6:
The Code View, ready to run the Date Calculator.

Managing text input with the TextBox

Clearly, the number of days (now set at seven) that the Date Calculator uses to calculate the new date should be variable. Follow these steps to accept input from the user, specifically the period in number of days:

1. **Add a** TextBox **control to the form.**

   Change the name of the TextBox control to DateNumber using the Properties window. This text box is the control where the user enters the number of days to add to the selected date.

2. **Align the text box with other objects on the form.**

   Drag the text box around until the left side aligns with the left side of the date DatePicker — use the guidelines to help make that alignment, as shown in Figure 4-7.

You can also use the Align feature on the Format menu. This feature makes laying out your forms the way you want them a lot easier by giving you options such as Align All Controls Center and Even Spacing Between Controls.

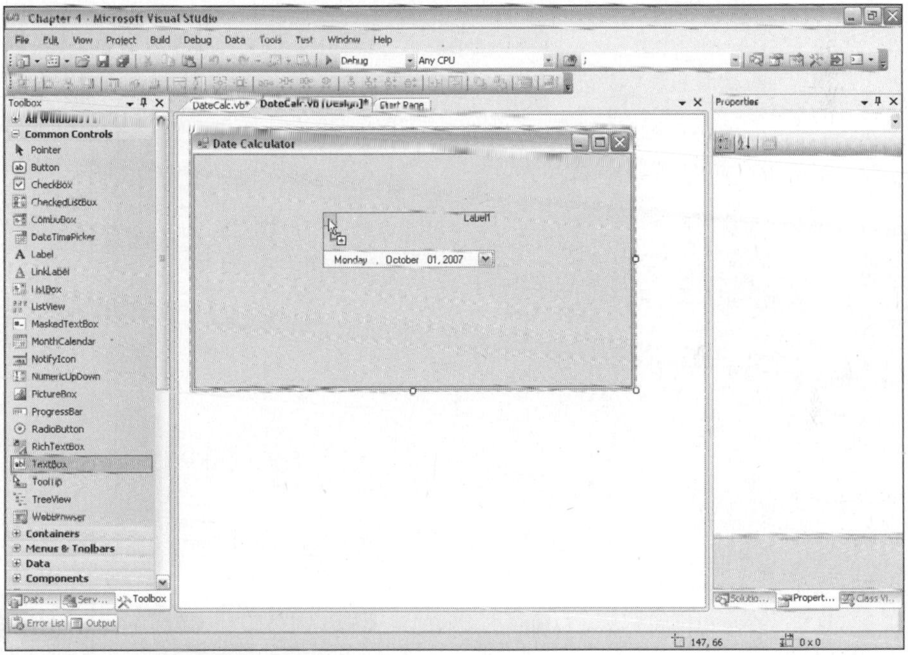

Figure 4-7:
Guidelines
that help
you line
up your
controls.

TIP

At this point, you should have two tabs at the top of the designer, `Date Calculator.vb [Design]` and `DateCalculator.vb`. The Design tab represents the form designer, which should be selected now. The other tab represents the Code View, which you opened before by double-clicking a control.

You need a default value for the number of days. If the user doesn't add anything in the text box, the application must be able to set the interval value to something. For now, define a new variable in the Code View. Under the `Inherits` class definition, add a dimension statement like the following:

```
Dim DateInterval As Integer = 7
```

Then replace the body of the `DateChooser_ValueChanged` event handler with the following:

```
Private Sub DateChooser_ValueChanged(ByVal sender As System.Object,
ByVal e As System.EventArgs) Handles DateChooser.ValueChanged
   If DateNumber.Text.Length > 0 Then
      DateInterval = CInt(DateNumber.Text)
   End If
   NextWeek.Text = DateChooser.Value.AddDays(DateInterval).ToString()
End Sub
```

What have you done here? You added a text box that allows a user to override the default number of days you are calculating from the date in the date chooser. Click the Start button to enter debug mode again and give it a try. You see something like the calculator shown in Figure 4-8.

Date Calculator	— □ ✕
5	10/22/2007 3:33:22 PM
Wednesday, October 17, 2007 ▾	

Figure 4-8:
The Date
Calculator
so far.

You now have an application that does the following:

✔ Accepts a starting date from the user or uses a default date

   ✔ Accepts a span (number) of days from the user or uses a default number
      of days

   ✔ Calculates and displays the date that falls the entered span of days from
      the input date

Next, you just need to add a few of the features that users will expect of a
Windows application, and you'll just about be done.

Communicating with the user using the status strip

Now that you have the base functionality of the Date Calculator, you need to
add those features that users expect of a Windows application. Menus, status
strips, and mouseover ToolTips are part of the Windows experience. Visual
Studio 2008 supports all of these and more.

As I write this chapter using Microsoft Word 2007, a fairly complex status
strip appears at the bottom of the window, as shown in Figure 4-9. It shows
the current page, the section, the line and column, and what features I have
active, such as recording of macros or tracking changes.

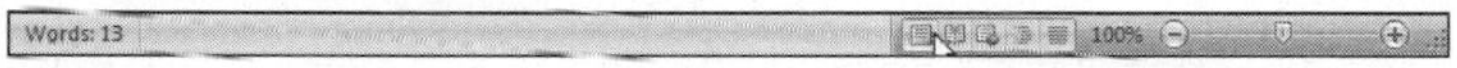

Figure 4-9:
The status
strip in
Microsoft
Word.

This status strip is another control provided by the team that developed
Visual Studio. Find the StatusStrip control in the Toolbox and drag it onto
the Date Calculator form, as shown in Figure 4-10. Rename it to something
like mainStatusStrip.

The StatusStrip is just a container for stuff. You can add stuff to the bar as
needed from the Properties window, in the property collection called Items. A
shortcut is available for adding these properties, in the form of a Smart Tag
(see Figure 4-10).

Also, note the Edit Items link in the Properties window. Clicking this link
opens the Items Collection Editor dialog box, as shown in Figure 4-11.

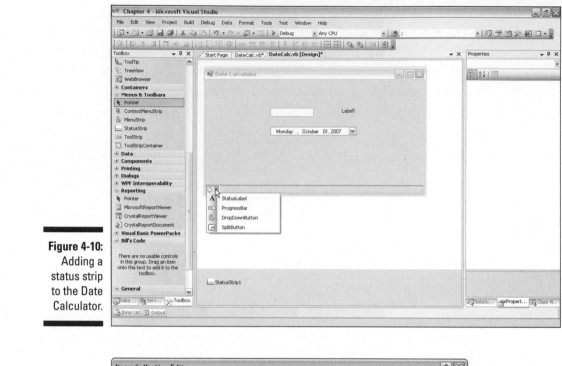

Figure 4-10:
Adding a
status strip
to the Date
Calculator.

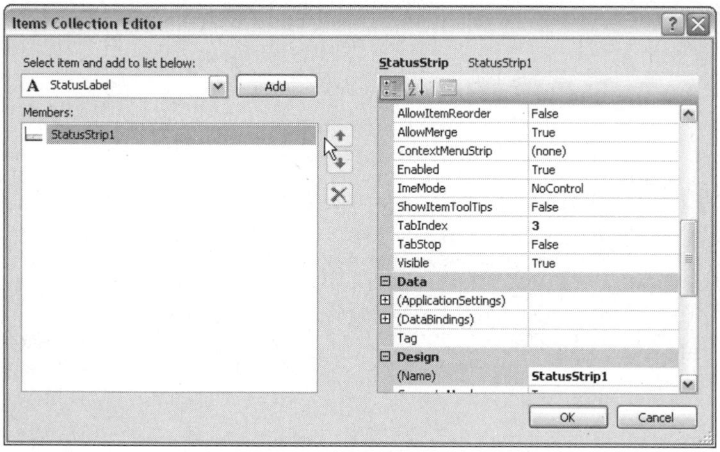

Figure 4-11:
The Items
Collection
Editor
dialog box.

The Items Collection Editor dialog box is a tool that will become very familiar — it is common throughout Visual Studio as a tool to edit items in collections. Next, you add some reference items to the StatusStrip just placed on the form.

1. **To add an item, click the Add button.**

   The instance will appear to the left, in the Members window, and the properties will appear to the right, in the Properties window.

2. **Add two** StatusLabels**, and name them** datePanel **and** userPanel**.**

3. **In the Properties window, set the Spring property to True.**

4. **Click the OK button to close the Items Collection Editor dialog box.**

To do something with these new members of your StatusStrip, you need to set that text value and other properties programmatically, when the form loads. You can do that in another event handler, called Form_Load. To edit the Form_Load event handler, double-click the form.

The Form_Load event handler is one of the first things to run when a new form is brought onto the screen.

In this type of single-form application, the Form_Load event handler will be close enough to the first code that runs that all your setup code should go here. Because you want to set up the StatusStrip instance when the form loads, you add the following code to that event handler:

```
Private Sub DateCalc_Load(ByVal sender As System.Object, _ ByVal e As
            System.EventArgs)
Handles MyBase.Load
    datePanel.Text = System.DateTime.Now.ToShortDateString()
    userPanel.Text = My.User.Name
End Sub
```

Giving hints with the ToolTip control

The ToolTip control gives you the ability to add a different ToolTip to every control on a certain page and control them as a collection. You can assign a ToolTip object to any set of objects, but each individual object can only be associated with one ToolTip object. Note that you can change the individual ToolTip.

Because you have a ToolTip referenced on the form, you have access to a ToolTip property in each control on that form. Drag a ToolTip object onto the Date Calculator form, and note that a component appears in the Component Tray. Click the component and change the Name property to primaryToolTips.

Of controls and values . . .

Look at the `DateCalc_Load` subroutine in this chapter's application, and see whether you can find some higher truths. When you create a control, it is an instance of an object. The control knows it can have a text value, and the control knows where to show the value, but it doesn't know what that value is until you set it. You can set the value at *design time* (when the code is written), or you can set it at *runtime* (meaning when the code is executed). Run-time versus design-time variables are an important development consideration, as in the following examples:

- ✔ Setting text at design time is handled like I handled setting the text date interval. You can set the text in the designer, and then largely leave it alone. This is great for titles of forms, labels on radio buttons, and stuff like that.

- ✔ Setting run-time text depends on more than your whim as a developer — it is based on

the environment at the time the program is executed on the user's machine. In the example for the status strip, the date and the current value of the period are set as the two panels. The date is obviously a run-time decision because that value changes day by day. To handle run-time changes, you set the value as I did in the `Date Calc_Load` event handler.

- ✔ But why set form width at run time? Because the actual size of the form is another variable that you have little control over. Various preferences that the user can set in Windows can control the size of new forms, such as requiring that they open maximized. The `StatusStrip` itself changes with the form. The panels, because of their static nature, do not. Thus, you will need to calculate the width of the panels when an application loads, not when you build the form.

Now if you look at the Properties window for, say, the `DateNumber` text box, you find a new property, `ToolTip on primaryToolTips`, as shown in Figure 4-12. Select the property value, type **Enter the number of days here**, and then run the program. When you hover the mouse pointer over the text box, the famed ToolTip appears next to the pointer, as shown in Figure 4-13.

ToolTips are only one of many ways an application communicates with the user in real time.

Some controls come with extras

Tips and context menus can be dragged the designer from the Toolbox, and the erties can be set in the Properties window electing the objects in the Component Tray.

a look at the `ToolTip` object, for exam- The `ToolTip` object, as do many unob- ble objects in the Windows Forms world, des additional functionality not usually ble to a given set of controls. Unlike the `StatusStrip` object, which specializes in user ction, or the `StatusStrip` object,

which specializes in user information, the `ToolTip` control gives Windows Forms controls extra properties.

Extra properties added to an object? How is that possible? Polymorphism. Visual Basic.NET is an object-oriented language, and thus it has to adhere to four rules — objects must be inheritable, extensible, relatable, and polymorphic. Therefore, you can define an object that redefines the properties of another, if you wish.

Navigating with the MenuStrip control

Throughout the history of Windows application development software, nobody has come up with a decent way to deal with the development of menus. Visual Studio 2008 uses a draggable control as the core visual representation of the menu, as shown in Figure 4-14.

Drag a `MenuStrip` control anywhere on the form in Design View, as shown in Figure 4-14, and rename it to `mainMenu`. The form designer provides you with a Type Here prompt, which brings you to the key part of developing Windows Forms applications and software with accepted standards.

Have you noticed that almost every application you run in Windows has a menu bar that shows "File, Edit, View, Insert, Window, Help" or something of the sort, as shown in Figure 4-15? Nothing forces developers to make such a menu bar, but they do it because this menu configuration is an accepted standard.

To beef up your main menu according to the accepted standard, follow these steps:

1. **To add a File menu, type** File **(after adding the** `MenuStrip` **control), as shown in Figure 4-14.**

    A prompt appears to the right of and below the new menu item just added.

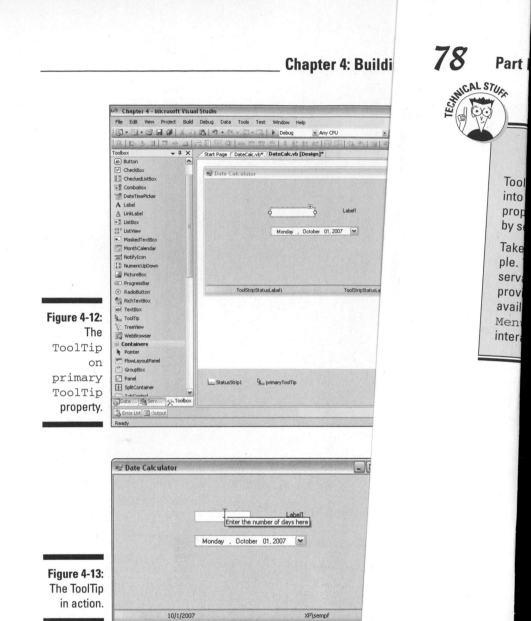

Figure 4-12:
The
`ToolTip`
on
primary
`ToolTip`
property.

Figure 4-13:
The ToolTip
in action.

Tool
into
prop
by s

Take
ple.
serva
provi
avail
Men
inter

2. **To add an Edit menu, click and type to the right of the last menu item added.**

   For this example though, just add an Exit option on the File menu.

   Notice that the MenuStrip object adds a component to the Component Tray at the bottom of the Design window, as shown in Figure 4-16. To access properties of the menu instance, you can click on the control instance rather than the menus at the top of the form.

3. **To add functional code to the menu, just click away from the menu; then go back and click the File menu to open the Exit item.**

   A lot of menu items have form-wide functionality, so you will make a lot of use of the Me object. Me is a useful Visual Basic alias that refers to the object that is currently the focus of the application. Double-click that item, and the already well-named item will create its own event handler.

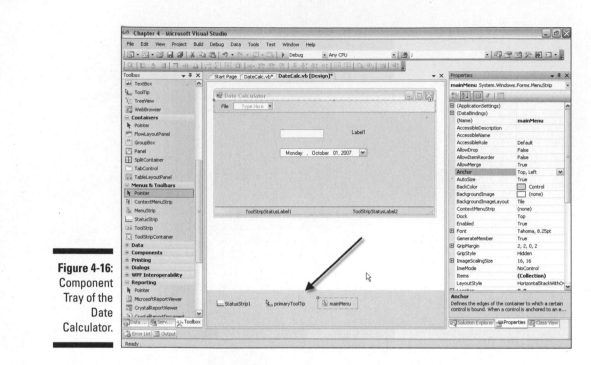

Figure 4-16:
Component
Tray of the
Date
Calculator.

4. **Double-click the Exit item and add the** `Me.Close()` **statement to the event handler for this item.**

This is the code's way of saying, "Run the close function of the container object" — in this case, the form — so that it closes the window when the menu item is selected.

Activating the right-click with the ContextMenuStrip

Another type of menu is the context menu, which is accessed by right-clicking a control in a running application.

You probably use context menus constantly, without even thinking about it. Right-clicking an image in a Web browser allows printing and saving. Right-clicking a scroll bar provides a Page Down and Page Up option. You can provide this functionality, like I did in the form shown in Figure 4-17, with the `ContextMenuStrip` object.

Like ToolTips, context menus are objects in the Component Tray, and they can be assigned certain properties. Like the `MenuStrip` object, you can assign a context menu to the `ContextMenuStrip` property of a form after using the neat little Menu Builder in the Design View.

Drag a `ContextMenuStrip` object from the Toolbox into the Component Tray and change the default name to `primaryContextMenu`. The `Context MenuStrip` builder appears in the form designer, and you can build it just as with the `MenuStrip`. Then, in the code, you can assign the property, just as with the `MenuStrip`. When you run the form, the `MenuStrip` appears in the upper-left corner, and the `ContextMenuStrip` appears when you right-click the form or other control. To determine what control gets what context menu, add a little code to the `Load` event of the form:

```
DateNumber.ContextMenuStrip = primaryContextMenu
```

You can use code like this to predefine a few context menus and assign them to certain user interface controls based on what options the user needs to see.

Chapter 5

Building Web Applications

*W*eb application programming has changed drastically since its origin in the '90s. But no matter how much programming characteristics may have changed, the applications still spring from a single concept: Based on a request from the Web application, a server passes data to a preexisting client (the Web browser), which then renders that data into an interface that the Web application user sees.

The addition of form elements and Common Gateway Interface (CGI) to the Web scene in 1993 boosted the Web servers' capacity to accept input from a user and return a processed response. Over the next 10 years, everything changed and remained the same. Currently, Web developers can use hundreds of preprocessing languages on dozens of platforms, but all these tools essentially use the CGI protocol to get information from the browser to the server and back again. ASP.NET — part of the .NET Framework — is the newest rendition of the original CGI protocol.

In this chapter about ASP.NET, I cover the difference between Windows and Web applications, and I tell you how the .NET Framework provides you with tools to simplify the difference for you as a developer. I explain how ASP.NET works and tell you about the problems that being disconnected (that is, not having a constant connection between the Web browser and the Web server) causes, specifically with the application issues of State and the reality of the PostBack.

You can build your first Web application — a Date Calculator, as designed in Chapter 3 — using Web tools and view it in a Web browser. And you find out a little about the immense power of ASP.NET through the details about hyperlinks, images, and the `HttpRequest` object.

Seeing How ASP.NET Works with Your Web App

ASP.NET is a preprocessor that works with Internet Information Server (IIS) 5.1 or higher to serve HTML to Web browsers. What you must remember — throughout this description of how ASP.NET works — is that it is essentially CGI for managing a request from browser to server and a response from server to browser. ASP.NET is built into the .NET Framework and is used to build Web Forms in Visual Studio 2008. For use on the Web, ASP.NET has several benefits over Windows Forms:

✔ **Clients using the Web Forms application don't need to have the .NET Framework installed** because information is returned to the browser making the request as only HTML — and not as some proprietary ASP format.

✔ **Clients don't even have to be using Microsoft Windows or Internet Explorer.** You can tell ASP.NET to render HTML that will work in any contemporary browser.

✔ **Complex processing or data access happens on the server,** which allows the browser to reside on a simpler workstation.

✔ **Code for an ASP.NET application is stored on the server.** Any change to an application has to be made in only one place.

Of course, ASP.NET has constraints as well:

✔ **The client computer must be able to access the server via a network connection.** This connection can come from a local network behind or through a firewall.

✔ **The server has little control over the software that the client uses to view the information.** Web Forms designs must remain simpler than those in Windows Forms so that the majority of users can get a satisfactory viewing experience.

✔ **Everything that the client needs to do is sent in clear text in the form of HTML.** The programmer must be very careful how forms are coded for stability and security reasons.

Two processes heavily differentiate the handling of Web Forms and Windows Forms. The first process is *PostBack,* which is how ASP.NET handles the CGI transmissions for transfer of information. The second process involves how ASP.NET manages the *State* of the application (that is, the way the server remembers what the client is doing inside your program).

PostBack: Not a returned package

The *PostBack* — a quasi-automated request from the browser to the server — is the magic behind the ASP.NET model. The PostBack communication process is how ASP.NET identifies a request for the same page in order to handle an in-page request by the user. Every user-initiated event — from typing in the initial URL, to clicking a button, to even changing a radio button selection — can cause a PostBack.

Visual Studio 2008 treats PostBacks as events, just like an event in a Windows Forms application. In Chapter 4, you find out about double-clicking a button to generate event handler code for that button. The process is much the same for Web Forms. If you are designing a Web Forms application and add a button, double-clicking that button in the Design View gets you event handler code, too. Although the coding process is very similar, the code that Visual Studio writes for you is different, and the amount of control you have is different.

The programmer really has no control over the way the browser makes requests to the server. If you have coded Web applications before — using ASP Classic or another preprocessor — the PostBack code that's automatically generated will feel very different. If you're coding your first Web application, using ASP.NET's automatic method will seem very easy. Either way, let Visual Studio do its thing and don't try to force the program to work the way you're used to. Like playing piano with a metronome, the framework that initially seems like a constraint will actually give you a lot of freedom.

A matter of State

Web applications differ from Windows applications in regard to managing the State of the application. The *State* of an application is characterized by what the application knows about itself at any given moment. For example, if you set a variable to a value in a Windows Forms application, the variable keeps that value until the application changes it or is closed (provided that the variable is declared in the program's Declarations section).

In a Web Forms application, however, the moment the server finishes rendering a page and sends it to the browser, the server promptly forgets any associated variable value until a request comes back from the client and the server looks up the State for that user. The Web Forms application itself has no State whatsoever unless the programmer specifically stores that variable somewhere.

Part of the power of ASP.NET is its capacity to save the application State in the server's memory until the browser makes another request. At that time, the server will remember the user session that the browser is referring to in the request, and it will call up the saved variable values.

ASP.NET saves different elements of your Web application in different ways, as follows:

✔ The values in Web Forms controls — such as text boxes and data grids — are saved automatically unless you specifically ask the values not to be saved.

✔ The values of your variables aren't saved unless you explicitly write code to save them and include it in your Web application.

✔ Details about the browser making the request are saved every time, but you have to know where to look for them. (These details are called *server variables,* and you can find out more about them in the documentation — you won't need them for this chapter.)

PostBack and State management may seem confusing in theory, but they become much clearer after you see them in action. I show you how these processes relate to the controls and structures that you use for the development of Web Forms applications.

Discovering the Web Controls

ASP.NET is more than just the sum of its form controls, but the controls do make up a significant part of the total. For example, take a look at Figure 5-1, where you can see the Date Calculator (the same one you find in Chapter 3) formatted as a Web application. The controls, like the calendar and the text box, look much the same as those found in the Windows Forms application that appears in Chapter 4.

Table 5-1 shows often-used Web server controls and their main uses. In addition to these and other core controls (such as a data grid and a button), Visual Basic offers a number of other controls that have less obvious visual impact on a page, but are just as significant in application development. Table 5-2 contains a list of categories for these less obvious controls.

Table 5-1	**Often-Used Web Server Controls**	
Control	*Toolbox Icon*	*Uses*
Button	ab	Submits a request (thereby causing a PostBack)

Control	Toolbox Icon	Uses
`Calendar`		Allows the user to select a date from a calendar
`RadioButtonList`		Offers easy access to a selection list like a DDL
`ImageMap`		Creates a dynamic version of the HTML classic
`FileUpload`		Handles the complexity of the multipart form
`Panel`		Acts as a collation mechanism for other controls on a page

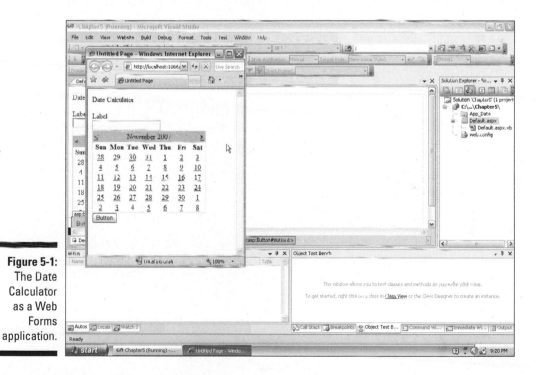

Figure 5-1:
The Date Calculator as a Web Forms application.

Table 5-2	Other Server Control Categories
Control Category	**Uses**
Web Forms	Page-level controls, such as the Crystal Report viewer, or PDF controls
Data	Data access providers, such as data sources and grids
Personalization	Web Parts, such as Business Intelligence tools, as developed for SharePoint
Security	Login functionality that integrates with other Windows security controls, for example, NTFS Security
Validation	Input validation controls that produce their own client-side script code
Navigation	Prebuilt systems for getting from page to page
HTML	Simply prewritten HTML for easy access

The goal of the ASP.NET developers was to reduce by 70 percent the amount of code that a Web developer (like you) must write. And giving you all these server controls to choose from goes a long way toward reaching that goal.

Outside the scope of server controls is the Web Forms namespace that is part of ASP.NET. Because Web application design is so outside the normal scope of a regular development effort, ASP.NET provides a significant number of classes to assist with the management of the application. For instance, the concepts of PostBack and State, described in the previous section, provide some challenges that ASP.NET is well suited to meet because of this added functionality. Table 5-3 lists some of these namespace classes.

Table 5-3	Some Classes in the System.Web Namespace
Class	**Uses**
`HttpApplication`	Defines properties of the entire application
`HttpSession`	Identifies properties of one session within an application
`HttpContext`	Offers access to the HTTP-specific properties of a specific request
`HttpBrowser Capabilities`	Gives access to the `Server_Variables` collection provided by CGI
`HttpCookie`	Reads and saves cookies to a client PC
`HttpRequest`	Grants access to the values sent by a request

Class	Uses
HttpResponse	Provides access to the values sent to the client in a response
HttpUtility	Defines generic utilities to encode and decode HTTP messages
HttpWriter	Allows passing values to an HttpResponse

Building Your First Web Application

The following sections take a look at building the Date Calculator (like the application appearing in Chapter 3) as a Web application. Essentially, the Web version of the Date Calculator works much the same way as the Windows Forms version discussed in Chapter 4. The difference in the Web Forms version is the extra code required to ensure that the application can forget and re-remember everything between refreshes of the form. That is, the application must save State every time the browser calls back to the server on a PostBack request.

Viewing the extras in Web Forms

As with Windows Forms (Chapter 4), you have a selection of views in the designer window, as shown in Figure 5-2. But unlike the views in Windows Forms, the Web Forms views have the names Design, Source, and Server. When you view the Design or Source, you have an option to view them together in a Split view, new in 2008.

The Server view is for the code-behind. These views show you the following:

- **Design View:** As you may expect from Windows Forms, Design View shows you Web Forms in What-You-See-Is-What-You-Get (WYSIWYG) format.

- **Source View:** Shows you the *display code,* which is essentially the HTML that the browser downloads. The exception to that is the ASP.NET server controls, which are rendered by IIS before they get to the browser. For those controls, you see special ASP.NET markup.

- **Server View:** Shows the Visual Basic 2008 code that is compiled and saved into a class library for use by the server in processing the incoming browser requests.

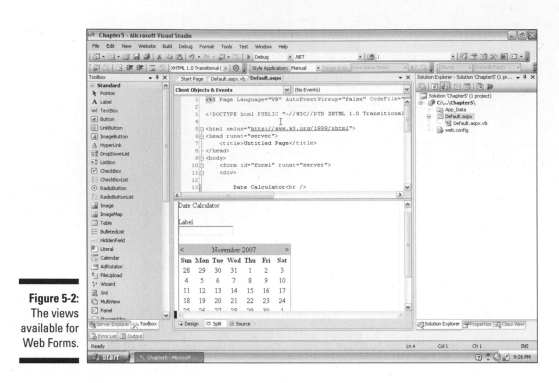

Figure 5-2:
The views
available for
Web Forms.

ASP.NET pages that accompany a Web application are actually represented by two editable files. The `.aspx` file contains the presentation code, that is, the HTML, which formats the material that shows up in the user's Web browser. The `.aspx.vb` file, which is called the *CodeBehind* file, contains the functional stuff (the Visual Basic code) that the user never sees. You can look at both files from the designer window, as you do with the Windows Forms.

Constructing the Web Forms application

Follow these steps to start your Web Forms application and populate it with the controls you need:

1. **Choose File⇨New Web Site from the Visual Studio main menu.**

   Web Forms are set up a little differently than Windows Forms projects: They appear as Web sites rather than projects. Visual Studio gives you a few template options in the New Web Site dialog box, as shown in Figure 5-3.

2. **Select ASP.NET Web Site from the Visual Studio Installed Templates list and type a name for the site in the appropriate text box.**

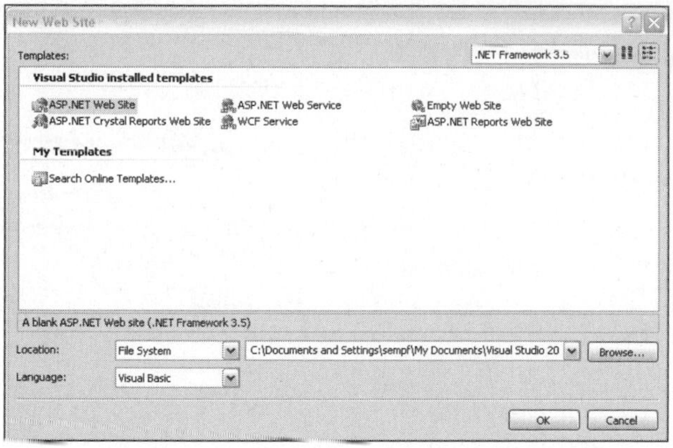

Figure 5-3:
The New
Web Site
dialog box.

In Figure 5-3, notice the Location drop-down list to the left of the file
selection drop-down list. This Location list gives you the choice to publish to an IIS site or an FTP site. If you use the local File System — which
I recommend during development — others won't be able to access the
site until after you publish it using the Copy Web or another deployment
tool. Search MSDN for the term *ASP.NET deployment* to find out more
about publishing your ASP.NET applications.

I named my Web site `DateCalcChapter5`, and I recommend saving the
site in the default location. Visual Studio creates a new Web site from the
template with the name you specify. The site includes a default page,
which I left with the name `default.aspx`. When you run the site from
Visual Studio for testing, it will run with a special custom Web server. If
you want other users to be able to see the site, you need to copy it to a
regular Web server.

3. **Click the Design tab to go to Design View and drag the controls you
need from the Toolbox onto the form.**

Layout in the Web designer is different than in the Windows designer.
Generally speaking, Web pages are laid out relative to the upper-left
corner of the screen. Because you as the developer don't control the
size of the users' screen (or the font size, or just about anything), the
design for a Web application has to be a lot more flexible than a
Windows application.

In this example, I start with a Label control. The Label control provides
server-controlled text on a Web page. Unlike with Windows Forms, Web
Forms allow you to type static text directly on a Web page, so you actually have two different ways to present text to the user.

When you place your first control, two characteristics become obvious
right away:

• The object in question aligns itself with the upper-left corner of the
form, no matter where you dragged it.

- The properties available when you work with a Web Forms control are very different from those of a Windows Forms control having the same name.

4. **To add all controls for the Date Calculator application, drag a Label, Calendar, and Button to your form.**

   Figure 5-1 shows the placement of these controls in my sample date calculator form.

5. **Format the Calendar control by selecting one of the formats and clicking the OK button.**

   When you drag the Calendar control onto the page, you see another feature of the SmartTags (which you may have discovered in the Windows Forms application built in Chapter 4) — the AutoFormat dialog box, as shown in Figure 5-4. The AutoFormat dialog box gives you the opportunity to quickly implement one of the predesigned looks for a given control. For my example, I choose the Professional 1 format from the Select a Scheme list. Make your choice, and the new design shows up in the designer.

6. **Click to place the cursor in front of the Label control you added at the upper left, and press Enter twice to add space.**

7. **Click to place the cursor back at the top of the page and type your application name.**

   In this example, I type **Date Calculator** to name my Web application. Highlight the text and use the first drop-down list on the Text Formatting toolbar to change the Block Formatting to Heading 1.

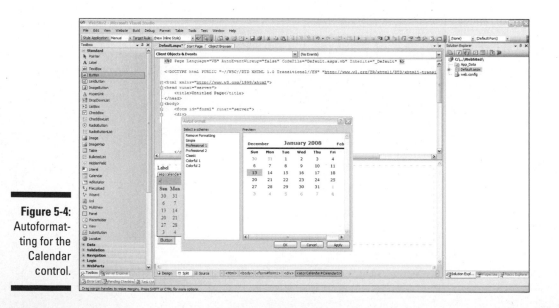

Figure 5-4:
Autoformatting for the Calendar control.

8. **Press F4 to open the Properties window; then click each control (the Label, the Button, and the Calendar) and change the ID property to usable names.**

   I used `NextWeek` for the Label, `SubmitButton` for the Button, and `DateChooser` for the Calendar.

When you add the Web Forms controls, you have made a good start on your first Web application.

In Visual Studio, developing Web applications with Web Forms is very different from developing Windows applications with Windows Forms. Web development adds another layer — ASP.NET — which is a central topic for the first several pages in this chapter. (But this is a book about Visual Basic, and don't worry, this chapter does relate ASP.NET to VB 2008.) If you are completely new to Web development, and you need to become very good very quickly, I recommend reading *ASP.NET 2 For Dummies* by Bill Hatfield (published by Wiley) in addition to finishing this chapter.

Viewing the results in Source View

To view your work in Source View and also add some functionality to your form, follow these steps:

1. **Click the Source tab to change to Source View.**

   You suddenly can see the specific layout of the form in HTML format. The HTML code for my date calculator application appears in Listing 5-1.

Listing 5-1: The HTML Code for Default.aspx

```
<%@ Page Language="VB" AutoEventWireup="false" CodeFile="Default.aspx.vb"
        Inherits="_Default" %>


<!DOCTYPE html PUBLIC "-//W3C//DTD XHTML 1.0 Transitional//EN"
        "http://www.w3.org/TR/xhtml1/DTD/xhtml1-transitional.dtd">

<html xmlns="http://www.w3.org/1999/xhtml" >
<head runat="server">
    <title>Untitled Page</title>
</head>
<body>
    <form id="form1" runat="server">
    <div>
        <asp:Label ID="Label1" runat="server" Text="Label"></asp:Label>
        <asp:Calendar ID="Calendar1" runat="server" BackColor="White"
            BorderColor="White"
          BorderWidth="1px" Font-Names="Verdana" Font-Size="9pt"
            ForeColor="Black" Height="190px"
```

(continued)

Listing 5-1: *(continued)*

```
            NextPrevFormat="FullMonth" Width="350px">
            <SelectedDayStyle BackColor="#333399" ForeColor="White" />
            <TodayDayStyle BackColor="#CCCCCC" />
            <OtherMonthDayStyle ForeColor="#999999" />
            <NextPrevStyle Font-Bold="True" Font-Size="8pt" ForeColor="#333333"
                VerticalAlign="Bottom" />
            <DayHeaderStyle Font-Bold="True" Font-Size="8pt" />
            <TitleStyle BackColor="White" BorderColor="Black" BorderWidth="4px"
                Font-Bold="True"
                    Font-Size="12pt" ForeColor="#333399" />
        </asp:Calendar>

    </div>
        <asp:Button ID="Button1" runat="server" Text="Button" />
    </form>
</body>
</html>
```

 REMEMBER

You can work with (add, delete, change, and so on) your controls in this view or in Design View — although you must know that a mistake in code in the Source View will cause a problem in Design View. Figure 5-5 shows the message resulting from an error made in the Source View.

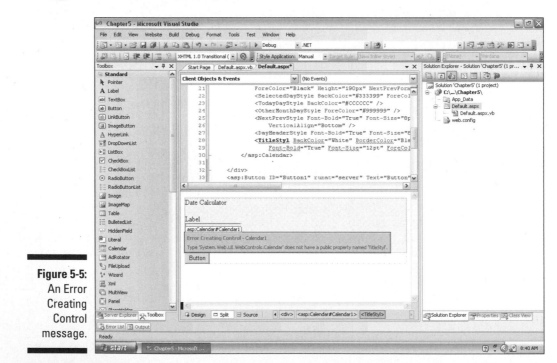

Figure 5-5:
An Error
Creating
Control
message.

Generally, I would advise that you focus on being either an HTML editor or a design editor. If your background is in Web design, use and stick with the HTML Source View. If most of your experience is in form designers like Visual Basic or Delphi, focus on using the Design View. Switching between the two is confusing and can cause logistical problems.

2. **Click the Design tab to go back to Design View.**

3. **Double-click the Button control to add a Click event handler.**

   Visual Studio changes to Server View, where you have the opportunity to add code to the instance of that click event. The methods, properties, and events for the Button control here are slightly different from those of the Windows application Button control because they need to support the PostBack model of the ASP.NET engine.

   For this example, I add code that increments the chosen date by seven days, as follows:

```
Partial Class _Default
    Inherits System.Web.UI.Page
    Protected Sub SubmitButon_Click(ByVal sender As Object, ByVal e As
            System.EventArgs) Handles SubmitButton.Click
        NextWeek.Text =
            DateChooser.SelectedDate.Add(TimeSpan.FromDays(7)).ToString()
    End Sub
End Class
```

After you complete these steps, you have the basics of a date calculator application. When you run the application, you can click a date on the calendar, click the button, cause a PostBack event, and get a refreshed Web page that displays the date a week hence as your result.

Running your Web application

Generally, Internet Information Server is required for running an ASP.NET Web application. When you develop the application with Visual Studio, however, that isn't the case. The Visual Web Developer (VWD) Web Server is an integral part of Visual Studio 2008 and makes development on a nonserver platform painless. You can take advantage of the close integration of these products and test out the Web applications you're developing on your local machine. With your application open in Visual Studio, follow these steps to run it in debug mode:

1. **Press F5 or click the Play button on the toolbar to launch the Web application in debug mode.**

   Debug mode is not automatically set up on a Web project, so you are initially prompted to set it up via the Debugging Not Enabled dialog box shown in Figure 5-6.

2. **Accept the default option — Modify the Web.config File to Enable Debugging — and click the OK button.**

   VWD Web Server appears in your system tray as hosting the site on the local machine with a random port number. See Figure 5-7.

   Your application runs with your Web page active and visible in the default Web browser you set up in the Visual Studio options. (See the Cheat Sheet at the front of this book for information on setting these options.) Figure 5-8 shows my Date Calculator application open in Internet Explorer.

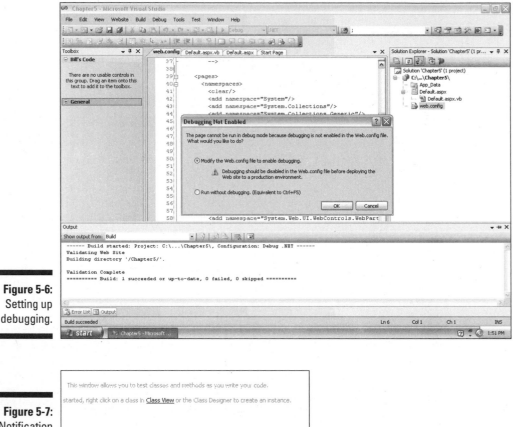

Figure 5-6: Setting up debugging.

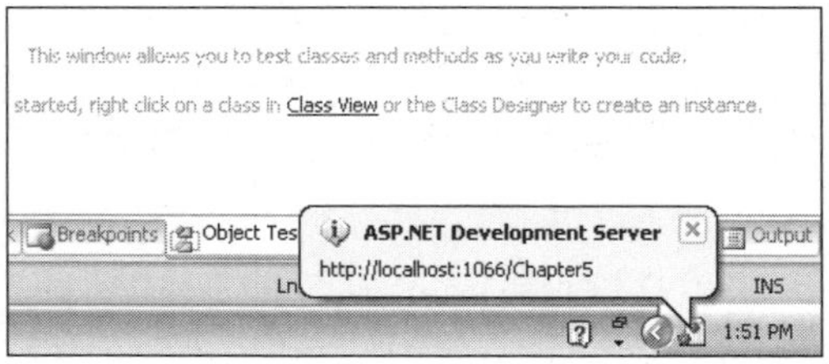

Figure 5-7: Notification of the VWD Web Server.

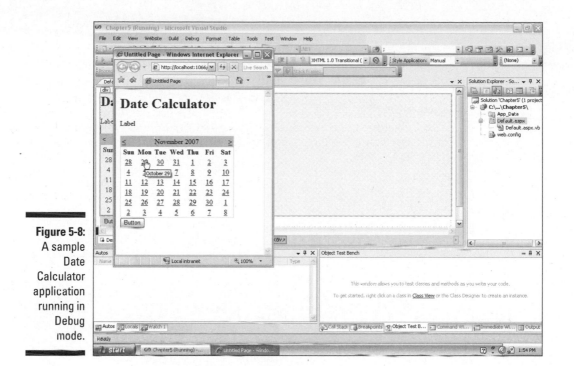

Figure 5-8:
A sample
Date
Calculator
application
running in
Debug
mode.

3. **Activate your Web application (by clicking a button, typing into a text box, or otherwise interacting with your program) and watch the results.**

   In my application, I click a date (October 29, to be exact) and click the button, and the calendar changes to highlight the date one week out (Remember, remember, the fifth of November), as shown in Figure 5-9.

4. **Close the Web browser that is running your application.**

   Visual Studio comes out of Debug mode, and the VWD Web server also closes.

Looking Below the Surface of Web Forms

ASP.NET is a framework within a framework — a comprehensive Web server management system provided for free as part of the .NET Framework from Microsoft. ASP.NET is insanely sophisticated and powerful, and it does much more than I can cover here. But I can help you with an important basic understanding of how ASP.NET encapsulates the CGI (Common Gateway Interface) functionality that has been around for ten years.

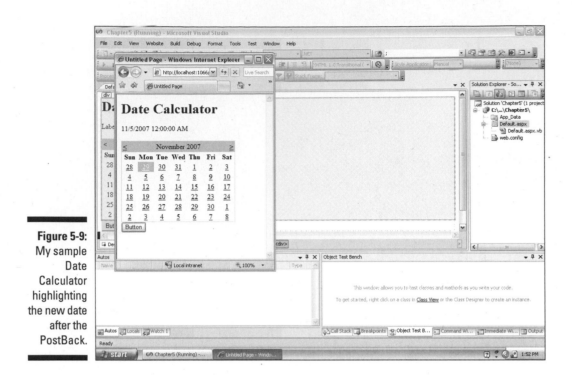

Figure 5-9:
My sample
Date
Calculator
highlighting
the new date
after the
PostBack.

Validating user input

User input controls on Web Forms look just like user input controls on
Windows Forms. Text boxes, drop-down lists, check boxes, and so on all
accept user input, and buttons submit that information to the application.
The difference between Web and Windows Forms comes from how the
forms handle user information under the hood.

From the development perspective, text boxes and other controls work simi-
larly to accept user input. For example, you can get to the value submitted by
the user using the Text property of a text box or the SelectedValue property of a drop-down list. One development issue that differs significantly
between Web and Windows applications is validation of the user input.
Because (for Web apps) the client is separated from the server, making sure
that the client requests are formatted correctly is something that developers
want to do on the client rather than the server. ASP.NET makes verifying
format simple with the Validation controls available in Visual Studio 2008.

You can find the Visual Studio Validation controls, as shown in Figure 5-10, in
the Toolbox under the (go figure!) Validation section. Web application users
may forget to provide all the data your application needs to work correctly;
they also may mistype an entry or enter the wrong type of data (for example,
entering text in a field where you expect numbers).

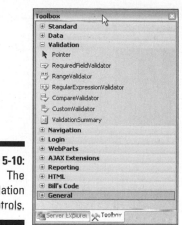

Figure 5-10:
The
Validation
controls.

Common reasons that you want to validate input include the following:

- **Confirming that required information meets the rules of the application:** For instance, checking to make sure that a date entered falls after the current date, if that is what your application requires.

- **Verifying the type of data entered:** Making sure that a date is formatted properly or that a number is entered in a numeric field.

To use Validation controls in your application, simply select the on-screen element that requires validating and drag the control (or controls) onto the page you're designing. I include a RequiredFieldValidator and ValidationSummary control on my Date Calculator page. The Required FieldValidator accepts a control to "watch" as a parameter, and reacts if the requirements set for that control are not met. The ValidationSummary sits at the top of the page and provides one of those nice bulleted lists of problems, without any code!

Drag a text box onto the page, select it, and change the ID property name to DateSpan. You can use this text box to do the same thing as the text box in the Windows Forms project (see Chapter 4). In this text box, the user specifies the number of days out to calculate from the selected date in the calendar. Figure 5-11 shows how my Web application's Design View looks after I added the RequiredFieldValidator and ValidationSummary controls (for which I set the ID to DateSpanValidator and DateSummary). I can set up this validation to look for users to enter a number and send them warning messages if they don't.

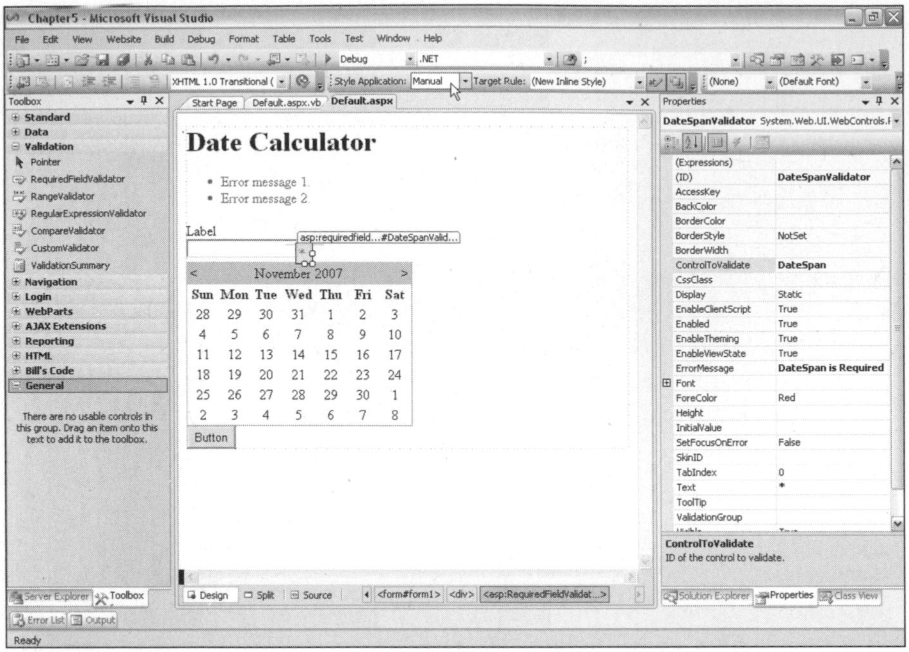

Figure 5-11: My application's Design View after putting in the text box and Validation controls.

You need to do three important things to set up a `RequiredFieldValidator` control. You can do all of these things in the Property panel with the validator selected in Design View:

1. **Type in the error message.**

   This message is what appears in the `ValidationSummary` control when the user misses filling in the field. I set my error message to "DateSpan is Required."

2. **Set the Text parameter.**

   This is what the validator itself shows when it is triggered. I usually use an asterisk (*).

3. **Set the Control to Validate parameter.**

   This setting shows the control that the validator is watching. In this case, the control is the `DateSpan` text box.

When I run my Date Calculator program and try to change the date without typing a number into the `DateSpan` text box, the user input validation that these steps put in place displays the error message shown in Figure 5-12.

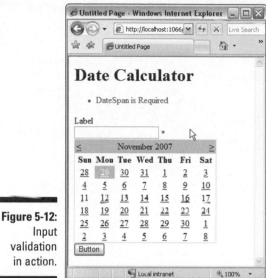

Dealing with State

As I mention in the introduction of this chapter, the State of an application is described by the current value of controls, variables, and object properties at any given time. When the server stops processing a page and sends it to the browser, the server gives up (forgets) almost all the elements that comprise the State. ASP.NET provides you with a few mechanisms to preserve State in a Web Forms application. The most useful of these are the ViewState and the Session objects, which I describe in the following sections.

ViewState

ViewState is a new concept for ASP.NET. In a nutshell, the server packages up the values of the form controls that were passed to it, compresses them, and saves them in a hidden form field that is rendered into the info that's sent back to the browser. The user doesn't know (or care) that the variable is there, but the server sure knows (and cares). This hidden form variable is passed back to the server when the user causes another PostBack (by asking for the same page again), and the server can decompress the variable to find out what values to set when it returns the page to the client.

Knowing the working details is less important than knowing how to use the ViewState object. In addition to the values of form controls, you can save noncontrol variable values to the ViewState as well. If your program needs to remember a variable from PostBack to PostBack, you can do so by saving and then retrieving the variable to the ViewState, as shown by the following two lines of code:

```
Me.ViewState("_NextWeek") = NextWeek.Text

NextWeek.Text = CStr(Me.ViewState("_NextWeek"))
```

In these lines, the Me object is just a shortcut that refers to the current object, which in this case is the Web page in general. You see this structure used a lot more in Part IV of this book. The CStr string conversion appears in this code because when a value comes back from the ViewState, it is just an *object* type, and your code needs to tell Visual Basic that the type value is a String. (For more on types, see Chapter 9.)

Session object

The ViewState object is great for saving a variable within a page, but what happens if you need to save a value across several pages? When a user changes pages, the ViewState object is lost. This situation makes sense if you think about it because your code refers to the ViewState object with Me, and that Me is the page. If the user moves to a different page, your program has a different instance of ViewState.

So to take care of this problem, enter the Session object. The Session object represents a particular user working with a particular application. While the Session object has several methods (which you can see if you check out the IntelliSense), the important method to know helps you save values — just like you do with ViewState object. But with the Session object, these values stay around until the user stops using the application, even if that use involves multiple pages.

The following two lines of code show that setting and getting variable values with the Session object are just as easy as using the ViewState object:

```
Session("_NextWeek") = NextWeek.Text

NextWeek.Text = CStr(Session("_NextWeek"))
```

Checking Out Some Cool Web Tricks

The Web has a ton of toys. Because the Web is a disconnected technology, and many of the toys are cross platform, they are kind of cool. Some of them are even expected — more or less — by users, and a few of them are worth knowing about.

Getting from one page to another

One of the most important capabilities of a Web application is allowing users to move from one Web page to another. If you are just creating straight navigation, you can use a simple Anchor tag and never even get involved with Visual Basic. The following line of code shows how an Anchor tag looks in the Source View, and Figure 5-13 shows how the coded link appears in the browser.

```
<A HREF="NextPage.aspx">This goes to the next page</A> and this does not.
```

Figure 5-13:
A hyperlink caused by an Anchor tag.

ASP.NET gets involved when you need to set the value of the HREF property of the Anchor tag in your .vb file (the file that contains your application's Visual Basic code). Suppose that you need to pick which page you want the user to reach during a PostBack. In Visual Basic, you could use a Hyperlink Web user control and set the value of the NavigationUrl property in the CodeBehind as needed. Following is an example of what that code would look like if you want to set the HREF based on input gathered from the user. In the case of the Date Calculator application (which you see in the section "Building Your First Web Application," earlier in this chapter), the DateSpan control (text box) retrieves the number of days to span from the user.

```
If DateSpan.Text > "7" Then
  HyperLink1.NavigateUrl = "thispage.aspx"
Else
  HyperLink1.NavigateUrl = "thatpage.aspx"
End If
```

This example shows an If-Then-Else statement used to handle the navigation decision. (I cover using the If-Then-Else decision statement in Chapter 10.) You can use this coding technique for site navigation (as depicted) or even for security. For example, you could look up an ID entered by a user in a database that matches the user ID with a list of Web pages (URLs) that the user is allowed to access.

Adding pretties

Web sites just aren't Web sites without images. Like anchors, images can be handled just with normal HTML, with an image tag that looks like this:

```
<img src="image.gif" height=100 width=100>
```

This tag refers to a Web-ready image (usually a GIF, JPEG, or PNG file) that is in the same directory as the HTML code file referring to it. The path can, of course, be changed in the src attribute to point to another directory in the project.

 Keep in mind that all paths are relative to the root of the project. If you always reference the location of images with a complete path from the root of the project — for example, with src="/images/navigation/image.gif" — no matter where your code is used, the browser will be able to find your image.

Just as the NavigateUrl property of the Hyperlink control changes the HREF attribute of an Anchor tag that it renders, the ImageUrl property of the image object changes the src attribute of the img tag it renders. So, if you drag an image object to a Web page you're designing and want it to render the tag as shown in the preceding line of code, you would write the following to add to the VB CodeBehind file:

```
Sub Page_Load(ByVal sender As Object, ByVal e As System.EventArgs) Handles
              Me.Load
  Image1.ImageUrl = "image1.gif"
  Image1.Height = 100
  Image1.Width = 100
End Sub
```

Getting information about the user

In the earlier section "Discovering the Web Controls," I discuss some controls that give server-based Web applications access to the browser environment. Sometimes browser information is very useful.

Take the security controls, for example. As part of its request to the server, the browser sends information about the user in the form of an object called a WindowsIdentity. Remember, because ASP.NET is disconnected, the server doesn't know which user is making a request at any given time unless it checks every request. You can use the `HttpRequest` object passed to your application from the server to get a `WindowsIdentity` object and then check the object for user information, including the username.

The following code is the Source View for a Web Forms page containing a little text and a label:

```
<%@ Page Language="VB" AutoEventWireup="false" CompileWith="ThisPage.aspx.vb"
          ClassName="ThisPage_aspx" %>
<!DOCTYPE html PUBLIC "-//W3C//DTD XHTML 1.1//EN"
          "http://www.w3.org/TR/xhtml11/DTD/xhtml11.dtd">
<html xmlns="http://www.w3.org/1999/xhtml" >
<head runat="server">
 <title>Untitled Page</title>
</head>
<body>
 <form id="form1" runat="server">
 <div>
 The current user is <asp:Label ID=ThisUserNameLabel Runat=server></asp:Label>
 </div>
 </form>
</body>
</html>
```

When you double-click the form in the Design View, you get the `Page.Load` event handler (see the following code), where you can add the VB code that lets your application access Web environment objects. This code gets a copy of the `WindowsIdentity` object from the `Request` object and then gets the `Name` property from the `WindowsIdentity`.

```
Sub Page_Load(ByVal sender As Object, ByVal e As System.EventArgs)
              Handles Me.Load
 Dim thisUser As System.Security.Principal.WindowsIdentity =
              Request.LogonUserIdentity()
 Dim thisUserName As String = thisUser.Name.ToString()
 ThisUserNameLabel.Text = thisUserName
End Sub
```

This method follows the general pattern for getting information out of the `http` objects. Generally, such objects return some kind of subobject that you need to declare in your application. For more information about getting information out of objects, check out Chapter 13.

You can use the `Request` terminology to refer to the current `HttpRequest` object because it is an artifact from earlier versions of ASP.

Suppose that your application has now received a request from the user, gotten the `Request` object fired up, and extracted a copy of its `LogonUser Identity`, which is an instance of a `WindowsIdentity` object. The `Logon UserIdentity` object has a `Name` property, which you have set equal to the text of a Label Web control (`ThisUserNameLabel.Text = thisUserName`). When you create and run this Web Forms application, you see a screen that (hopefully) has your machine and username, rather than mine, as shown in Figure 5-14!

The `HttpRequest` object offers a lot more than simply security; it passes information about cookies, the Header collection, the client's PC, and so on. For more details on what this object provides, you can heed my continued encouragement to read *ASP.NET 3.5 For Dummies* by Ken Cox (by Wiley Publishing, Inc.) and the MSDN documentation.

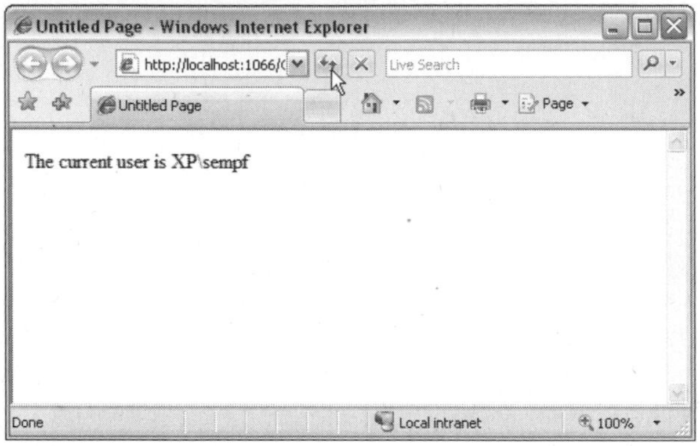

Figure 5-14:
The username in the Web browser.

Other good Web development things to know

You need to know more details to effectively write ASP.NET applications. Information on HTML, client-side scripting, and image development come to mind. ASP.NET — a server preprocessing platform — is just one piece of the whole, and a lot more technologies and practices go into making a good Web application. This chapter gets you started with ASP.NET, and this book deals with the CodeBehind VB language details you need to know. But you still have an opportunity to glean much more information about the workings of Web applications before you become an expert Internet application designer. Take a look at the following:

✔ Elements of HTML, such as tables and lists, that help you lay out pages

✔ The impact of image processing — including converting files to GIF, PNG, or JPEG — on the usability of the Web page

✔ Scripting languages such as JavaScript, to provide interactive functionality on the client that isn't otherwise provided by ASP.NET

✔ Configuration and management of a Web server, specifically Internet Information Server, to help maintain the environment for your applications

Chapter 6

Building Class Libraries

· ·

· ·

*T*o say that understanding class libraries is important would be a gross understatement. (A *class library* is a collection of reusable code organized into groups.) The entirety of the .NET Framework is a class library. All the groups of controls discussed in Chapters 4 and 5 are class libraries. In fact, all of Windows is a set of class libraries, even before .NET.

I cover a lot of details on a very complicated topic in this chapter. I describe how to use a class library to encapsulate logic, save on memory usage, and share code between applications. You should understand the parts of the class library and the parts of the class itself after reading this chapter.

In this chapter, you build a simple class that handles the logic of the Date Calculator designed in Chapter 3. The class you build here could be part of a larger class library (libraries usually have multiple classes). I discuss the difference between a class and an object. Also, I talk about some of the in-depth features of class libraries in this chapter.

I hope that classes and class libraries will become a significant part of your development pattern. You can, of course, write perfectly functional software without creating class libraries, but you really shouldn't. You should design your application first so that you can decide whether your software has no reusable code or anything that can be componentized before you dispense with the class libraries. Even if you just build them into the project and do not create separate DLLs, as described in this chapter, you should use class libraries for code encapsulation. Code encapsulation and reuse (covered in detail in Chapter 12) makes your code much more maintainable and easy to build other software with — you can even reuse the same code in Windows and Web applications this way.

Past to Present: DLLs Defined

Flash backward to November 1985. Microsoft has just released Windows 1.0, based on work at Xerox and Apple. At the time, Windows was really just a monolithic application for MS-DOS 2.0, meaning that all the code for the application was compiled into one executable file. When you wanted to use Windows, you ran the program. When you closed it, you went back to DOS, and the computer forgot all about it.

Windows 1.0 applications, in sum total, required more memory than the hardware was able to give them. To get all the features in place, stay within the memory constraints, and give the users a seamless experience, Microsoft built its software in component pieces. When Windows needed a particular feature, it loaded only the piece that was needed, as shown in Figure 6-1. These pieces are called Dynamic Link Libraries, or DLLs.

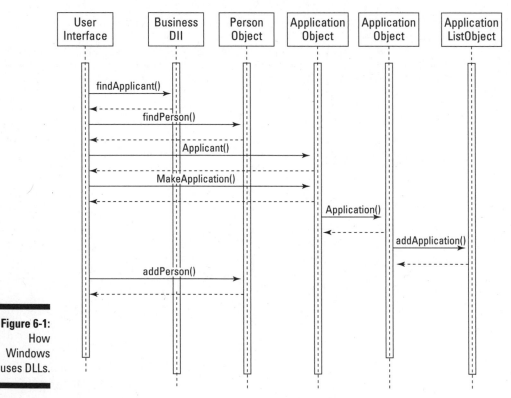

Figure 6-1:
How
Windows
uses DLLs.

As it turned out, DLLs are good for more than memory management. They are good for encapsulation of functionality. *Encapsulation* is the localization of knowledge within a module, and it is one of the core tenants of object-oriented programming, as well as a handy feature to have when writing an operating system. When you need to upgrade a function, you need to replace only the DLL, not the whole program. If a particular function needs to be secure, isolating the DLL helps to secure the function. If you have several programs that use the same function, they can share a DLL.

Note that DLLs aren't executable programs — you can't double-click on them and run them. They're designed to be referenced by other programs that are executable and provide extra functionality. In the programming world, it's common to have a Windows or Web Forms program in Visual Studio alongside a class library project in the same solution. The class library is providing necessary shared functions to the Windows or Web program.

A DLL is just a particular kind of class library that's specific to the Windows operating system. You can build class libraries for other platforms. When you build a class library for the Windows platform, the end result is a DLL.

As it turns out, the DLL thing stuck. DLLs are used to build all of Office, contemporary Windows, the .NET Framework — more or less everything in the Windows world. DLLs are just the best way to make software for the Windows platform.

Designing a Library

A *class library* on a Windows computer is a component of a program and is implemented as a DLL file, as described in the preceding section. The following sections cover how and why you can build a class library.

In the .NET world, class libraries are used to encapsulate functionality. For instance, take the Date Calculator that I discuss in Chapter 3. This application has some functionality involving adding a number of days to a date. (This functionality has nothing to do with the user interface, which is covered in Chapters 4 and 5. No matter what the user interface looks like, the program changes the date in the same way.)

Ideally, you write the code that makes the program work, or *business logic,* in a separate DLL file and include that file by reference in the calculator project. This separates the logic and the user interface and brings all the benefits I talk about in the previous section of this chapter.

That is an example of functionality that can be encapsulated. Though it is obviously a simple example, a well-structured Windows program — either a Windows Forms or Web Forms application — should encapsulate this functionality in a class library. An application that uses a class library references that library as part of the code. It then uses the functions and subroutines of that class library just as though they were part of the original program.

Objects and classes

So you have a class library, and classes are in it, as one would expect of a class library. You expect that, because it is a library, you can check out the classes within like you check out books from a regular library, and you can do exactly that. The difference is that when you check out a class from a class library, you get a copy of the class, so the original class remains in the library. This copy is called an *object,* and it is an instance of that class.

Classes are more or less like molds. They have holes in which to put information. When you get information together, you can get an instance of the class — an object — to hold the information. Take the Date Calculator example. You can define a class, called `DateCalcClass`, that has two properties and a subroutine. At design time, those properties are empty, and the subroutine is just a tool. When you instantiate the class in another program, however, it becomes an active vessel.

The program can put things in the object, because it is a three-dimensional vessel, whereas the class was only a two-dimensional mold. When the user sets the initial date — the first property — the subroutine `Calculate` is called. That sets the second property to the answer, which you can then use elsewhere in the application. The benefit is that after you are done, you can remove this logic from the computer memory, and of course if you need the logic elsewhere in the application, you don't have to rewrite it; you just add a call for the class library.

The parts of a class library

From the development perspective, the class library starts with a file, just like all the other projects. In the case of VB 2008, it is a `.vb` file that contains the following:

- **Classes:** The formal description of an object
- **Namespaces:** An abstract container of classes, as opposed to a class library, which is a concrete collection of classes
- **Functions:** A sequence of code that performs a specific task and returns a specific value

- ✔ **Subroutines:** A sequence of code that performs a specific task but doesn't return any values

- ✔ **Properties:** The qualities of an object

The structure of a .vb file is shown in Figure 6-2. Contained within the .vb file are namespaces. Within the namespaces are classes. Finally, within the classes are functions, subroutines, and properties, among other things.

This structure makes a lot of sense when you go to use a class file. For instance, take the method System.String.Compare(). The namespace is System, the class is String, and the function is Compare. The following code demonstrates this structure:

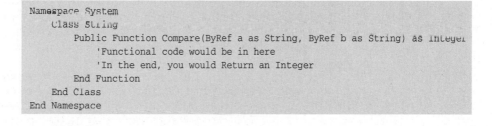

```
Namespace System
    Class String
        Public Function Compare(ByRef a as String, ByRef b as String) as Integer
            'Functional code would be in here
            'In the end, you would Return an Integer
        End Function
    End Class
End Namespace
```

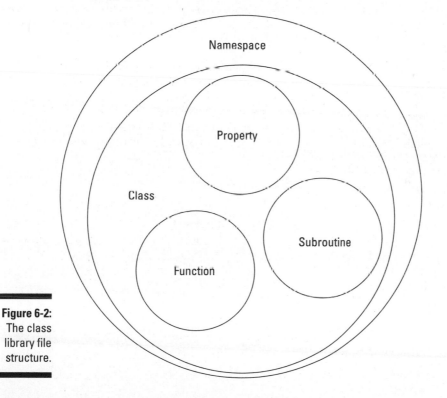

Figure 6-2:
The class
library file
structure.

Namespace

Class

Property

Function

Subroutine

Inside the class are the code-building parts of the VB 2008 language. Instead of using them now, however, you are building them:

- ✔ **Functions return a value.** Generally, functions accept input and return output. The Date Calculator would use a function that accepts a date as input and returns a date one week into the future as output. Functions are denoted by the `Function` keyword.

- ✔ **Subroutines don't return a value.** Generally, subroutines modify something else about the system, such as properties within the class. If you wrote code to set the value of a label, it would be a subroutine because it wouldn't return a value when you called it. Instead, it acts on something else in the system. Subroutines are denoted by the `Sub` keyword.

- ✔ **Properties maintain a value.** An instance of a class maintains its own data in properties. For instance, when you set the value of a label in a Windows Forms or Web Forms application (as discussed in Chapters 4 and 5), you modify its text property. Properties are denoted by the `Property` keyword.

Don't let me fool you. There is a lot more to a class in any language than functions, subroutines, and properties, but those are enough to get you started.

Coding a class library

The following list describes some of the important things you need to know about a class library:

- ✔ Class files are, by nature, code-heavy devices.

- ✔ Class libraries are designed and built with a language, and they are meant to be used in a language.

- ✔ Class libraries are not generally built using a designer, as are Windows and Web Forms.

- ✔ Class libraries make use of the same .NET Framework tools that Windows or Web Forms use in the Code View. In fact, the code for Windows or Web Forms is actually a class library.

A class library has three parts that are important to understand right now:

- ✔ **The class definition:** This is where you define one of what might be many classes in your library.

- ✔ **The operation declaration:** Here you define something about that class for later use. These are the functions, subroutines, and properties that I define in the previous section.

✔ **The functional code:** This is the innermost piece of the puzzle, and it goes inside an operation declaration. Here you write the code that does the work.

Listing 6-1 shows the parts of the class.

Listing 6-1: The Parts of the Class

```
Class Sample

    Public Function SampleFunction(ByVal input as String) as String
        'Functional code goes here
        'The function returns a string
    End Function

    Public Sub SampleSub(ByVal input as String)
        'Functional code would be in here
        'No return value because it is a subroutine
    End Sub

    Public Property SampleProperty() as String
        Get
            'Code to get the value goes here
            'Returns a string based on property return type
        End Get
        Set(ByVal value As DateTime)
            'Code to set the value goes here
            'Uses the value parameter to set the base property
        End Set
    End Property

End Class
```

The difficulty in coding class libraries becomes apparent when I say, "That is all you need to know." The fact is, nearly anything can go in the functional code, as long as it doesn't depend on other code elsewhere in the program. The procedures can be defined however you wish. The classes can be structured in practically any way. You have lots of room for doing things poorly, and the only way to find out how to code class libraries efficiently is to practice and review code from other programs.

Creating a Class Library

A good place to start when you're creating a new class library (perhaps your first) is to write a piece of code that manages the functionality of the Date Calculator. (See Chapter 3 for more about the Date Calculator.)

Getting started

To get started building a class library, follow these steps.

1. **Open Visual Studio and choose File⇨New Project.**

2. **Select VB.NET Class Library from the project templates.**

3. **Rename the default class file, `class1.vb`, to something more appropriate to your project.**

   For example, I named the library `DateCalc2008.vb`.

4. **Add appropriate code inside the Class block.**

   In this case, I added the code described in the following section of this chapter.

5. **Choose Build⇨Build Solution to create the DLL file.**

   The DLL file is the file that you use with the user interface to implement the code that you write.

The process of building a class library is very simple. Because the majority of the code is designed to make your program run, you won't always get a lot of guidance from Visual Studio. This makes figuring out what goes into the class library all the more difficult, and puts the burden on you. The only guidance you have in creating a class library comes from the design of your application (see Chapter 3), which points to one reason why design is so important.

Building the Date Calculator

When you have a design, you know what procedures you need to define and what functions the code needs. If you followed the steps in the preceding section, you're looking at a blank class like the following code, one of the scariest things in all of Visual Basic programming — or one of the most liberating:

```
Public Class DateCalc2008

End Class
```

To start, you need three properties: the start date, the end date, and the span you want between them. To create properties, you need local storage for the values of the properties, in the form of private variables.

A *private variable* is a variable that is defined outside of an operation and that is available to all the procedures within the same class file; private variables are sometimes called *fields*. By convention, private variables that provide local storage to properties use the same name as the property, but start with an underscore character, as follows:

```
     Private _startDate As DateTime
     Private _endDate As DateTime
     Private _span As Integer
```

Next, you need the properties themselves. Start by typing **Public Property StartDate as Datet** between the lines of the class declaration, and the IntelliSense feature pops up with DateTime selected. Press Tab to complete the statement.

Then press Enter to finish the line, and enjoy one of the nicest, simplest features of class library development with Visual Studio. The code template for the property is completed for you by Visual Studio, as follows:

```
     Public Property StartDate() As DateTime
         Get

         End Get
         Set(ByVal value As DateTime)

         End Set
     End Property
```

This feels a little more like Visual Basic. All you have to do is finish the code. Visual Studio built two mini-procedures for you, which are predefined parts of a property — Get and Set. They work exactly as expected: Get has the code that gets the value of the property, and Set has the code that sets the value of the property. The finished property declaration looks like the following:

```
     Public Property StartDate() As DateTime
         Get
             StartDate = _startDate
         End Get
         Set(ByVal value As DateTime)
             _startDate = value
         End Set
     End Property
```

Make two more properties by following the same procedure, but substitute EndDate and Span for your names. Remember that the value for Span should be Integer.

Doing math with a subroutine

Next, you need to teach the library to do the math necessary to use the properties. As described in Chapters 4 and 5, this code is fairly simple, and nothing has changed. Instead of using the values of DateTimePickers and Labels, you use the properties, and instead of an event, you use a subroutine.

A *subroutine* is an operation that doesn't return a value — it only affects internal values. In this case, the internal values are the private variables in the class. An example of how the subroutine works is as follows:

```
Public Sub IncreaseDate()
    EndDate = StartDate.AddDays(Span)
End Sub
```

The logic to this is a little convoluted. It assumes that the user of the system sets the properties, so by the logic in the `Set` statement, the private variables are set as well in the instance of the class the user is working with.

You use the private variables to do the math and set the private `_endDate` variable. When the user goes to get the finished value — the `EndDate` property — the logic for the `Get` statement is called, and the user gets the current value in the private property.

These properties are a simple example of a very complex, powerful idea. This may seem like a lot of extra code to do something so simple, but when you're developing applications, you rarely create a program as simple as the Date Calculator. And as a developer, you'll often find — in a real project — that a little extra code makes the project much easier to write.

When you build the project, you have a class library that calculates a given number of days from a given date. What's more, the class library is compiled into a DLL file usable by any .NET application. In the next section, I show you how to use your DLL file.

Running a DLL file

As I mention at the beginning of this chapter, a DLL needs to be used by an application with a user interface, such as a Windows Forms application.

To run your new DLL file, you need to add a project with a user interface to the same solution that holds your DLL project. The following steps help you get this working:

1. **Choose File⇨Add⇨New Project.**

2. **Select a new Windows application and give it an appropriate name.**

    I named mine `DateCalcShell`, representing that it is a shell around the DLL it will reference.

3. **Rename the default form to something appropriate**.

    Naming strategies never cease. I named my form `Calculator`.

4. **Right-click the new project and select Add Reference.**

    The Add Reference dialog box appears.

5. **Click the Projects tab, select the project that appears there, and click the OK button.**

   In this example, `CalcClass2008` appears in the list under Project Name, as shown in Figure 6-3.

6. **Double-click the My Project file in Solution Explorer, and when it opens in the Design View, click the References tab.**

   `CalcClass2008` appears in the References grid, as shown in Figure 6-4.

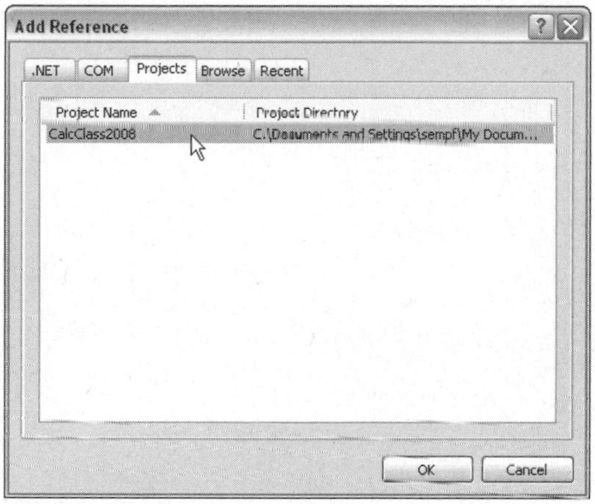

Figure 6-3:
Calc
Class
2008
in the Add
Reference
dialog box.

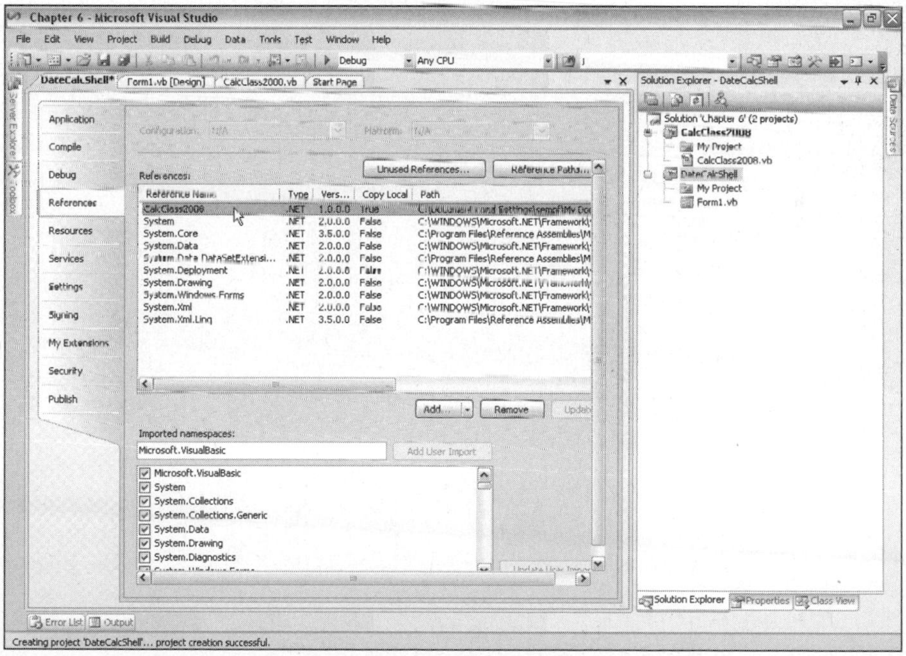

Figure 6-4:
The
References
tab of the
My Project
file.

7. Go back to the form file and move appropriate controls to the form.

Add a `Label` and a `DateTimePicker` control. (See Chapter 4 for more about these controls.)

8. Change the names of the controls to something appropriate.

I used `StartDatePicker` for the `DateTimePicker` control and `EndDate` for the `Label` control.

9. Instantiate your class from your class library as a new object in Code View.

Getting a new `DateCalc` object is the same as getting a new instance of the `String` object. Remember, everything is an object in .NET. A simple dimension does the trick: `Dim myCalc as New DateCalcClass Chapter6.CalcClass2008()`.

10. Double-click controls to add code.

In this case, double-click the `StartDatePicker` control to add a `Value Changed` event handler. Then use the new component that you defined in Step 9. You can set the `StartDate` property from the value of the `DateTimePicker` control, set the `Span` property to 7 to represent a seven-day span, and then call the `Calculate` method so that the object sets the `EndDate` for you. Finally, set the `EndDate` label text to the `endDate` property of the `myCalc` object. This code is as follows:

```
Private Sub StartDatePicker_ValueChanged(ByVal sender As System.Object, _
    ByVal e As System.EventArgs) Handles StartDatePicker.ValueChanged
    Dim myCalc As New 2008DateCalsClassChapter6.CalsClass2008()
    myCalc.StartDate = StartDatePicker.Value
    myCalc.Span = 7
    myCalc.IncreaseDate()
    EndDate.Text = myCalc.EndDate.ToString()
End Sub
```

11. Click the Start button to test the application.

Set the `DateTimePicker` control to some value and watch the label change. For a cheap thrill, use the debugger, which is covered in Chapter 8. Set a breakpoint in the DLL file, and use the debugger to watch the code walk through two projects. It's neat. You might need to right-click the Project file for the Windows Application and set it as the Startup Application.

Delving Deeper into DLLs

There is more to discover about DLLs than I can put in this chapter. However, you should understand a few more points about DLLs before you start using them.

Telling between friends and foes

Throughout this chapter, you use the `Public` keyword to describe class procedures. This is not the only way to describe procedures, however, and the differences among the procedures are notable, especially when it comes to the touchy subject of security. I discuss security in depth in Chapter 14, but I discuss accessibility keywords here briefly.

Five accessibility keywords can be used to describe procedures. They describe a gradually more restrictive security outlook. Generally, you want to pick the most restrictive accessibility possible for your expected use of the procedure in question:

- ✔ **Public:** These methods essentially give no restrictions. Any application with physical access to the DLL can use `Public` methods.

- ✔ **Protected:** These methods are only available from other methods within their own class, or a class that is derived from their class.

- ✔ **Friend:** These methods work anywhere in the application where they are declared.

- ✔ **Protected Friend:** These methods are a combination of the `Protected` and `Friend` keywords, so they are available only in an application where the class and calling program are in the same class and assembly.

- ✔ **Private:** These methods are accessible only from within their own scope.

Be nice and share

Shared functions are handy because the programmer doesn't have to instantiate the class into an object with a dimension statement to use it. You can just directly call the functions — but you don't have the benefit of a stateful object with properties and so on. Using the *shared* keyword is another tool in your programmer's toolbox.

To build a shared function, you need to accept and return values. For this example, I built a shared function that accepts the `StartDate` and `Span` values and returns a value for `DateTime`, which should be the end date.

This shared function is completely different from the subroutine because you don't use the properties. It is a separate function altogether. I am showing you for the sake of example: This shared function and the subroutine/property solution are two ways to do the same thing.

So, as you do with the properties in the earlier section "Building the Date Calculator," type the beginning of the function declaration, and IntelliSense picks up that you are declaring variables, as shown in Figure 6-5.

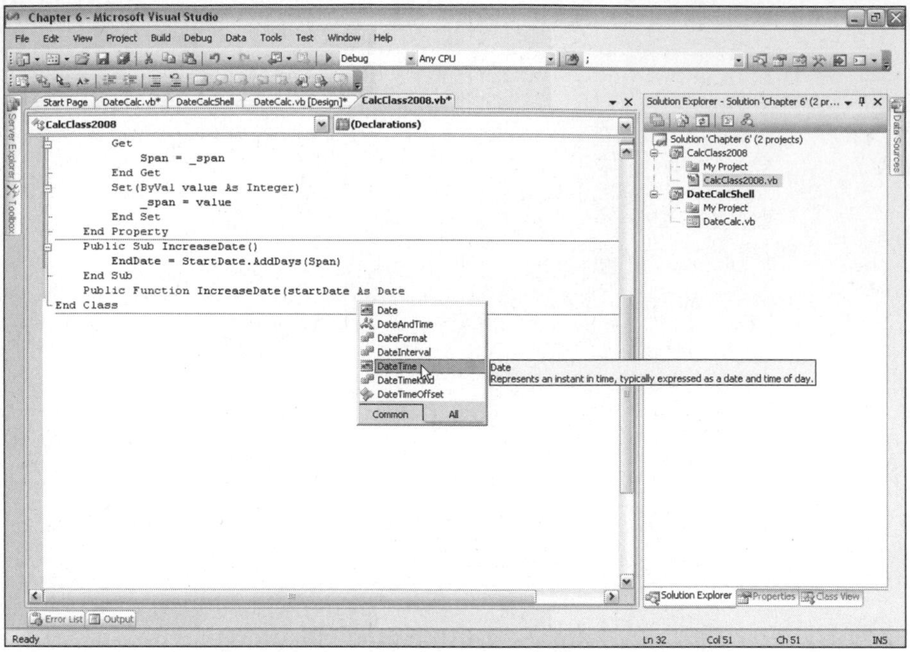

Figure 6-5:
Declaring a
function.

The functional code then takes the StartDate and Span values that are passed in, does the date math, and sets the value of the function equal to the result. The code looks like the following:

```
Public Function IncreaseDate(ByVal startDate As
        DateTime, _
        ByVal span As Integer) As DateTime
    span = CDbl(span)
    IncreaseDate = startDate.AddDays(span)
End Function
```

Getting more out of less

Without saying anything, I used one of the more useful features of VB 2008 class design in the playbook — functional overloading. Notice something interesting about the finished class, especially the IncreaseDate function . . . oh, wait, was it a subroutine? No, it was *both!* How is this possible?

It is possible through *overloading.* To simplify class design, two methods can have the same name if they have a different *method signature,* meaning parameter types and number. In this case, you have a function that doesn't use the properties, so it accepts the start date and span as parameters, and then returns the end date. A subroutine has the same name, but it has zero parameters and returns nothing.

Because of the different signatures, you can have two methods that do approximately the same thing, but in a different way. The IDE is even prepared to handle this with a special feature of IntelliSense, as shown in Figure 6-6.

When you call the method in the code, after you type the first parenthesis, you can see that the method is described with two lines. Use the arrow keys to move between them. You don't have to choose a specific one explicitly; the IntelliSense is just there for reference.

Figure 6-6:
Overloading in the IDE — IntelliSense shows two overloads.

Chapter 7

Building Web Services

*T*his chapter covers the fourth of what I consider the four most significant project types: the XML Web service. In the grand scheme of things, an XML Web service is an open-source version of the class library (described in Chapter 6). It can be used in a Windows or Web application (see Chapters 4 and 5, respectively) as needed.

The two main parts of developing a Web service are producing and consuming. *Producing* a Web service is what you do as a programmer: develop a service for users' consumption (as with the class libraries built in Chapter 6). *Consuming* a Web service is what the end user does: make use of the service in your application.

This chapter also examines how you bridge the gap between producing and consuming Web services — for example, documenting your service so that the default page that IIS creates for it will actually make sense to the reader. The players in XML Web services show up in the final act of the chapter, including a parade of the great acronyms — XML, SOAP, WSDL, and UDDI — and what they mean.

Getting to Know XML Web Services

If creating a Web service seems a little familiar, it's no accident; if not, no problem. An XML Web service is to a DLL what Web Forms are to Windows Forms — and (like a DLL) it's a class library — only more so. A Web service is more versatile than a DLL or Windows Forms — after all, those are compiled only for use on Microsoft Windows computers. XML Web services and Web Forms can be used on any platform because they follow open standards. Figure 7-1 sums up the similarities and differences of these project types.

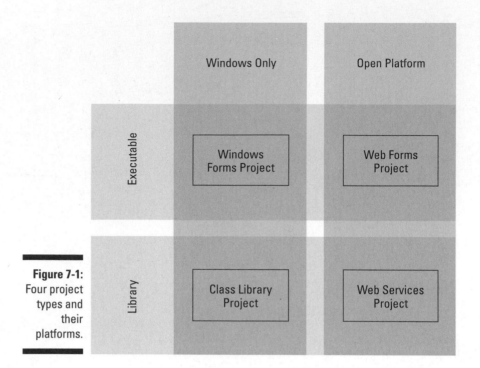

Figure 7-1:
Four project
types and
their
platforms.

The figure shows the extension of familiar Windows concepts into open-source versions that XML makes usable on the Web:

- Windows Forms have their equivalent in Web Forms (detailed in Chapter 5), which create a user interface that can be viewed on any platform.

- Windows DLLs are compiled from class libraries (see Chapter 6) to help build applications on Windows platforms; a Web service is an open-source equivalent of a DLL.

- XML Web services represent a novel combination of the best features of class libraries and Windows Forms. What's new here is XML; it gives Web services a standard format that is available to a variety of platforms — including (but not limited to) Windows.

Of course, this basic relationship between XML Web services and their ancestors is just scratching the surface. Properly used, they could be the Next Big Thing in application development. To produce a solid Web service and have it used (consumed) correctly, however, you have to get a handle on a lot of practical details — such as security policies, the management of transactions, and the availability of system resources. The next sections give you a closer look at what makes a Web service tick.

Web services: Characteristics

DLLs have broad functionality within Windows; it makes sense that as their talented offspring, XML Web services are broadly usable. If you're designing a broad enterprise system, this flexibility means that you can (and probably should) develop a complete suite of tools for a wide range of users. Remember, however, the following four vital characteristics of XML Web services:

- ✔ **Architecture-neutral:** Web services don't depend on any proprietary wiring configuration, cable type, file format, schema description, operating system, or discovery standard.

  Discovery is how other consumers can find out what your Web service does.

- ✔ **Ubiquitous:** Web services are "all for one and one for all," everywhere. Any Web service that supports the standards can support the service you're creating.

- ✔ **Simple:** Creating Web services is easy, quick, and even (sometimes) free. That's partly because the description of the data is human-readable, making for a better development experience. Any programming language can participate.

- ✔ **Interoperable:** Because the Web services all follow the same standards, they can all speak to one another.

Web services: Quirks

Designing Web services feels like designing class libraries because (basically) that's what they are. These particular class libraries are Web-driven, though, so here are some design differences to watch for:

- ✔ **All communication between an application and the service happens over the Internet.** That means you incur at least some overhead to send each individual message; the wise developer reduces the overall number of messages.

- ✔ **Chunky beats chatty.** Sending fewer messages means making fewer — and larger — function calls. Rather than make several calls to get pieces of a document, for instance, you make one call and get the whole document. This practice is called making *chunky* rather than *chatty* calls.

- ✔ **These class libraries aren't stateful.** There are no properties (or anything like them) in a Web service–based class library; in effect, all operations are shared.

✔ **Because functions are shared, subroutines are not very effective.** After all, no properties or local variables are available for the subroutines to alter when called. As with Web applications, the problem is a lack of statefulness. Your service, then, ends up as a set of tools, implemented as functions with return values.

Designing for Web Services

The overall goal of building Web services is to get your business logic exposed to the masses. (*Business logic* is the code that sits between your user-interface form and your data source or file and that tells the program what to do; you can read more about it in Chapters 3 and 6.) Because a standard exists for consuming Web services, as well as for creating them, you can focus your development on providing tools for a very broad range of applications.

Planning the design strategy

The root of Web-service design is a basic contrast: DLLs are stateful — and Web services are not. When you instantiate a DLL with a `Dim` statement in your application code, you are creating an in-memory representation of the class. Not so with Web services; they are using IIS to support themselves, so you can't instantiate them in the same way. Treat them as though you were developing a bunch of static functions, rather than a group of stateful objects.

This strategy actually has a name — *Service-Oriented Architecture,* or *SOA.* When you're designing for SOA, the approach is different from what you may be used to: In effect, you treat it more like a toolbox and less like a living piece of software.

It's no surprise that designing for SOA requires a sort of thousand-yard view. Fortunately, Visual Studio provides this big picture — one that system architects can use to tie Windows and Web Forms applications into the same bundle with class libraries built from both Web services and DLLs. From this bird's-eye view, the map looks like Figure 7-2.

Okay, Figure 7-2 lays out the basic frame of reference for your design strategy. What turns your project into an actual Web service is another consideration that's just as important to software development: how you use your programming language. Stay tuned.

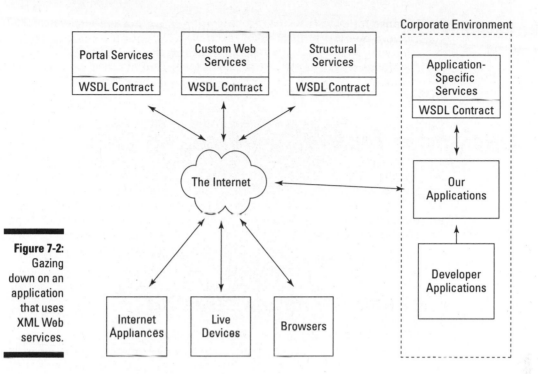

Figure 7-2:
Gazing
down on an
application
that uses
XML Web
services.

Getting a grip on the tactics

Developing a Web service requires two very different sets of tactics: one set
for producing the Web service and one set for controlling how the service is
consumed. Some specific — but probably familiar — tactics come into play
when you use Visual Basic 2008 to create tools that work within SOA:

- The tactics you use to produce Web services will be just like those used
  to create class libraries and compile them into DLLs.

- The tactics that control how a Web service is consumed are similar to
  referencing a DLL and using its methods and properties in a Windows
  Forms project (as described in Chapter 6).

Building a Web Service

The whole process of creating a Web service and setting it up for use
involves three stages: producing the service, viewing the service to make
sure that it'll do what you want, and making the service available to the users
who consume it.

Producing a Web service begins with (surprise, surprise) a project template. Use these steps to get one started:

1. **Open Visual Studio and choose File⇨New⇨Web Site.**

   The output of a Web service project is a Web site, just like the output of a class library project is a DLL file.

2. **Under Visual Basic, select ASP.NET Web Service as the Visual Studio installed template.**

   You'll also notice that a WCF service is available. More about that later.

3. **Under Location, change the name to something appropriate for the project.**

   Here, I changed my sample project's name to `Chapter7DateCalc`. I changed the solution name to `Chapter7`.

   Visual Studio creates a project template for you. The new template includes a default service file called `Service.asmx.vb`, a Data folder, and an ASMX file called `Service.asmx`. The `Service.vb` file contains your class library code. The `Service.asmx` file contains display code that the Web server will use to make an automatic page of documentation for your Web service.

4. **Add a new Web Service file, and rename the files and class to something appropriate for the project.**

   Here, I used `DateCalc`, so my class is `DateCalc`, my ASMX file is `Date Calc.asmx`, and my class file is `DateCalc.asmx.vb`.

5. **Write code in the class as Public Functions, overwriting the sample method.**

   Notice the default code in Listing 7-1.

Listing 7-1: The Default Web Service

```
 1: Imports System.Web
 2: Imports System.Web.Services
 3: Imports System.Web.Services.Protocols
 4: <WebServiceBinding(ConformanceClaims:=WsiClaims.BP10,
            EmitConformanceClaims:=True)> _
 5: Public Class Service
       Inherits System.Web.Services.WebService
 6:    <WebMethod()> _
 7:    Public Function HelloWorld() As String
 8:        Return "Hello World"
 9:    End Function
10: End Class
```

Is that all there is to a Web service? Well, yes, but more is going on here than meets the eye. Here's a closer look:

- ✔ After the `Imports` statements and before the `Class` statement, a `Web ServiceBinding` statement (on line 4) serves as a compiler directive. It tells the .NET Framework that this particular class will be used as a Web service.

- ✔ The standard-looking `Class` statement on line 5 is followed by an *inheritance statement* that gives you as the programmer of the class access to the methods, properties, and events of the Web service classes.

- ✔ Another compiler directive appears on line 6 — the `WebMethod` directive, which gives you a few documentation choices later on and also shows the compiler that this specific method will be exposed to the service when you have it up and running.

- ✔ Lines 7, 8, and 9 are pretty standard in Visual Basic 2008: just a function that accepts nothing and returns a string: `"Hello World"`. The `End Class` statement completes the class. It is just a test line of code, to make sure that the wiring works.

You can replace lines 7 through 9 with most any VB function. In the Microsoft world, such a function can return any object in the .NET universe. But let's not get too far afield here. In reality, you must consider that a UNIX or mainframe computer might call this service. If cross-platform (or backward) compatibility is an issue, it might be necessary to limit the return value to a primitive type. (I cover types in Chapter 9.)

When you have your completed project template in hand, you're ready to build the Web service.

Building the DateCalc Web service

This section of the chapter builds the `DateCalc` Web service as a detailed example. I have replaced the sample code in lines 7 through 9 with a function for the class library in your DLL file (see Chapter 6 for details of this function). Listing 7-2 shows the sample code for the finished service.

Listing 7-2: The DateCalc Service

```
1: Imports System.Web
2: Imports System.Web.Services
3: Imports System.Web.Services.Protocols
4: <WebService(Namespace:="http://services.vbfordummies.com/")> _
5: Public Class DateCalc
      Inherits System.Web.Services.WebService
```

(continued)

Listing 7-2: *(continued)*

```
 6:    <WebMethod(Description:="A Web Service implementation of the Date
            Calculator")> _
 7:    Public Function IncreaseDate(ByVal startDate As DateTime, ByVal span As
            Integer) As DateTime
 8:      IncreaseDate = startDate.AddDays(CDbl(span))
 9:    End Function
10: End Class
```

Okay, I admit it, I changed a few things here (that was the point):

- ✔ **Line 4** has changed from a `WebServiceBinding` directive to a `Web Service` directive. I did that so that I could easily describe a default namespace. *Default namespaces* are important for the consumer; they validate the expected location of the service with its actual location. (The `WebServiceBinding` directive is more often used for enterprise-level services, which aren't of interest here.)

- ✔ **Line 6** now includes a `Description` property so that the service is more self-documenting.

- ✔ **Line 7,** the function declaration, now accepts a `startDate` and `span` as input.

- ✔ **Line 8** contains the code that has a starring role in all four chapters in Part II — the date math that increases the start date.

When the appropriate Web-service features are in place, give the new service a test drive before you send it out there to meet the users.

Viewing the DateCalc service in action

Click the Play button to start the service. (Now, there's something you can't do with a DLL.) Web services come with a default display page; in this case, I have named it `DateCalc.asmx`. IIS will create a nice page for you (as shown in Figure 7-3), with some documentation as described in the `WebMethod` directive.

When you click the `IncreaseDate` link, you see the test page for the function I created, as shown in Figure 7-4.

You don't get this if you aren't working with the built-in development Web server. If you are using IIS, it will block the test code because it is a security concern.

At this point, enter a starting date and a time span in the startDate and span text boxes, respectively. (I entered **7/25/75** in the startDate text box and **13** in the span text box.) Click the Invoke button, and your browser opens a new window with the answer in its full date format glory, as shown in Figure 7-5.

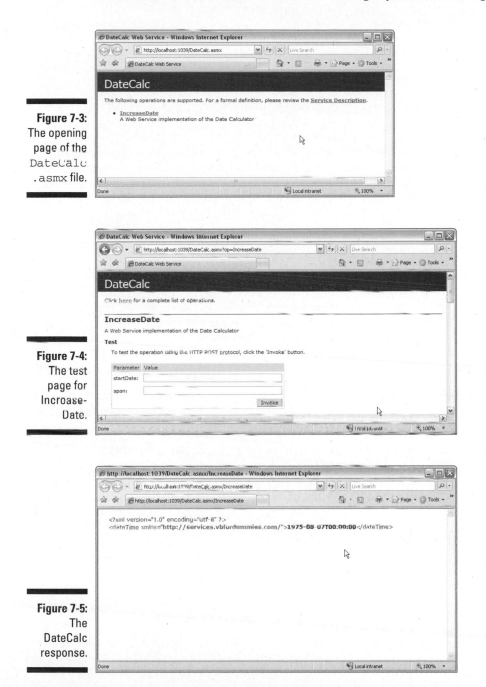

Figure 7-3:
The opening page of the DateCalc .asmx file.

Figure 7-4:
The test page for Increase-Date.

Figure 7-5:
The DateCalc response.

Pretty cool — but this exercise is not really the point of the XML Web service I created. It's just a simple way to test a Web service — even a sophisticated set of services — regardless of whether you've written them yourself or have tried someone else's handiwork.

The goal of any Web service (as I mention in the section "Designing for Web Services," earlier in this chapter) is to provide other applications with access to your business logic. Notice that all these sample pages are shown in a Web browser — and that the namespace of the service is at a Web address. Neither of those choices is an accident. If this function is published, I want it to be available at a URL on the World Wide Web — like this one:

```
http://yourMachine/Chapter7DateCalc/DateCalc.asmx
```

With the Web service built and tested, the next step is to consume the service in an application. The next section shows you how.

Consuming a Web Service

At first, building an application that consumes a Web service seems similar to building a test application for a class library. You start by building a Windows Forms application similar to the one described in Chapter 4 — but then you reference the Web service in much the same way as you reference a DLL (see Chapter 6).

In fact, Visual Studio treats a Web service much the same as it treats a class library in development. When you reference a Web service and then compile a project, Visual Studio actually builds a small DLL file that remembers the details of the Web service. (Fortunately, this happens automatically, as you can see in the upcoming steps.)

To build an application that consumes a Web service, follow these steps:

1. **Create a new project of any type.**

   Here I use a Windows Forms application called `DateCalcConsumer`, but any .NET project can consume a Web service.

2. **Right-click the project file and select Add Service Reference.**

   The Add Service Reference dialog box shown in Figure 7-6 appears, offering to help you reference the service.

3. **Type the URL of the service you are trying to reference into the Address text box.**

   Okay, if you are doing the exercise in the previous section, you don't actually type in the URL. You click the Discover button, then open the tree view to show `DateCalc`, and then select `DateCalcSoap`. Select

`DateCalcSoap`, and the `IncreaseDate` function shows in the right side of the window. Finally, change the Namespace to `Chapter7`.

If you don't want to run the service from your local machine — and you want to try running the service from the Internet — try the service I have running on `www.vbfordummies.com`. The URL for that service is as follows:

```
http://www.vbfordummies.com/Chapter7/Services/DateCalc.asmx
```

After the browser locates the service, the screen changes to the reference format, as shown in Figure 7-7. I used the Discover button to find the other project in the solution here.

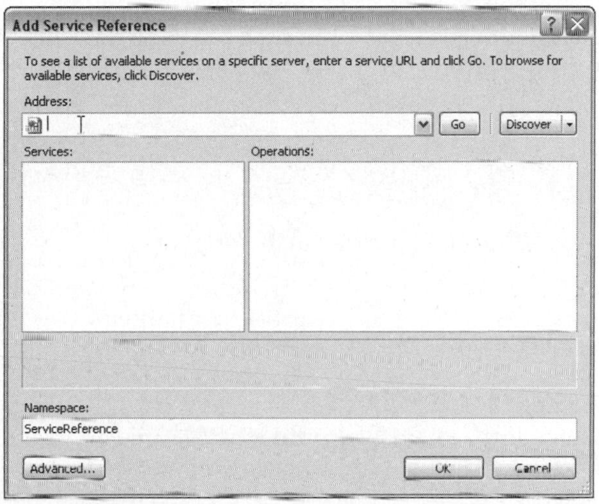

Figure 7-6:
The Add
Service
Reference
dialog box.

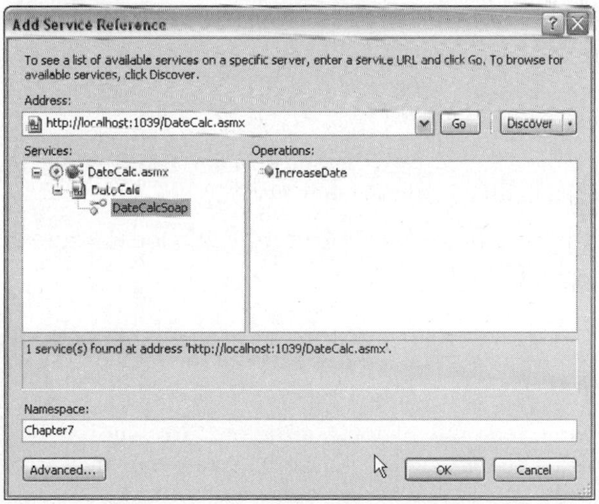

Figure 7-7:
Adding a
reference
to the
DateCalc
service.

4. **If you want, change the name of the Namespace in the box at the bottom to something appropriate for your project and then click OK.**

   Keep in mind that Visual Studio creates a class file for this, just like you do manually in Chapter 6. Naming is important so that you can find the service easily later in your code. After you click OK, Visual Studio creates a proxy class and gives you a reference to it in the Service References folder. An example appears in Figure 7-8.

5. **Add code to your project that references the Service Reference you just added.**

   In my case, I have a Windows Forms application, so I add a `DateTime Picker` and a `Label`, and then double-click the `DateTimePicker` to get the `ValueChanged` event handler.

6. **Reference the Service by instantiating a new copy of the proxy class.**

   In my sample project, here's what this looks like:

   ```
   Dim myDateCalc As Chapter7.DateCalcSoap
   ```

7. **Call the methods of the Web service, just as you would for any other function in VB.**

   The finished code for the Date Calculator that uses the Web service looks like Listing 7-3.

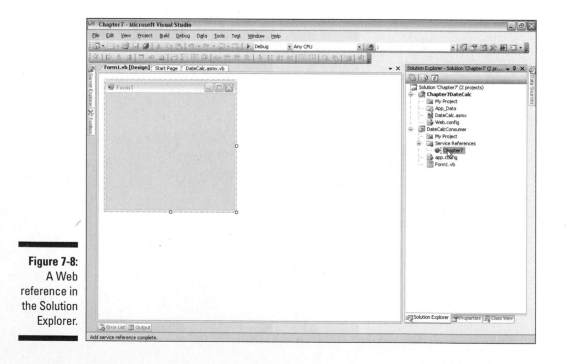

Figure 7-8:
A Web reference in the Solution Explorer.

Listing 7-3: The Date Calculator Using the Web Service

```
Public Class DateCalc
    Private Sub StartDatePicker_ValueChanged(ByVal sender As System.Object,
            ByVal e As System.EventArgs) Handles StartDatePicker.ValueChanged
        Dim myDateCalc As Chapter7.DateCalcSoap
        Label1.Text = myDateCalc.IncreaseDate(StartDatePicker.Value, 13
    End Sub
End Class
```

The proxy class has a state, but that doesn't mean that the service itself has any sense of state. If you want to get fancy, you can use this fact in ways that make the Web service emulate a class — but you are still dealing with a disconnected Web service; it doesn't keep track of its own state.

Web Services in More Depth

Ah, Web services — now, there's a topic that could fill several books (in fact, I've written a few that you can still find floating around). Though you don't have to understand how all the players (systems, policies, applications, and users) use Web services, it helps if you are working on a team of developers to make sure that you are all speaking the same language.

From the serene bird's-eye perspective of Web services (refer to Figure 7-2), you generally won't have to deal with a few parts of the big picture as a developer — for example, actually presenting your completed Web service to the users. Internet Information Services (IIS) is the Microsoft Web server application that makes these services public. Four protocols — XML, SOAP, WSDL, and UDDI — are what make that minor miracle possible:

✔ **IIS:** Internet Information Services plays the same role with XML Web services as it does with Web Forms. The page that you see when you run a service from Visual Studio, or type the URL into a browser, is automatically generated by ASP.NET and passed to the browser by IIS. You can see this flow in Figure 7-9.

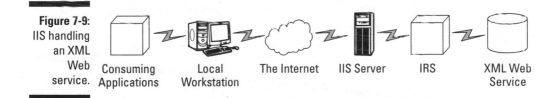

Figure 7-9: IIS handling an XML Web service.

Consuming Applications   Local Workstation   The Internet   IIS Server   IRS   XML Web Service

IIS treats a Web services application just like a Web Forms application. Bottom line: It needs the same tender loving care from your administrator. Remember, you're exposing your business logic to the world. Security is important and is covered in Chapter 14.

✔ **XML:** Of the four protocols that make Web services work, eXtensible Markup Language (XML) is the one you're likeliest to run into. Generally considered a data-storage protocol, XML is the backbone that supports all the messages passed as part of Web services.

✔ **SOAP:** Simple Object Access Protocol describes the messages that are passed. It's a meta-language of XML. The .NET Framework spares you (almost completely) from having to deal with SOAP.

✔ **WSDL:** Web Services Description Language is the XML meta-language that describes the service's input and output parameters for public consumption. Again, the .NET Framework shields you almost completely from having to hassle with WSDL. Almost.

Occasionally, however, a Web services directory will need a link to your WSDL for listing purposes. To get the WSDL from any ASMX-based service, add ?WSDL to the end of the URL. For instance, the WSDL for the URL I list here would be at:

```
http://www.vbfordummies.com/Chapter7/Services/DateCalc.asmx?WSDL
```

✔ **UDDI:** Universal Discovery and Description Language is another XML meta-language that assists consumers with the discovery of your Web services. More information about UDDI can be found at http://uddi.microsoft.com.

UDDI could easily take up an entire new book, and in fact it has. I at least get you started by telling you how to enable UDDI. The industry standard is a DISCO file — an XML file with a set of standard tags that tells a UDDI server what services are in your project.

The process in which a UDDI or other server gets Web services (in this case, from a DISCO file) is called *discovery*.

To create a DISCO file, follow these steps:

1. **Create a new XML file in your Web service project by right-clicking the project and selecting XML File.**

2. **Add the standard discovery tags to the document.**

   For this purpose, this process can be as simple as the one shown in the following code, though it will be tougher as the services get more complex. (All that you would need to change for another project would be the two tags ending in Ref, which I set in boldface in the following code.)

```
<?xml version="1.0"?>
<discovery xmlns="http://schemas.xmlsoap.org/disco/">
<discoveryRef ref="/Folder/Default.disco"/>
<contractRef ref="http://TheServerUrl/DateCalc.asmx?WSDL"
             xmlns="http://schemas.xmlsoap.org/disco/scl/"/>
</discovery>
```

3. Rename the file.

In this case, base it on the DISCO file by using `default.disco`.

Now, when you register this service with UDDI — for example, on a Universal Business Registry on a Windows 2003 server — the site there knows where to browse. Then your service appears in the listing for everyone to use.

UDDI is unusually handy for large-scale deployments of company-wide services, or public services of any size. Remember, if you are in a multiserver environment, you can create UDDI servers that go find functions they need by using DISCO files. Potentially, that's a very powerful system.

Chapter 8

Debugging in VB 2008

. . . .

In This Chapter

▶ Using visual tools to squash bugs

▶ Implementing debugging with tools from the .NET Framework

▶ Finding bugs in different types of projects

. . . .

*I*n the examples in Part II, you play your code to see it run in a Web browser or as a Windows application. As you may have guessed, there is more to this functionality than meets the eye.

Debugging is the process of finding and fixing problems in an application of any type. Often, debugging code takes as long as writing it did in the first place, according to most software development lifecycle systems, such as CMM (Capabilities Maturity Model). One of the most significant reasons for using an integrated development environment to build applications is to take advantage of the included debugging tools.

Visual Studio 2008 is replete with debugging tools that work in some of or all the project types. Throughout this chapter, I give you a blow-by-blow description of what debugging tools are available — both visual tools and tools in the .NET Framework. I then show you how to debug each project type.

Cool Visual Tools for Debugging

Debugging is so important that it has its own menu in the Visual Studio environment. The ability to watch your code run, review values in variables, and check the contents of objects is the primary reason why experienced developers use an IDE such as Visual Studio instead of just writing their code in a text editor.

Before you can use the visual tools, you must meet the following requirements:

- **You must have a runnable project open to debug.** Class library projects such as the ones I discuss in Chapter 6, for instance, will not run without some kind of visual shell. See the later section "Class libraries" for instructions.

- **Visual Studio must be in Debug mode (also called Paused or Break mode).** When you press F5 or click the Play button to run your project from Visual Studio, you are putting the project in Debug mode.

- **The project must be paused to see runtime variables.** You pause the project with a breakpoint, which I talk about in the next section. Also, you can enter a project in Break mode, which I cover in the later section "Debugging the Projects."

Visual Studio provides a number of debugging tools of varying complexity. I cover the three most often-used tools:

- **Breakpoint:** A marker that you place on a line of code to pause the execution of a program.

- **Watch window:** A window that shows the runtime values of variables and objects.

- **Immediate window:** A command window that lets you type in runtime VB 2008 commands and see potential results.

Breakpoints

The breakpoint is your friend.

Allow me to suggest a scenario. You have a complicated algorithm that generates a final price for a user. Two object properties and three variables are used to create the final price. When you test your application, the price is wrong.

How do you figure out what the problem is? You know what line it is in, but you don't know the values of the variables. You could laboriously put five labels on your form and set the values of the labels equal to the two properties and three variables. Then, when you find the problem, you need to delete all the labels. A better way to find the problem is to set a breakpoint at that line and check the variables while the application is paused.

TIP

To view the values of variables, your application must be in a paused state, such as provided by a breakpoint. If you try and look at variable values while the application is running, you won't get what you expect. This is why developers use breakpoints.

Setting up breakpoints

When you play your applications from Visual Studio, you are actually entering Debug mode. From this mode, you can ask Visual Studio to pause the execution of the application at a specific line of code with a breakpoint.

You create a breakpoint by clicking the gray bar to the left of the line of code at which you would like the program to stop. This action leaves a little red dot on the gray bar, as shown in Figure 8-1.

When you play the project, the execution stops at that location. Press F5 after putting in a breakpoint, and you see execution stop at that line of code, as shown in Figure 8-2. Pressing F5 again continues execution of the program from that point.

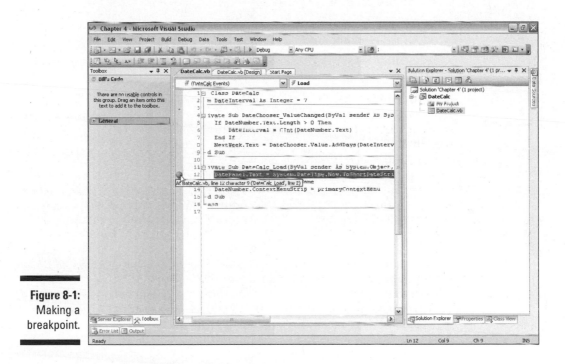

Figure 8-1:
Making a
breakpoint.

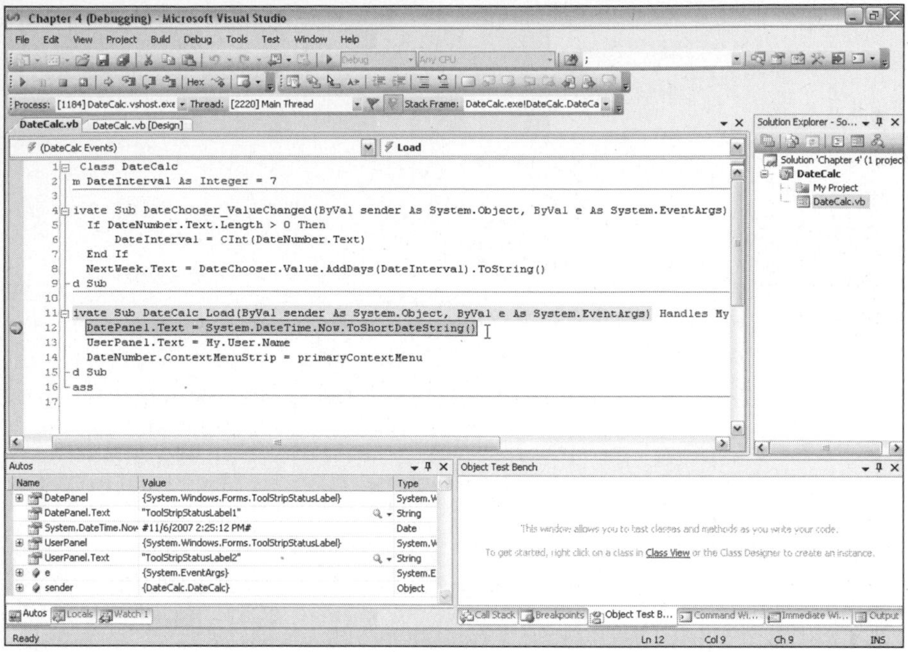

Figure 8-2:
Stopping
at a
breakpoint.

Managing breakpoints

Fast-forward to the middle of the development project, and you may find that you have way too many breakpoints to be useful. Visual Studio provides a tool for you to manage them all — the Breakpoints window, shown in Figure 8-3, which you invoke by pressing Ctrl+Alt+B.

The default Breakpoints window is useful when in a paused state, or just in normal development mode. The default columns include the Hit Count column, which describes when the breakpoint is hit during the execution of the code, and the Condition column, which describes an expression that must evaluate as true for the execution of the application to stop. Other considerations for deciding how to work with breakpoints include the following:

- ✔ You can add other Breakpoint window columns by selecting them from the Columns drop-down list, including columns that show what function the breakpoint is in, the Language, and When Hit. The When Hit column allows you to define a message to print or a macro to run when the breakpoint is reached.

- ✔ You can edit debugging functions — such as Hit Count, Condition, and When Hit — by right-clicking the breakpoint marker to the left of the code or by right-clicking the breakpoint in the Breakpoints window. The context menu that appears contains selections for each of these options that enable you to manage breakpoint functions.

Figure 8-3:
The
Breakpoints
window.

> ✔ Breakpoint properties simply make breakpoints quicker to use. While debugging, you can easily just set a breakpoint and go look at values to see what the problems are. Using the options, though, reduces the number of steps you need to go through to get the answer you need.

A breakpoint strategy becomes like a standard set of chess openings over time. Experience dictates how you use the debugging tools, based on your personal programming style.

The Watch window

Watches are little programmatic spies that you can place on objects to keep an eye on their values while stepping through code. Visual Studio provides four Watch windows, and on a project-by-project basis, they remember what you have chosen to watch.

To show the Watch window, choose Debug⇨Windows⇨Watch while in Debug mode, and then select one of the four Watch windows. The Watch window itself is essentially a table that shows the name of the object being watched, its type, and its value, as shown in Figure 8-4.

Figure 8-4:
The Watch
window.

To add a watch to the watch list, follow these steps:

1. **Pause the project, either by reaching a breakpoint or by clicking the Pause button on the toolbar.**

2. **In Code View, right-click the object that you want to watch and select Add Watch from the context menu.**

To see the value of a variable, it must be in scope. A variable is *in scope* when it exists within the block of code currently running. For instance, if you declare a variable within an event handler for a button, only when you click that button do the values of that variable become available to watch.

When in Debug mode, a variable is either with or without a value, just as it is when a program runs. The Watch window shows this very well, as shown in Figure 8-5.

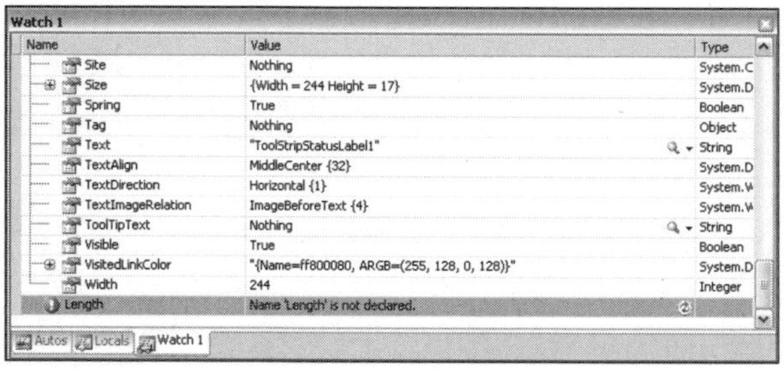

Figure 8-5:
Variables
in and out
of scope.

When the variable is without value, it appears with the error icon and the following text:

> *Variable.Name* is not declared or the module containing it is not loaded in the debugging session.

When the variable has a value, it is described with all properties.

The Watch window is a great way to watch whole objects, rather than just values in variables. Collections, such as arrays and datasets, often have a wide variety of properties and values that you need to check on every break. The Watch window provides a simple method for a structured check on values.

The Immediate Window

Sometimes a watch isn't enough, and you need to run a command while the application is paused. The Immediate Window, shown in context in Figure 8-6, is designed for just such a situation.

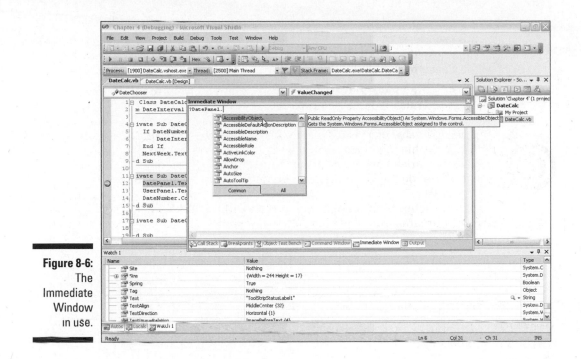

Figure 8-6:
The
Immediate
Window
in use.

The basic syntax for the Immediate Window is that of writing the values of expressions to the window using the `Debug.Print` method, which I cover in the next section. The shortcut for this method is the question mark.

To use the Immediate Window, as with most other debug tools, your project must be paused. To write the value of a variable to the screen, then, you simply type **?*VariableName*** into the window. In the example in Figure 8-6, I typed **?DatePanel.** to get the value of that property. If the value is out of scope, I would receive the same out-of-scope error as displayed in the Watch window.

Using the Immediate Window is more of a spot check than using many of the other debugging tools. If you are using conditional breakpoints that only break when variables contain certain values, you will find yourself using the Immediate Window to see what brought about the stoppage.

Using the Debugging Tools in the .NET Framework

Visual Studio provides great tools for debugging, but the .NET Framework itself also has some fantastic features that make debugging easier. These tools are more code-based and less visual. I go over a few of them here, and then cover a few more when I discuss debugging specific project types later in this chapter.

The Debug class

What would debugging be without a Debug class, right? Just like the windows earlier in this chapter are sort of the Windows Forms implementation of debugging, the Debug class is the DLL implementation of debugging.

The Debug class has a whole host of methods, properties, and events that assist you in seeing what your application does while it runs. The simplest example of a method in the Debug class is the Write method. The following steps get you started:

1. **In Visual Studio 2008, choose File⇨Project/Solution to open a Windows Application project.**

    For example, I opened the DateCalcChapter4 from the Sample applications.

2. **Double-click an empty place on the form to create a Form_Load event handler.**

    This example creates a DateCalc_Load function that handles the form load event.

3. **Insert a Debug.Write statement in the DateCalc_Load function, as follows:**

```
Private Sub DateCalc_Load(ByVal sender As System.Object, ByVal e As
            System.EventArgs) Handles MyBase.Load
    Debug.WriteLine("Loading Form")
End Sub
```

4. **Click the Play button in Visual Studio to enter Debug mode.**

5. **The Output window displays your message.**

There is more to the Debug class than the Write statement, but the most common use of the class is to track program execution, and the best way to track program execution is to drop breadcrumbs as parts of the program execute.

Error handling

Error handling and debugging go hand in hand. Debugging is the act of tracking down errors, and error handlers are designed to, well, handle errors!

Error handling is a big part of debugging, because the errors that are created by bugs in software should be caught and handled. An interesting phrase describes error handling in Visual Basic — Try-Catch. You *try* a piece of code. If a problem occurs, Visual basic throws an error, and you can *catch* that error.

The Try-Catch block looks like the following code. Visual Studio writes most of it for you. Just type **Try** in a function and press Enter, and Visual Studio automatically inserts the rest of the block.

```
Try

Catch ex As Exception

End Try
```

You can see that the `Catch` statement is catching something in particular that deserves a closer look — the `Exception` object.

The `Exception` object is what you get back from Visual Basic in runtime when an error occurs. It is what Visual Basic throws to you so that you can catch it with your error handling.

For instance, follow the steps in the previous section to get a `Form_Load` event handler method, except insert the code in Listing 8-1. Inside the `Try` block (line 2 of Listing 8-1), an `Integer` is set equal to a `String`, which you cannot do. (For more information, see Chapter 9.)

This test causes an error to occur, and an `Exception` object is the result. In the `Catch` part of the block (line 3 of Listing 8-1), you can get to the `Exception` object with its declaration ex.

Listing 8-1: Causing an Error in the Form_Load Event Handler

```
Try
    Dim bugInCode As Integer = String.Empty
Catch ex As Exception
    Debug.Write(ex.Message)
End Try
```

In Debug mode, you can look at the contents of the `Exception` object by typing **?ex** in the Immediate Window. Set a breakpoint on the `Debug.Write(ex.Message)` line and run the project. For the code in Listing 8-1, the `Exception` object returns all this useful information in the Immediate Window:

```
Data: {System.Collections.ListDictionaryInternal}
HelpLink: Nothing
HResult: -2147467262
InnerException: {System.FormatException}
IsTransient: False
Message: "Conversion from string "" to type 'Integer' is not valid."
Source: "Microsoft.VisualBasic"
StackTrace: "   at Microsoft.VisualBasic.CompilerServices.
             Conversions.ToInteger(String Value)
             at DateCalcChapter4.DateCalc.DateCalc_Load(
             Object sender, EventArgs e) in C:\Documents and Settings\sempf\
             My Documents\Visual Studio\Projects\OSIA\DateCalcChapter4\
             DateCalcChapter4\DateCalc.vb:line 9"
```

The `Exception` object returns a wealth of information about what went wrong. Some details may be hidden in objects that you need to look at separately, but two main pieces of information are front and center: The `Message` property (of the `Exception` object, which you name `ex`) has the error that occurred, and the `StackTrace` property has the line number. With those two pieces of information and the date you originally sent to the method, you have what you need to know 80 percent of the time.

All of this information can be used in application-level error handling. You can e-mail this information to yourself, return it to the user, or write it to a log file. More information on the various ways to get this done can be found on the Web. I would recommend the Microsoft Exception Management Blocks component, available from the Microsoft Patterns and Practices Web site at `http://msdn2.microsoft.com/en-us/practices/default.aspx`.

Debugging the Projects

Each of the projects I cover earlier in Part II — Windows Forms, Web Forms, class libraries, and XML Web services — have a similar set of debugging tools. The details I talk about earlier in this chapter work for all projects, but each of the project types has its own specific tweaks. I cover these in the following sections.

Windows Forms

Windows Forms applications are the most straightforward to debug, because they are stand-alone applications over which you have complete control. A few tricks are required when debugging Windows Forms, but I take this opportunity to cover the debugging feature you use most often — stepping through code. You can apply this feature to all project types, but it is best shown as part of a Windows Forms application.

The "Breakpoints" section, earlier in this chapter, describes how to use break-points and demonstrates how powerful they are. You can use this power to execute your code one line at a time and keep an eye on the specifics of object properties and variable values. The following steps get you started stepping through code:

1. **Load a Windows Application project by choosing File⇨Project/Solution and selecting a project file.**

   For example, I use the DateCalcChapter4 project.

2. **Press F10 to start debugging the project.**

   This starts running the project in Debug mode and stops the project on the first breakpoint found. For the DateCalcChapter4 example, you can set one at the Form_Load handler.

3. **To continue stepping through the code, press F10.**

   This walks through the code one line at a time in Break mode. You can use the Immediate Window, or you can mouse over variable names to see their values.

4. **To step over a method call, press F10.**

   This passes over the internal code of a method so that you stay in the flow of the original program.

5. **To step into a method, press F11.**

   This enters the functional code of a method call and may change the file you are looking at.

6. **To continue running the program in Run mode (that is, to exit Break mode), press F5.**

   This continues to run the program outside of Debug mode.

Using a combination of the breakpoints and stepping through code, you can solve most of the logic and execution problems that your program may have.

Web Forms

Web Forms are different, as I mention in Chapter 5, because they are running on an Internet Information Server (IIS) rather than directly on your workstation. While you can be running a Web Forms application on your workstation using either IIS or Visual Web Developer Web Server, it is still considered remote debugging, because the application is being handled by a separate system.

This brings whole new problems to debugging. First, you may need to debug a Web Forms application that is not running on your workstation. Second, environment variables (such as Session variables, which I discuss in Chapter 5) can make a large impact on your application. Knowing the values of these variables is important — in Break mode *or* Run mode.

Remote debugging

Remote debugging is necessary because if you are running a Web Forms application on a server that doesn't have Visual Studio installed, it won't have the necessary program to allow debugging. To install that program, follow these steps:

1. **Insert the Visual Studio 2008 Remote Debugger CD in the remote machine.**

2. **The Remote Debugger Setup program should run automatically.**

   If not, open the CD drive from Windows Explorer and launch the Remote Debugger Setup program.

Often, to debug on a remote machine, you need to have an Administrator account on that machine. When you open a Web project with a remote address, you can debug the project as if it were running locally on Visual Web Developer Web Server.

Trace

Some information about Web applications is not best gathered through debugging in Break mode. Sometimes if a page can be viewed in Run mode, but with comprehensive information about the execution of the page available, your problems can be solved.

Trace enables just that. Trace is enabled by changing the @Page directive at the top of an ASPX file. To do this, follow these steps:

1. **Open a Web project by choosing File⇨Project/Solution and selecting an ASP.NET project file.**

   For this example, I use DateCalcChapter5.

2. **Open a page by double-clicking it in the Solution Explorer.**

   I use the `default.aspx` page that I created with the Date Calculator in it.

   Note the `@Page` directive at the top of the page, like the following code. This appears on every ASP.NET page, and it is what the Web server uses to link the page to the code-behind file and set the language, among other things.

   ```
   <%@ Page Language="VB" AutoEventWireup="false"
           CompileWith="Default.aspx.vb" ClassName="Default_aspx" %>
   ```

3. **Add a `Trace` attribute to the `@Page` directive, setting `Trace="true"`, as follows:**

   ```
   <%@ Page Language="VB" AutoEventWireup="false"
           CompileWith="Default.aspx.vb" ClassName="Default_aspx"
           Trace="true" %>
   ```

4. **Save your changes, and then compile the application by choosing Build⇨Build Web Site.**

5. **Right-click the file you changed and select View in Browser.**

   The information provided by Trace appears at the bottom of the page.

Trace works great for XML Web services too!

Like the `Exception` object that I discuss earlier in this chapter, Trace has a whole host of information, well organized by ASP.NET. Sections include the following:

- **Request Details:** Gives the basic information about the request made to the server.

- **Trace Information:** Details the timing from step to step in the request, which is very important for discovering performance problems.

- **Control Tree:** Shows every `Server` and `User` control being used by the application.

- **Session State and Application State:** Displays the contents of the `Session` and `Application` variables at response time.

- **Request Cookies Collection and Response Cookies Collection:** Details the collections of cookies at response time.

- **Headers Collection and Response Headers Collection:** Shows the standard HTTP headers, usually used for debugging Web server problems. The Headers Collection is what came into the server, and the Response Headers Collection is what went to the client.

- **Form Collection:** Gives the values of all the form fields sent to the server.

> ✔ **QueryString Collection:** Displays the values of variables sent to the server in the URL.
>
> ✔ **Server Variables:** Shows a standard set of variables passed between all clients and servers, independent of platform or middleware.

You can see that this information is invaluable when debugging problems with Web applications. There is even more, too, because with the `Trace` class in the .NET Framework, you can insert notifications into your code that only appear in the Trace mode. Because changing a page to Trace mode just requires a change to the ASPX file, you can even do it in a production system. It is a very powerful tool; more can be discovered by searching for *ASP.NET Trace* in the MSDN Library at `http://msdn.microsoft.com/library`.

Class libraries

Class libraries are an interesting debugging problem just because they are not runnable by themselves. As I mention in Chapter 6, class libraries are used by other applications to componentize functionality. For this reason, they are only usable as part of other applications.

Chapter 6 describes how to use two projects in one solution. That is what you need to do to debug a class library. If you run a Windows Forms application that references a class library, and you have the project for the referenced class library in the same solution, when you step through the code in the Windows Forms application, the app steps right into the class library when you call a method or property of that class library.

To make this happen, follow these steps:

1. **Open a class library solution in Visual Studio.**

   For this example, I use the class library that I developed for Chapter 6, `DateCalcClassChapter6`.

2. **Add a project to the solution by choosing File⇨Add⇨New Project.**

3. **Select a Visual Basic Windows Application project from the Add New Project dialog box, name it something appropriate, and click the OK button.**

   I call mine `DateCalcShell`.

4. **Right-click the new project and select Add Reference from the context menu.**

5. **Click the Project tab, select the class library file project, and then click the OK button.**

6. **Double-click the** `Form1` **form to get a** `Page Load` **handler.**

7. **Add the code that calls a function of the class library project.**

   In my example, I just added a quickie variable called myDate that I set to a week from now using the IncreaseDate function, as follows:

```
Private Sub Form1_Load(ByVal sender As System.Object, ByVal e As
        System.EventArgs) Handles MyBase.Load
    Dim dateCalculator As New CalcClass2008.DateCalc()
    Dim myDate As DateTime
    myDate = dateCalculator.IncreaseDate(System.DateTime.Now, 7)
End Sub
```

8. **Press F10 to step into the application. Continue pressing F10 to move line by line through the code.**

   As you step into line 4 of the preceding code, the debugger opens the class library project and steps you through the code of the Increase Date function, and then returns you to the Form_Load event handler.

If you used Visual Basic 6 or 7, you may recognize this feature — it has been around for a while. The new object-oriented flavor of Visual Basic makes it look a little different, but it is really very much the same thing.

Web services

Web services are by far the most challenging to debug. Like with class libraries, you have to use some tricks to debug Web services. After you get past those tricks, it is very much like debugging any other type of project.

The key thing to remember about debugging Web services is that you can't debug unless you have access to the source code of the service itself. If you are using someone else's service, for instance, and a bug is in the code, your debugging doesn't show you all the advanced debugging information. If you have the code for both the Web service and the client application, you can debug both.

If you are debugging a Web service that you have developed locally — as described in Chapter 7 — you can just press F10 and enter Break mode to step through the code, just as in the preceding examples in this chapter. If the service is already running on a Web server, you may need to attach to the process that is running on that server.

To attach to a process to debug a Web service, do the following:

1. **Open a Web service project.**

   For this example, I use the project I developed for Chapter 7 called DateCalcChapter7.

2. **Choose Tools➪Attach to Process.**

   The Attach to Process dialog box appears, as shown in Figure 8-7.

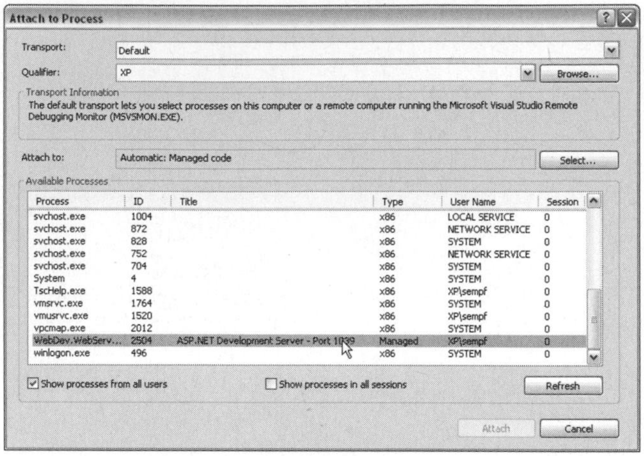

Figure 8-7:
The Attach
to Process
dialog box.

3. **Select the server running the Web service from the Qualifier drop-down list.**

4. **In the Available Processes box, choose either** `aspnet_wp.exe` **or** `w3wp.exe`.

   The `aspnet_wp.exe` file is used on Windows XP and 2000 servers; `w3wp.exe` is for Windows 2003 servers.

5. **Click the Attach button.**

6. **Click the OK button.**

When you press F8 to step into the project, Visual Studio can watch code running on the remote server that you have selected in the Attach to Process dialog box.

TIP

This method is also useful for other debugging actions. For more information, search for *Debugging Deployed ASP.NET Applications* in the MSDN Library at `http://msdn.microsoft.com/library`.

Part III
Making Your Programs Work

The 5th Wave   By Rich Tennant

"You might want to adjust the value on
your 'Nudge' function."

In this part . . .

Much of programming is about the details of *business logic* — the rules of the program you are writing. This part covers how to make decisions, do things more than once, and use and reuse code that is already out there, ripe for the picking, to make your job easier.

Chapter 9

Interpreting Strings and Things

*T*he core of an object-oriented programming language such as Visual Basic is the movement of information. Some other programming languages specialize in maintaining a link with hardware and some specialize in the management of machinery, but Visual Basic specializes in information.

How Visual Basic stores information internally is of great importance to you, the developer. Words, numbers, digital pictures, and locations inside the computer each have their own special *types*. These types all have their own methods, properties, and events because they are treated as objects in Visual Basic 2008.

In this chapter, I describe this feature of the language by showing how words, numbers, and dates (all types) are treated when referred to in programs. I discuss the functionality that an integer automatically acquires as part of a program, and the cool things that you can do with text the user enters.

I go over how to use types to your best advantage, too. For instance, validation of type is essential for making sure that the user enters the correct information (numbers, text, and so on) into your application. You can also manipulate information in interesting ways by using fantastic tools called regular expressions.

I briefly cover dates and date math in this chapter. You have a lot to understand about dates. To get there, though, you need to start at the beginning — by discovering the differences among types.

Changing one type into another is also covered in this chapter. For example, you can handle changing a number to a word in several different ways. Some of these methods are best used in specific situations, which I describe in this chapter.

Types of Information in Visual Basic

Computer programs, at their most basic, have two kinds of storage: volatile and nonvolatile. *Volatile storage* is the storage that the program uses while it is running; when the program stops, the stored information is gone. It is physically stored in the random-access memory (RAM) of your PC.

Nonvolatile storage is permanent storage, such as databases and text files; I cover nonvolatile storage in Part IV. Nonvolatile information is usually stored on the hard drive.

Volatile information is stored in "buckets" labeled by the kind of information that can go in them. Words, numbers, and dates, for instance, are different kinds of information. They are stored in volatile memory in buckets called variables, which are sorted by type.

Some of the types of information you frequently need to store in variables include the following:

- ✔ **Text:** Words are usually stored in the `String` type.
- ✔ **Dates:** Time and dates are stored in the `DateTime` type.
- ✔ **Numbers:** Numbers can be stored in several different ways — if you are a math specialist, you'll appreciate the `Integer` and `Double` types. *Integers* are whole numbers, and *doubles* are fractions stored as decimal numbers.

When working in Visual Basic, most of your programming time is spent writing the code to accept input from users, figuring out what type to put the input into, and putting it there.

Understanding types in Visual Basic

To create a new variable of a certain type in Visual Basic, you use the `Dim` statement. `Dim` stands for *dimension,* and it refers to the old days when you needed to set aside a parcel of memory to store the contents of the variable. That is actually what is still happening, so programmers still use the term. For instance, to declare a new string, you would code the following:

```
Dim MyNewString as String = "This is the content of my string variable!"
```

String values are surrounded by quotation marks. If you need to have a quotation mark in a string, use two quotation marks; for example, `"I use the word ""bucket"" too much in this chapter"`. Using two quotation marks is called *escaping the mark.* Other type values, such as numbers and dates, are referenced without quotation marks.

A *string* is an object, like all types, and sometimes the value of another object is of a `String` type. This can get confusing when enough objects are on the page. Essentially, you only need to dimension a new string object when you need to handle it individually.

The types, such as string and integer, available for use are many and varied. Table 9-1 covers the most often used types. You should know that more types exist and that you can create your own.

Table 9-1	Intrinsic Types in Visual Basic
Typo	*Description*
`Byte`	A single-digit number, such as 8.
`Char`	A single character, such as *r*.
`DateTime`	A date and time together, such as 3/4/2004 12:45:54 PM.
`Double`	A decimal number, such as 4.534.
`Integer`	A whole number, such as 56386.
`Object`	Anything. An object type can hold anything in the .NET Framework.
`String`	Words, such as *This is a string*

When you get data from a user or another source, such as a database, it will already have a type, usually `String` or `Object`. To use the data to do math, for instance, you need to change that string or object into the `Integer` or `Double` type. That is done with `CType`.

Changing types with CType

`CType` is Visual Basic's way of letting you change the type of a variable. Seeing how this works is best done by using a real-world example. Follow these steps to change the type of a variable:

1. **Open Visual Studio 2008 and choose File⇨New⇨Project.**

2. **Select a Windows Application project, and name it in the Name text box.**

   I named mine `StringsAndThings`. You could also use a Web Forms project for these steps.

3. **Change the solution name to Chapter 9 and click the OK button.**

   This isn't a requirement, but it will help to keep things organized if you choose to add other projects related to this chapter.

4. **Put two text boxes, a label, and a button on the default form, as shown in Figure 9-1.**

   You can use the Format➪Center in Form➪Horizontal function to center the fields, if you so desire.

   For this and all the chapters in Part III, I leave the default names for simplicity. *Never* do this in a production application. It makes the application hard for you to debug and impossible for someone else to maintain.

5. **Double-click Button1 to create an** `OnClick` **event handler.**

6. **Put the following code in the event handler for Button1:**

```
Label1.Text = TextBox1.Text + TextBox2.Text
```

7. **Press F5 to run the program.**

8. **Enter** 4 **in the first text box and** 56 **in the second text box.**

9. **Click Button1.**

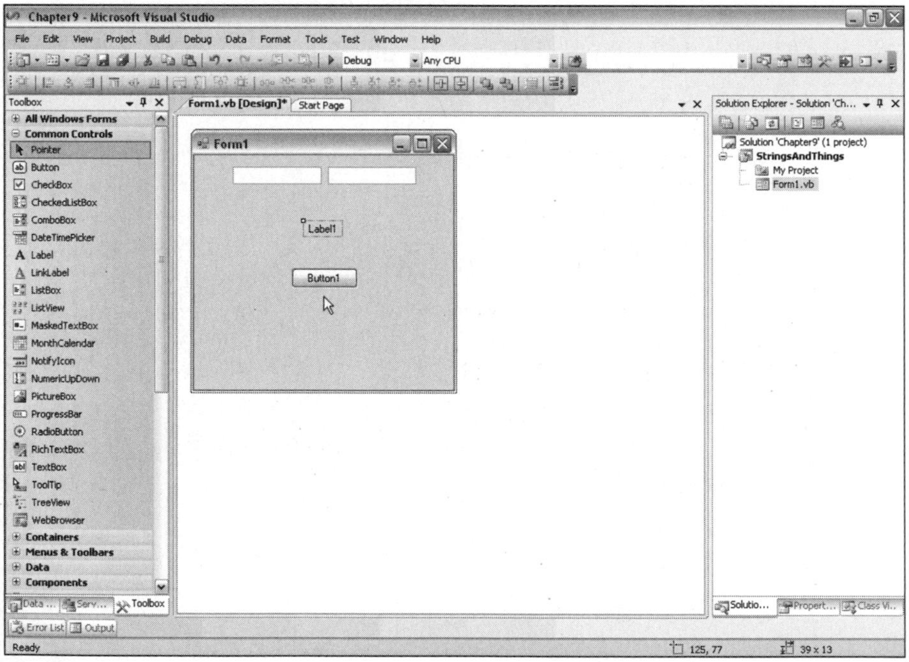

Figure 9-1:
The
StringsAnd
Things
sample
application.

Figure 9-2 shows the results. Whoops. Must be new math: 4 + 56 = 456? What happened?

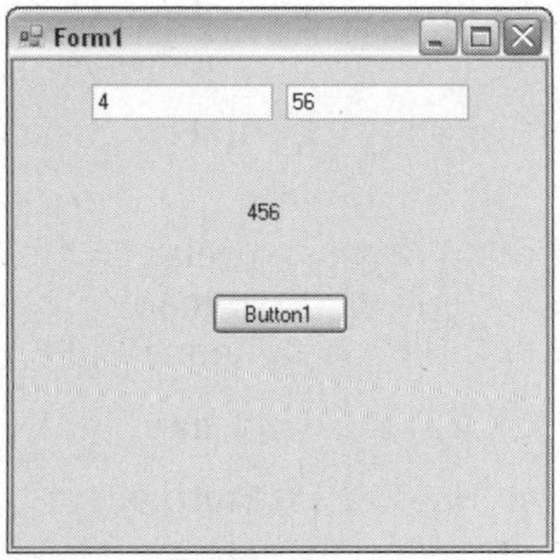

Figure 9-2:
New math.

What happened was that the program *concatenated* two strings (put them one after another) instead of adding two numbers. Visual Basic assumes that — because you didn't tell it differently — the two pieces of information entered into the text boxes were strings. This is usually a good assumption, but in this case, it was incorrect.

So what do you do? You need to tell Visual Basic that those values are integers. To do that, you use the aforementioned CType function. Try putting the following code in the event handler for Button1:

```
Label1.Text = CType(TextBox1.Text, Integer) + CType(TextBox2.Text, Integer)
```

The CType statement tells Visual Basic that it can expect integers from the Text property of TextBox1 and TextBox2. When you run the application again and enter the same values in the text boxes, you get the correct value in the label when you click the button.

Some shortcuts to the CType statement are throwbacks to earlier versions of BASIC:

- ✔ CStr casts from an object to a string. (To *cast* is to describe the action of using a CType.)

- ✔ CInt casts from a string to an integer. You could use CInt in the preceding code line if you wanted to, as follows:

```
Label1.Text = CInt(TextBox1.Text) + CInt(TextBox2.Text)
```

- ✔ CDate casts strings to dates.

- ✔ CBool casts a string or integer to a *Boolean* — a true or false value.

✔ CObl casts anything to an object — useful if you are interacting with an older language.

✔ CDbl casts types to a *double,* which is a decimal number.

Using a CType statement has certain implications, though. What happens if the user enters a few letters or words in those text boxes instead of numbers? In that case, Visual Basic gives the error message shown in Figure 9-3.

Visual Basic throws an InvalidCastException error because you can't change a letter to an integer easily — or at all. As they say, you just can't do that.

So what do you do? You have to force the user to only enter integers in this case. That is handled on the user interface side of things. What's more, it gives me the chance to introduce another new idea in types — using the Type as a static class.

In the following example, you are going to use a method of the Integer object, called TryParse. It's just like any other function, except it accepts its return value as a parameter, called an Out Parameter. I discuss classes and methods in more detail in Chapters 12 and 13.

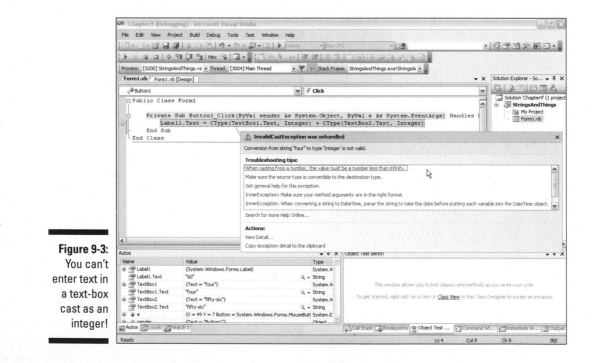

Figure 9-3:
You can't
enter text in
a text-box
cast as an
integer!

Controlling types with validation

You can do validation in Windows forms in many different ways — and in Web Forms for that matter. I have selected one of many ways because it works well in simple applications. To restrain the user to entering only a specified type of information (integers, in this case), follow these steps:

1. **In the** StringsAndThings **project you have been using, change to Code View.**

2. **Add two new variables in the Declaration section, right under the Form statement:**

```
Dim firstnumber As Integer = 0
Dim secondNumber As Integer = 0
```

3. **Change the** Button1_Click **event code to the following:**

```
Try
    'Check for integers first
    If Not Integer.TryParse(TextBox1.Text, firstnumber) Then
        Throw New ApplicationException( _
        "The first number must be an integer")
    End If
    If Not Integer.TryParse(TextBox2.Text, secondNumber) Then
        Throw New ApplicationException( _
        "The second number must be an integer")
    End If

    'Do the math if we haven't errored out.
    Label1.Text = firstnumber + secondNumber

Catch ex As Exception
    MessageBox.Show(ex.Message, "Error in entry", _
        MessageBoxButtons.OK, MessageBoxIcon.Error)


End Try
```

4. **Choose Debug⇨Start Debugging to run the program.**

5. **Try and enter something other than an integer in one of the text boxes.**

    The new code will warn you with the error message that you entered.

Obviously, I have added a whole lot of code to this simple example. An unspoken rule says that for every line of functional code, four lines of code make sure that it works. When you add in the code, you have to add more code to make sure the user hasn't entered bad data . . . well, you get the idea.

How this works is pretty straightforward. It follows principles that programmers use in even more complex examples:

- ✔ **Start by setting up holding variables for the values that you want to work with.**

- ✔ **Test the values in the text boxes, and if the values are valid, set the holding variables equal to the tested values.**

  `TryParse` is very convenient for this, because it returns False if the change to an integer doesn't work and leaves the holding variable that was passed in unchanged. I discuss `TryParse` at the end of the chapter.

- ✔ **If all of that worked, do the original function code, using the holding variables.**

  You are done with the text boxes.

- ✔ **If it didn't work, you have wrapped the whole thing in a Try Catch block.**

  This informs the user of the problem and could implement any global error handling that you have set up.

Making Words Work with the String Type

When you do want words, not numbers, you are dealing with the `String` type. Traditionally, the BASIC languages — Visual Basic included — were weak in string handling. Because of the .NET Framework backing up Visual Basic 2008, many of those problems have disappeared.

The fantastic tools built into strings

When you declare a string and fill it, the string becomes an object with its own methods, properties, and events. To get started using strings, open a new Windows Forms application and add a button, two text boxes, and a label, as described in the earlier section "Changing types with CType." Then add a title string to your program by following these steps:

1. **In Design View, drag a second label to the form.**

2. **Double-click a blank part of the form to switch to Code View with a** `Form1_Load` **event handler.**

3. **Enter the following code in the** `Form1_Load` **event handler:**

```
Dim TitleString As String = "This is my sample program."
Label2.Text = TitleString
```

When you run the application, it should have a title on the form where you dropped the second label. Now that you have a `String` object in your program, you have the opportunity to look at some of the cool things that you can do with a `String` object.

For instance, look at the `ToUpper` method. Instead of `Label2.Text = TitleString`, enter the following:

```
Label2.Text = TitleString.ToUpper.
```

The form shows the uppercase version of the string without changing the original string! To replace a specified character with another character, use the `Replace` method, as follows:

```
Label2.Text = TitleString.Replace("i", "!")
```

The `String` object has 46 methods, properties, and events built in, and all of them are available to any declared string. Find out more by searching for "String class, methods" in the Help files.

I would be remiss if I didn't mention `String.Format`. It is a tool that is built into the `String` type itself — not any particular string. It uses a string-formatting basic: referring to an argument with an ordinal. For instance:

```
MessageBox.Show(String.Format("The text in Label2 is {0}",Label2.Text))
```

The ordinal in the curly braces refers to the first argument. If another argument followed the `Label2.Text` statement, it would be referred to as `{1}`.

Essentially, this is a yet another way to build text strings, just like concatenation and the `StringBuilder` class. (For more about `StringBuilder`, see the section "Constructing strings with the StringBuilder class," later in this chapter.) `String.Format` is great for building URLs in ASP.NET pages.

Emptiness — handling nulls

Because strings are objects, they can be set to various values that one would not think of as strings. Primarily, these values are different ways to say that the string is empty.

For instance, one preset value is called `String.Empty`. What is it equal to, you ask?

```
""
```

Yup. Nothing. A whole property to refer to nada. Why? In case the value of nothing changes. It is a little more elegant than coding `MyString = ""`.

The worst of these empty values are *nulls,* variables full of nothing, not even zero or an empty string. Nulls come in two flavors — those assigned by the .NET Framework and those given to you by databases. The database nulls, additionally, come in one flavor for each kind of database. (No, I am not kidding.) I cover databases in Chapter 15.

The nulls used by the framework are pretty simple. Setting a string to the value of null is just like saying that it equals nothing — not `String.Empty`, not `""`, not 0, but actually nothing.

To see whether a string contains a null value, you can use the `IsDbNull` method built into Visual Basic. I cover If-Then statements in Chapter 10, but here is a preview:

```
If IsDbNull(MyString) Then
        MessageBox.Show("That string is null")
End If
```

Frankly, null values should be avoided because of the need to check for them at every turn. You don't need to use null values to code good programs. In the flow of your application, make sure that every variable has a type and a value.

To further confuse matters, not just any variable can be set to be nullable. I don't recommend this, because a null variable is usually a mark of a problem and should be handled like the error that it usually represents, a `Null ReferenceException`. Nonetheless, if you do need it, just add a question mark to the end of the declaration, like this:

```
Dim MyString as String?
```

This is actually shorthand for the following generic expression:

```
Dim MyString as Nullable(Of String)
```

Both do the same thing. Now in addition to being empty, `MyString` can be null, or Nothing in VB dialect. It is more or less the same as the database null, except you can test for it like this:

```
If IsNothing(MyString) Then
        MessageBox.Show("It is nothing")
End If
```

Finding Tools for Managing User Input

Continuing on the thread of discussing getting values from users, you may need to manage the input you get from the users after the input becomes values inside your system. Strings, especially, are subject to manipulation, either by building new strings for output or by changing existing strings for storage.

The StringBuilder class is a fantastic tool that was new for the .NET Framework 1.0, and it has been updated for the 3.5 version of the .NET Framework. It allows you to systematically make decisions about how to make big strings out of many little strings.

Several high-end programming books are devoted entirely to *regular expressions,* which is a special language devoted to handling string patterns. I don't cover even 10 percent of what there is to know about regular expressions here, but I give you enough information so that you can read a book about regular expressions without being lost.

Constructing strings with the StringBuilder class

StringBuilder is a class that is designed to help you manipulate strings. Often, it is used for creating output strings from various sources of input, such as a database, an input file, or user input.

The StringBuilder class is part of the .NET Framework that isn't included in the default project. To use it, you need to add a new line of code to the very top of the Code View. The new line 1 is as follows:

```
Imports System.Text
```

You need to add this line because the StringBuilder class is really the System.Text.StringBuilder class. To reference it, you need to use the Imports statement. You can reference an object with the entire path, but it's simpler to just add the System.Text reference.

After you have that, you can create a new StringBuilder object in the code for the Form1_OnLoad event handler. Then you can build new strings!

The great little functions available in the `StringBuilder` class include the following:

- **Append:** Adds the provided text to the end of the original string.
- **Insert:** Places the provided text into the original string at the specified location.
- **Remove:** Takes a range of characters from the string.
- **Replace:** Similar to the `Replace` method I describe in the section "The fantastic tools built into strings," earlier in this chapter, this method replaces specified instances of strings with the string you supply.

The `StringBuilder` class performs string manipulations that you can do other ways. However, it is a very elegant solution to a problem that you will face all the time: Visual Basic programmers must constantly stitch strings together and then go back and make changes based on changed requirements. The `StringBuilder` class makes implementing changes to strings easier if you use it to start with.

For instance, take a look at the code that you could use to construct a new title string, as described in the earlier section "The fantastic tools built into strings." Replace the lines of code that assign the title . . .

```
Dim TitleString As String = "This is my sample program."
Label2.Text = TitleString
```

. . . with the following lines:

```
Dim sb As StringBuilder = New StringBuilder
sb.Append("This ")
sb.Append("is ")
sb.Append("a ")
sb.Append("title.")
sb.Insert(10, "new ")
Label2.Text = sb.ToString()
```

This code writes a title in `Label2` that reads "This is a new title." The `Insert` statement puts the word *new* in the middle of the string — something that is notoriously difficult to do in the course of programming logic. The `StringBuilder` class does this for you — and does it faster and better than any other method.

Manipulating strings with regular expressions

After a string is built, you often need to search or modify the string. *Regular expressions,* a traditional part of the Perl language, are a complex way to manage strings using fantastic, intricate, innovative coded strings to describe what you need to change.

Regular expressions are based on patterns. *Patterns* are just what they sound like — combinations of characters that are recognizable by a definition, such as [a-z] for all lowercase letters. The complexity comes in when you try and make the definition.

Regular expressions are used for a number of wonderful things:

✔ Searching a string for values, right within your code

✔ Editing strings using a pattern

✔ Validating user input against values too complicated to be shown as a string

Two major components make up a pattern:

✔ **Literals:** Exact representations of a string that you are looking for — like the examples earlier in this chapter. "0" is a literal, as is "Sample."

✔ **Metacharacters:** Descriptions of categories of characters. Metacharacters are normally defined by using square brackets and dashes. For instance, the range of numbers from 0 to 1000 would be described as "[0-1000]".

For instance, if you wanted to make sure that TitleString contained the string "sample," you could do it using Regular Expressions. You just generate a new Regex object and use the Match function, as follows:

```
Dim myPattern As New Regex("sample")
If myPattern.IsMatch(TitleString) Then
    MessageBox.Show("The title is Valid")
End If
```

You will probably need to add Imports System.Text.RegularExpressions as the first line of your code — above the class declaration — for regular expressions to work.

Regular expressions aren't just for validation, either. For instance, you can split a string using a pattern, breaking another string into parts using the characters and metacharacters specified in the pattern.

You can also replace characters using a pattern. The Replace method of the Regex object tells the string, "Hey, replace anything that matches this pattern with this new text." This is astonishingly powerful, as I am sure you can imagine. When working with data manipulation, you are constantly asked to change large strings. "Replace all integers with an X" is a common one. The following code actually works:

```
myPattern.Replace(newString, "[0-9]", "X")
```

I spent one section on a topic that could — and does — fill an entire book. If you are into string manipulation, regular expressions will be a powerful tool for you. For more information, search for "regular expressions" online.

Things That Aren't Strings — Numbers and Dates

Though you spend most of your time in Visual Basic with words and strings, sometimes you need to work with other types. Numbers and dates have a big place, and they are fairly tough to work with.

Integers and reals and imaginaries, oh my!

Numbers are covered by a whole host of types. For the purpose of this discussion, I cover only two — whole numbers and decimals. Whole numbers use the `Integer` type. Decimals use the `Double` type.

Numbers are really fairly simple — the main thing to remember is that unlike strings, you do not refer to them using quotation marks. When setting a variable equal to an integer or a double, you just directly refer to the number, as follows:

```
Dim myInteger as Integer = 65
Dim myDouble as Double = 6.555
```

Any number type can be manipulated with operator symbols, as shown in Table 9-2.

Table 9-2	Operators
Operator	*Description*
+	Addition
–	Subtraction
*	Multiplication
/	Division
%	Modulo (the remainder of a division)

To add two numbers using an operator, you build code that looks just like the code used to concatenate the input from two text boxes, as described in the earlier section "Changing types with CType." It is just myAnswer = my Number + myDouble. Numbers of any sort can usually be added together, as long as the variable for the answer is of a type that can handle it. In this case, myAnswer has to be a Double type, or the numbers after the decimal point in myDouble will get lost.

Just like all the great tools that are built into strings, numbers have a few built-in methods that assist with making sure that they are as expected. For instance, the Integer type has a MaxValue and MinValue method, so you can make sure that an operation won't overload the variable.

Variables are just memory locations and have a specific amount of space allocated. Integers can only be between –2,147,483,647 and 2,147,483,647. This sounds like a big range for numbers, but you will be surprised how easily you can overwhelm that range.

Doubles have a few other methods that represent wild math values. You can test for values that represent PositiveInfinity, NegativeInfinity, and Epsilon — that wonderful number approaching zero but not reaching zero that your freshman-year calculus teacher kept talking about. Because all of these imaginary numbers are possible outcomes to mathematical equations, it is great to be able to test for them.

Working with dates and date math

Dates are a whole different story. Not only does a whole separate category of applications use dates — as compared with heavy numerical applications — but it also takes a different mind-set to use the DateTime types in Visual Basic.

Let me start with one straightforward fact — whether you need a date or a time or both, Visual Basic essentially stores the whole bunch in a single type. The type that you use most often is DateTime; as you may expect, it holds both a date and a time.

In Part II, I show you date math by building the Date Calculator program that finds the difference between two dates using a method built into the Date Time type, just as you use the ToUpper and ToLower methods to manipulate the content of the string variable.

The DateTime type has a blue million built-in methods. The following list describes just a few of the most powerful:

- ✔ **Add:** You can add any type of span to a date in a DateTime type. For instance, Hours, Minutes, and Days are some of the spans available in the Add method.

✔ Component: The Component properties allow you to just get a part of a DateTime type. For instance, the Month property gets just the month out of a date.

✔ Conversion: The Conversion methods help you to change a date to another common format. For instance, the ToUniversalTime method converts the date in the DateTime object to UTC universal time — handy for international applications.

In addition, a few methods and properties don't fall into any category; instead, they do something specific. For example, the IsDaylightSavingsTime determines whether the date depends on daylight saving time in the United States.

To get a better idea of how the DateTime type works, take a look at the chapters in Part II. I use it extensively while designing and building the Date Calculator application.

You can find a lot more to dates than this, though. For instance, to get the current date in a DateTime variable, you can use the Now function, as in the following code line. It gives you the current date down to the nanosecond.

```
Dim myDate as DateTime = Now
```

You can also get the string representations of dates and times. For instance, say that you need the name of a month that you uncovered using one of the Component categories of DateTime type methods. The MonthName function gives you a string that contains the actual name of the month:

```
Dim MyMonth As Integer = 4
Dim Name As String
Name = MonthName(MyMonth)
MessageBox.Show(Name)
```

You get a message box that says "April" — a very handy tool for user interface creation, because users don't want to see a number; they want to see a word!

One last thing on dates — format providers allow you to show dates in any wonderful way you want. The DateTimeFormatProvider is a global tool that allows you to format dates in a flexible, universal way. The most common way to use the format provider is with the ToString method. The following code returns "Saturday, August 7, 1971 12:00:00 AM":

```
Dim myDate As DateTime = "8/7/1971"
MessageBox.Show(myDate.ToString("F"))
```

Some of the other format providers for dates include those shown in Table 9-3. Notice that the case of the value used in the ToString method is important. More can be discovered by searching for "DateTime.Parse method" at the MSDN Library Web site.

Table 9-3	DateTime Format Providers
Format Provider	*Sample Output*
D	8/7/1971
D	Saturday, August 7, 1971
G	8/7/1971 12:00 AM
G	8/7/1971 12:00:00 AM
S	1971-08-07T00:00:00
Y	August 1971

Changing Types with Parse and TryParse

Parse is a term used by system architects when they need to get something from one format to another, but they don't really know how. In Visual Basic, the Parse and TryParse methods give you a way to get a value into a new format while controlling exactly how it is done.

To use the Parse method, you need to understand something complex about Visual Basic — types are objects, too. Just as a variable can be declared as a DateTime type, the DateTime type itself is an object of Type type. That means types have their own methods, properties, and events.

Note that every object has a ToString() method. The ToString() method isn't always what it seems. Ostensibly, it is designed so that you can see the object as a string, but it isn't always obvious what should be shown when you ask for a string version of an object (such as the ToString() method of a Graphics object, for example). Don't depend on the ToString() method — use Parse, ConvertTo, or CStr instead, and allow the system to throw an error if it gets confused. Better that than bad data.

One of the most common problems is taking a string from the Text property of a TextBox and making it into a usable type such as a date. When someone enters "8/7/1971" into a text box, it is just a string, not a DateTime type. Strings are useful, but you can't add a number of days to a date entered as a string because, according to Visual Basic, it isn't a date!

To make, for instance, a string into a date, you use the Parse method of the DateTime type. Logically, you follow a number of steps:

1. **Get a date as a string,** myString, **from a database or user input.**

2. **Declare a new** DateTime **type called** myDate **to handle the new date.**

3. **Use the** `DateTime.Parse` **method to make a new** `DateTime` **variable from the string, as follows:**

```
Dim myString as String = "8/7/1971"
Dim myDate as new DateTime
myDate = DateTime.Parse(myString)
```

The `TryParse` method is very much the same, but it is more useful if you aren't sure that the value in `myString` is a date. Because `TryParse` doesn't return a value, but instead accepts a value such as a subroutine, it will not throw an error if the value in `myString` is not able to be parsed. Instead, it will return a null. The following code shows what the preceding code would look like using `TryParse`:

```
Dim myString as String = "8/7/1971"
Dim myDate as new DateTime
DateTime.TryParse(myString, myDate)fv
```

Chapter 10

Making Decisions in Code

*T*hey don't call the code in business applications *logic* for nothing. Many applications that you write in Visual Basic involve logic, and much of logic involves making decisions. In fact, making decisions represents the single most important process in business. You can't proceed with producing business applications without understanding the complexities of replicating the human decision-making process using Visual Basic 2008 code.

In this chapter, I give you a design procedure to follow when describing a business process for your applications. This process, which is a derivative of basic flowcharting, assists you in all decision-making designs — not just programming code.

Then I show you how to work with the three decision-making tools in Visual Basic — single process, multiple choice, and exceptions — which are utilized in the Visual Basic code by the `If-Then-Else`, `Select-Case`, and `Try-Catch` constructs, respectively. You see how these three constructs can be used to assure that your business applications most closely replicate the human decision-making processes you are trying to replace.

Designing Business Logic

I have a client who describes all business process logic as *those if-then-goto diagrams*. Given the number of degrees this client has under his belt, I always assumed that he really knew what he was talking about. And I was right! When I showed this gentleman a four-page, sophisticated process flow (the diagrams I present in this chapter), he picked out the only flaw in my logic in about 15 minutes. (Wouldn't I love for all my clients to think like that?)

I use this example to illustrate that outlining the business logic is the single toughest situation that a programmer deals with on a daily basis. The business logic serves as the basis for the mechanical code between the user interface and the data in an application. This code determines how the user views the information he or she is after, and how that information gets manipulated when saved.

Before I delve into each example of code in the following sections, I discuss a process for designing business logic using a flowchart. I go over the basics of application design in Chapter 3, but the problem of logic design is a specific situation that not all business applications encounter.

The reason for using a flowchart to describe business logic is straightforward. Modeling the *process⇨decision⇨direction* system using a flowchart is exactly what you will need to do when modeling program logic. Even with a large system, it benefits you as the programmer to model complex loops and decisions using flowcharts.

Depicting Logic with Flowchart Components

A *flowchart* is a "pictorial representation of an orderly step-by-step solution to a problem," according to Indiana State University. I couldn't agree more. A flowchart is simply lines that connect three structures representing communication, processes, and decisions. Flowchart magic — that is, the business or application logic — is depicted by how you combine these components (also known as *nodes*).

For example, a comprehensive flowchart that describes a morning routine might look something like Figure 10-1. This particular flowchart uses the process and decision components, depicted by rectangles (like *Wake Up*) and diamonds (like *Shower last night?*), respectively. Obviously, this morning routine is something that you would not replicate in code, but because you have hopefully performed a similar process in the last 24 hours, it makes a great example!

Communicating with the user

Of the three components of an application flowchart, communicating with the user becomes the part of the program visible to the outside world. To the user, this communication may come across as a message written to the screen, or a printout. Program flow for user communication is represented by a box with rounded corners, as in the In/Out diagram shown in Figure 10-2.

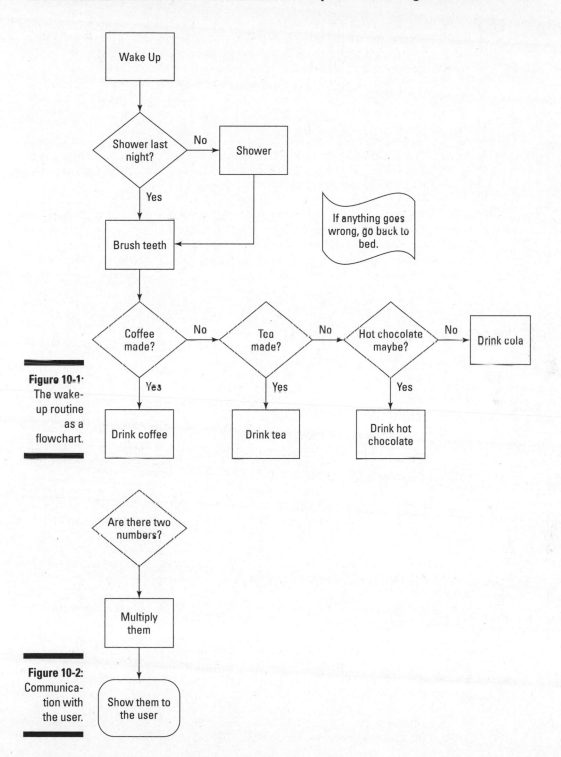

Your program successfully communicates with the user when the following happens:

✔ The output is tangible.

✔ The program produces a printout, even if it's just printed to the screen.

The user would expect feedback from the program at this point.

Defining the process

A process component of a program flowchart depicts a block of code that handles a single interaction with an entity. For example, acquiring input from the user and updating the database are processes that may be depicted in a flowchart. Process components (like the drinking processes from the morning routine depicted in Figure 10-1) are represented by rectangles, as shown in Figure 10-3.

Figure 10-3:
Morning
routine
processes.

The following three characteristics identify a process component:

✔ The node has no output.

✔ It represents a business rule.

✔ It describes a function that would usually be performed manually.

Making a decision

The core of the flowchart is the decision component, which has associated branches that allow the chart's flow to change direction. *Branching* (that is, following a branch in the flowchart) is that magic that adds flexibility and substance to the program logic. Without decisions to make, the flowchart is just a list of things to do (processes) and stuff to show to (or ask of) people (communication).

The decision node is physically very simple; it's a diamond in the diagram that requests a yes or no answer. Figure 10-4 shows the decision diamond and its branches. One branch comes in with the input, and two branches go out — one for yes and one for no.

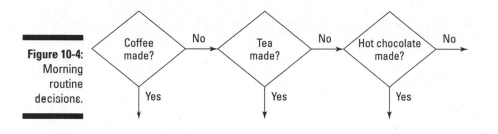

Figure 10-4:
Morning
routine
decisions.

A decision component

- ✔ Has one input and two outputs.
- ✔ Is phrased as a question (like a contestant's "answers" in *Jeopardy!*).
- ✔ Requires a feat of logic to pass the node.

You can think of the decision component as management input to the normal processes of business. Suppose you have a bunch of staffers who perform a set of processes day in and day out. If this group suddenly needs to deal with a single unusual decision, a multiple-choice question, or an exception, it may call in the managers to make a decision. Such a situation would constitute a decision node in a human process flowchart.

A computer process has similar decision-making situations, which you can divide into three categories:

- ✔ **Single process:** A simple "If this, then that; else go on as usual" sort of decision. An example of a single-process decision would be driving on the highway: "If the car in front of me stops, then I should hit my brakes; else I keep going."

- ✔ **Multiple choice:** A process that has a lot of options. "If she wants it blue, then buy blue paint; if she wants it green, then buy green paint; if she wants it red, then buy red paint; else drink beer."

- ✔ **Exception:** A special kind of single process. This is a decision when you didn't want to make a decision. "Go on as usual. If it breaks, call the manager."

Implementing These Processes in Visual Basic

To describe the processes in code, you need to know what the processes look like in a diagram. Properly designed, the diagram tells you what you are describing in code.

Single process

The single process is fairly simple — a single decision, isolated within a flow, is usually a single process. In some cases, you are actually looking at an exception. Largely, though, if you are looking at an image like Figure 10-5, it is a single process.

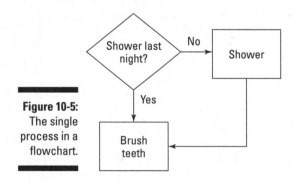

Figure 10-5:
The single process in a flowchart.

Single-decision processes execute a block of code if a statement is true. In Visual Basic, you need to provide the program's decision point with a *Boolean statement* — that is, something that can be evaluated as either true or false — to decide whether the code is to be executed. For example, check out these steps for a quick single-decision project:

1. **Open Visual Studio and create a new Visual Basic 2008 Windows Application project.**

2. **Drag a** `Textbox` **control and a** `Button` **control from the Toolbox to the form.**

3. **Double-click the** `Button` **control to have Visual Studio generate its** `OnClick` **event handler.**

4. In Code View for the `OnClick` **event handler, add the code that gives your program a single decision to make.**

In my example, I add the following code to display a message box if the right word is typed into the text box:

```
If TextBox1.Text = "Showered" Then
        MessageBox.Show("Brush Teeth!")
End If
```

Notice that this code shows an `If` statement followed by an `End If` statement. An `If` statement requires an `End If` statement only when you have multiple statements to execute. A single statement can be put on one line, like so:

```
If TextBox1.Text = "Showered" Then MessageBox.Show("Brush teeth!")
```

But in general, every control-flow statement in Visual Basic has a start and an end line. Also, the start line (the `If` condition is this example) can become more complex. If either of two possible answers can cause the message box to show, you can generate a Boolean statement by connecting exactly two statements with a conditional operator.

For example, if you want to support showers or baths, the code can be written as follows to mimic the English in this requirement:

```
If TextBox1.Text = "Showered" OR TextBox1.Text = "Took Bath" Then
        MessageBox.Show("Brush Teeth!")
End If
```

You can link two conditional `If` statements. Use two linked `If` statements when two possible results to the decision can cause two different lines of code to be executed in an exclusive way. You can link two conditional `If` statements with an `Else` statement, which works just like the English "If this, then that; else the other."

The `Else` statement is for the "No" branch on the decision box in your flow-chart. An `Else` statement shows up in the following code:

```
If TextBox1.Text = "Showered" Then
        MessageBox.Show("Brush Teeth!")
Else
        MessageBox.Show("Shower.")
End If
```

You can also link several `If-Then-Else` statements to handle a multiple-choice process. The `ElseIf` statement can help with that, as follows:

```
If TextBox1.Text = "Showered last night" Then
      MessageBox.Show("Brush teeth!")
ElseIf TextBox1.Text = "Showered two nights ago" Then
      MessageBox.Show("Shower again!")
Else
      MessageBox.Show("Shower!")
End If
```

This example is startlingly like the next in a series of conditional statements that are available in Visual Basic — proving once and for all that you can accomplish the same task in more than one way in Visual Basic. For many multiple-choice environments, the best choice in code is the Select-Case statement.

Multiple choice

Multiple-choice processes are equally obvious to code if you are very honest in your diagram. The fact is that few designers are honest enough to write a diagram like that shown in Figure 10-6. This tiered structure, though, is the unquestionable signature of a multiple-choice process.

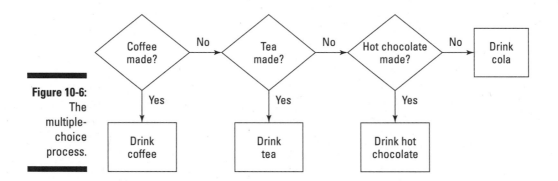

Figure 10-6: The multiple-choice process.

Effectively, this diagram shows several single-process diagrams in a row. Visual Basic 2008 provides you with a structure that handles this kind of situation. A good software design takes advantage of as much of the language in question as possible.

Whereas an `If-Then-ElseIf` statement evaluates a number of different answers, the Select-Case statement evaluates the same variable against a number of possible answers.

For example, the `If-Then-ElseIf` statement shown in the previous section compares the same text box to two different values. It could have just as easily compared two different text boxes to two different values.

The Select-Case statement is designed to compare the same variable to several possible values. The following code shows how to write a Select-Case statement that accomplishes the same thing as an `If-Then-ElseIf` statement.

```
Select TextBox1.Text
     Case "Coffee Made"
          MessageBox.Show("Drink Coffee!")
     Case "Tea Made"
          MessageBox.Show("Drink Tea!")
     Case "Hot Chocolate Made"
          MessageBox.Show("Drink Hot Chocolate!")
     Case Else
          MessageBox.Show("Drink Cola!")
End Select
```

The code in a Select-Case statement can do exactly the same thing as the code in an `If-Then-ElseIf` statement (as in the preceding code and the code shown in the previous section), but the Select-Case statement is much easier to read, and it actually runs a little faster.

You can also put a comma-delimited list of values in each case to give almost a two-dimensional grid feel to the process. Using a comma-delimited list that way is pretty slick, and an elegant way to code the multiple-choice process as designed in the preceding code.

The Select-Case statement isn't the only process that is similar to the `If-Then-ElseIf` statement. Another process is the exception process, where you find yourself writing a flow that says, "Try to go on unless something goes wrong; then do this." In VB 2008, this is called a Try-Catch statement.

Exception

The *exception* is a special case of the single-process model. When you're writing a flow, and you suddenly need to put in a process that says "If this isn't as expected, do that," you're dealing with an exception. Figure 10-7 shows what an exception looks like in a flowchart.

Figure 10-7:
How I handled an exception.

If anything goes wrong, go back to bed.

An exception is different from an error. An *error* is a flaw in one of the layers of an application — for example, a bad database row or a failed network connection; or in the worst case, an error is a bad piece of code. An exception is an expected error. It is something that you figure might happen, though you don't want it to, and you have a piece of logic to deal with it. For more about exceptions, see Chapter 12.

The Try-Catch statement is different from the other two decision structures. It assumes the following:

- ✔ You have a list of processes that you want to perform.
- ✔ You want to redirect the process flow if an error occurs.
- ✔ You have processes to follow if an error is encountered.

The Try-Catch statement is best for that process that is hard to diagram — "Do this unless something goes wrong; then do that."

The list of things to do goes under the `Try` statement, and each expected error goes with a `Catch` statement. Each `Catch` statement includes the process that is to be run if that `Catch` statement is reached. If no errors occur, the code in the `Catch` statements is ignored.

The following code shows an example of a Try-Catch statement based on Figure 10-1, just to keep things consistent. The `MorningRoutine` function would consist of all the decision code in the chapter so far.

```
Try
    MorningRoutine()
Catch somethingWentWrong as Exception
    MessageBox.Show("Something went wrong - go back to
            bed")
End Try
```

When using a Try-Catch block to catch a logic exception (like the data is in error) rather than a technical error (like the database is broken), use an `ApplicationException` rather than an `Exception` with the `Catch` clause.

The following code is a much more common use of a Try-Catch statement. Notice how I use the `Message` property of the exception that is caught to tell the user what went wrong:

```
Dim smallNumber as Integer
Dim largeNumber as Integer
Try
     smallNumber = 4534
     largeNumber = 7654
     largeNumber = smallNumber * LargeNumber
Catch badNumber as InvalidCastException
     MessageBox.Show("The number was bad - " & badNumber.Message)
```

```
Catch somethingElse as Exception
    MessageBox.Show("Something else went wrong - " & somethingElse.Message)
End Try
```

The exceptions that make up the Catch statements are an exciting part of the .NET Framework and a little beyond the scope of this chapter — or even this book. When something unexpected happens, such as an error, the framework throws an exception, and that exception is what you are catching with the preceding code.

I should mention Finally. After a Try-Catch statement, sometimes you need to do things regardless of whether an error occurred. If that is the case, put the code in a Finally statement. For instance, if you are dealing with a database, you should close the connection to the database on success or failure. That instruction would appear in a Finally block, after your last Catch block.

You can find hundreds of exception types, and you can write your own. For more on exception management, see Chapters 8 and 12; for further research, search for "Exception Management" in the MSDN library.

Chapter 11

Getting Loopy

● ●

● ●

*T*here are two kinds of control structures in Visual Basic — decisions and loops. In Chapter 10, I cover *decisions,* which are all about branching the flow based on some input to the program.

Looping, the second type of control structure, is about repeating the same command (or series of commands) until a certain condition is met. Business applications, especially, have to repeat program logic for a certain amount of time or a certain number of iterations — resulting in the programming equivalent of "lather, rinse, repeat." Of course, you wouldn't want to wash and rinse your hair all day, so this phrase really should read "lather, rinse, and repeat once." A sequence of events like this is analogous to a looping structure — known as the For-Next loop — in a Visual Basic program.

Programmers often use looping and decisions together. Visual Basic provides a construct for that, too. The Do-While loop is an example of this — the program loops through a command or series of commands (the Do part) as long as a certain condition (the While part) is true. As soon as the condition becomes false, the looping stops.

In this chapter, I go over the design and code for the four kinds of loops in Visual Basic 2008:

- ✔ For-Next
- ✔ For-Each
- ✔ Do-Until
- ✔ While-End

All of these looping control structures have some common characteristics. They repeat a block of code, and they make a decision about when to stop. The differences among them are completely based on counting logic.

Dealing with Zero

Making decisions about which loop to use is tough. Using the wrong loop can significantly change the processing of the program, and it can really mess up the user experience. So the following sections help you determine which looping structure to use and where to start counting your loops.

Starting at zero

Everything important about loops can be broken down by looking at counting. Ever tried to count the number of hours between the end of lunch and the end of the workday? You count, "One o'clock, two, three, four, five! Five hours!"

But your workday afternoon isn't five hours long; it's four hours long. To count the right number of hours, you need to skip the first time increment. What you need to count are the spaces between hours, as follows: "One to two, two to three, three to four, four to five. Four hours."

Looping through code in a program is similar: If you're counting the spaces between the numbers, you skip the first number. That is, you always run the loop the first time, and then check the condition at the end.

Figure 11-1 shows two diagrams. The one on the right is the wrong way to count the hours after lunch. This diagram starts counting at 1:00 PM. The diagram on the left starts counting at 2:00 PM, which is the same as counting the spaces between the numbers.

Comparing specific loops and indefinite loops

Another difference among the different types of loops is whether the loop repeats for a specific number of times or repeats for an indefinite number of times. A *specific loop* is looped a definite number of times; an *indefinite loop* makes a decision, either at the beginning or the end of the loop, to stop.

A loop that runs a specific number of times is like "ten lashes with a wet noodle." This concept is implemented with a For-Next or For-Each loop. Effectively, you are translating the example to, "For each in a collection of ten, lash with a wet noodle." This example is shown in Figure 11-2. That seems a bit overboard, but it makes a lot of sense in context.

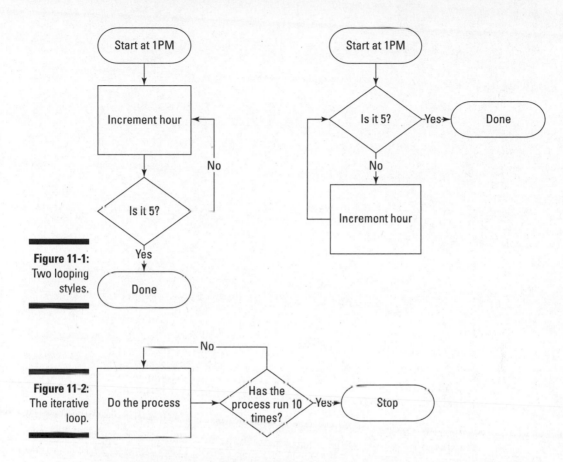

Figure 11-1:
Two looping styles.

Figure 11-2:
The iterative loop.

A loop that has an indefinite quantity is like "lather, rinse, repeat." How many times to repeat? Well, that's the joke in the example — you don't know. You assume that it means repeat until clean, but you don't really know.

Assuming that the goal is to repeat until clean, you're back to the counting problem. Do you assume that it is dirty, and then start with the lather? Or do you check first before you lather the first time? Figure 11-3 shows you how Figure 11-1 could be changed to show those two options for the shampoo example.

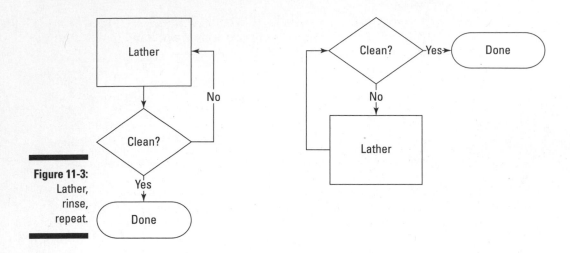

Figure 11-3:
Lather,
rinse,
repeat.

Writing Loops with For-Next

The For-Next loop is an iterative loop. At the beginning of the loop, you define a quantity, and the loop repeats that many times. When the loop is done repeating, the code after the loop runs. The following is an example of a simple For-Next loop that shows the number in a message box:

```
Dim Counter as Integer
For Counter = 1 to 5
     MessageBox.Show("The number is " & counter)
Next Counter
```

You can do a lot with a For-Next loop. Whenever you are manipulating something a set number of times, when you need to make sure that something happens a set number of times, or when you must retrieve a set number of items from a group, this is your loop.

For-Next loops can do a few neat tricks, too. For instance, imagine that you need to do something to every other line of a collection. You could test in the middle of the loop to see whether your counter is even, or you could use the Step statement the way I do in the following code:

```
Dim Counter as Integer
For Counter = 2 to 10 Step 2
     MessageBox.Show("The number is " & counter)
Next Counter
```

This code block shows you 2, 4, 6, 8, and 10 in the message box. Pretty slick. You could use this to access every other item in a collection by using Counter in the collection index.

Also, the Step statement can be used to count backward, like I show in the following code. When you do this, make sure that the first number is bigger than the second, or the loop won't run!

```
Dim counter as Integer
For Counter = 5 to 1 Step -1
    MessageBox.Show("The number is " & counter)
Next Counter
```

As I'm sure you guessed, this code gives you 5, 4, 3, 2, and 1. I suppose this adds another use — counting down for a rocket launch or something.

One last thing about For-Next loops: Sometimes you need to get out of a loop before the loop is done. This situation usually happens when the start and end values are variables, and you don't know going in exactly what they are.

For example, say you don't want to go below 0 in the following example. You can use an If-Then statement and an Exit-For statement to stop the loop.

```
Dim Counter as Integer
Dim startValue as Integer = 5
Dim endValue as Integer = -1
For Counter = startValue to endValue Step -1
    If counter < 1 Then Exit For
    MessageBox.Show("The number is " & Counter)
Next Counter
```

This code will stop when the counter gets to 0 and moves to the line after the Next Counter statement.

Using the For-Each Listing with Collections

A *collection* is a special construct of the .NET Framework that contains a number of objects and is accessed with an index that refers to the item in the collection. Although a collection isn't found only in the Windows world, the specifics are rather unique to the .NET Framework.

I don't have enough space in this chapter to go into the specifics of collections. You see them in examples in the book, usually as a plural property of an object. For instance, all the controls in a form (such as buttons and text boxes) are held in a collection called ControlCollection.

The collection is implemented using an interface called `IEnumerable`. This library of code specifies that the code using `IEnumerable` must be able to be iterated using the For-Each listing. If you need to know whether you can use For-Each to iterate through a collection, look at the documentation of the object to find out if it implements `IEnumerable`. For instance, the `Control` collection — which is iterative — looks like this in the documentation:

```
Public Class Control.ControlCollection _
     Inherits ArrangedElementCollection _
     Implements IList, ICollection, IEnumerable,
          ICloneable
```

To loop through the `Control` collection using the For-Each listing, you need to set up a little sample application by following these steps:

1. **Open Visual Studio and start a new Windows Application project.**

2. **Drag four text boxes to the form.**

3. **Drag a button to the form.**

   The application should look like Figure 11-4.

4. **Double-click the button to fire up the** `OnClick` **event handler.**

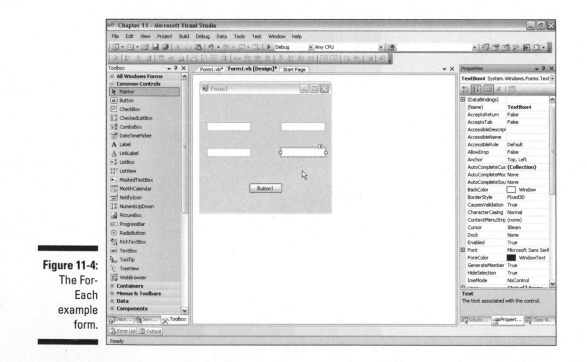

Figure 11-4:
The For-Each example form.

5. Add the following code to the method created:

```
Private Sub Button1_Click(ByVal sender As System.Object, _
        ByVal e As System.EventArgs) Handles Button1.Click
    For Each myControl As System.Windows.Forms.Control In Me.Controls
        If myControl.GetType Is TextBox1.GetType Then
            myControl.Text = myControl.Location.ToString
        End If
    Next
End Sub
```

6. Click the button to start the code in the method.

Note that the text is changed in each of the text boxes.

Although you didn't tell the loop how many times to run, it was still a constrained number of times, because the collection contains a discrete number of form controls. Also notice how I further isolated the number of controls acted upon by checking the type in the loop with an If-Then statement.

Why did I have to do that, you ask? Because no collection of text boxes exists, just a collection of form controls. If you only want the `TextBox` controls, you need to filter using an If-Then statement the way I did.

Writing Indefinite Loops with Do-Loop

Indefinite loops are loops that aren't counted, but that continue infinitely until something happens. Indefinite loops are a little tougher to write, because two things can happen to lock up your application — forgetting to move to the next item in a group, or setting the criteria for when to stop the loop to a condition that will never be true.

You can use the Do-Loop in four ways:

- Loop while something is true, checked before you start.
- Loop while something is true, checked after the first iteration.
- Loop until something becomes true, checked before you start.
- Loop until something becomes true, checked after the first iteration.

The Do-Loop is by far the most flexible looping construct because it handles almost everything. In fact, with a counter that you manually increment, a Do-Loop can replace a For-Next loop.

Generally, though, programmers use the Do-Loop as a last resort because it is so prone to error. A Do-Loop is so very broad that it is very easy to create a situation where the loop would end prematurely, never run, or go on endlessly.

The Do-Loop is a very useful construct, however, and worth learning to use well. I discuss each of the four options, first in a flowchart and then in code.

Do-While loop, checked at start

The following example of using the Do-While loop describes running a routine for every day in a month when you aren't sure whether you are in the month you want. For instance, say you had a process that you wanted to run once for every day of the month, but only in the month of December. Charted out, this would look like Figure 11-5.

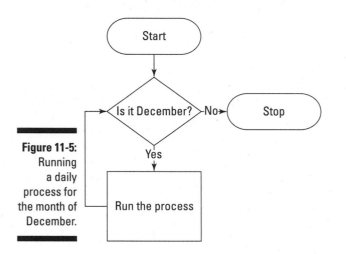

Figure 11-5: Running a daily process for the month of December.

Running this would look like the following code:

```
Dim myDate as DateTime = Date.Now()
Do While myDate.Month = 12
     RunTheProcess()
     myDate = myDate.AddDays(1)
Loop
```

Don't forget to increment your loop iterator!

Do-While loop, checked at end

Taking the opposing perspective of this daily-process example entails a process that you know you always want to run once, no matter what the month. For instance, say the process runs at least once for every month, in every month, and you just want the loop to stop when the day counter doesn't fall in December, as shown in Figure 11-6.

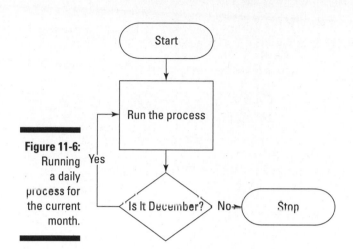

Figure 11-6:
Running
a daily
process for
the current
month.

Building Figure 11-6 in code would look like the following:

```
Dim myDate as DateTime = Date.Now()
Do
        RunTheProcess()
        myDate   = myDate.AddDays(1)
Loop While myDate.Month = 12
```

Do-Until loop, checked at start

Following along with the date theme, say you have a process you want to run every day of the week until Saturday. If it starts on a Saturday, though, it shouldn't run, right? So the logic reads like this: "Run the routine once for every day until Saturday."

Running this would look like the following code:

```
Dim myDate as DateTime = Date.Now()
Do Until myDate.DateOfWeek = DayOfWeek.Saturday
        RunTheProcess()
        myDate   = myDate.AddDays(1)
Loop
```

Do-Until loop, checked at end

You can run the routine at least once every time, and run it until the day shows as Saturday. This means that if it starts on a Saturday, it would run until the next Saturday, meaning eight days total. Maybe that is what you want — but make sure first!

Running this routine would look like the following code:

```
Dim myDate as DateTime = Date.Now()
Do
     RunTheProcess()
     myDate  = myDate.AddDays(1)
Loop Until myDate.DateOfWeek = DayOfWeek.Saturday
```

Checking at the Beginning with While

In the code in the "Do-While loop, checked at start" and "Do-While loop, checked at end" sections, earlier in this chapter, you can see the `While` statement in the Do-Loop. Why, then, is there a While-End loop?

The difference is the `Exit While` statement. You can't exit a Do-Loop. The While-End loop can be exited like a For-Next loop can by using the `Exit While` statement. Other than that, as you can see in the following code, the differences between a Do-While loop and a While-End loop are minimal:

```
Dim myDate as DateTime = Date.Now()
While myDate.Month = 12
     RunTheProcess()
     If MyDate.DayOfWeek = DayOfWeek.Saturday Exit While
     myDate  = myDate.AddDays(1)
End While
```

Chapter 12

Reusing Code

A lot of functionality is floating around out there. Old VB 6 programs, DOS apps, other people's DLL files, and even module files that the last programmer left are all potential sources of code to reuse for your new VB 2008 application.

In Chapter 6, I show you how to write library programs, called Dynamic Link Libraries, or DLLs. And although I recommend a DLL as the project type to turn to when you need to write reusable code, it is far from the only way to reuse your code's functionality. You can also create reusability by writing functional code within your programs themselves. That is, you can easily add helper subroutines and functions to your programs without having to use a DLL project.

A program that is losing prominence but is still out there is the old Disk Operating System, or DOS. Many people who started with early personal computers still swear by the command-line interface. Admittedly, some things are much easier using the command line, and .NET allows you to touch the old DOS commands right from your VB 2008 code.

In this chapter, I cover how to get values into and out of functions and subroutines. You also find out where to find the hooks for outside programs and when to use DOS.

Reusing Code to Build Software

Every piece of code in any program in Visual Basic must be inside a procedure like a function or a subroutine. The event handlers that show up throughout the programs in this book (see Chapters 4 and 5 for examples) are all functions. However, controlling program operation by using event handlers is not the only way to build software. Moving repeated code — that is, the same lines of code that show up in more than one event handler — into auxiliary procedures is the accepted way to build applications. The reason for this is simple: Debugging and maintaining an application that was built this way are quicker and less prone to introduced errors. Specifically, making changes to code lines that appear in one place (the reusable procedure) is much more efficient than making changes to the same code lines that appear in several places (the individual event handlers).

Creating reusable functions or subroutines is not more difficult that coding specific event handlers, but it does require a little different approach. You construct reusable code by building a stand-alone function or subroutine in a class file and then calling it from the event that requires it. Keep the following items in mind when you set out to make truly reusable code:

- ✔ **Know the difference between encapsulating code and creating reusable code.** *Encapsulated* code is common code that you put in a file or location away from your main program — within a class file, for example — for convenience and logical separation. Encapsulated code keeps a specific piece of logic together for the use of a specific set of functional code. *Reusable* code is code that you encapsulate and use again without changes. A company-wide data library is an example of reusable code that can be used in several programs.

- ✔ **Understand that good reusable code contains an element of abstraction.** That is, the reusable code must not depend on the specific names of controls that call it or, in fact, on controls at all. Being *abstract* means that the reusable code operates on passed parameters and returned values. It needs to accept base types (like integers and strings) or known constructs (like datasets and collections) and return the same.

- ✔ **Make the reusable function part of a separate file,** rather than placing it within the project that calls it. This is the encapsulation part. You want to encapsulate your code so that you can easily move it from one project to another.

Building functions with reuse in mind

To show you how reusable code looks in a real application, I start with code from the Date Calculator built in Chapter 4 and alter it to meet the requirements of reusability. The Date Calculator contains event-handler code — `LateDate_ValueChanged` and `EarlyDate_ValueChanged` — which is the actual code that does the date math and sets the returned value. The following code shows both event handlers:

```
Private Sub EarlyDate_ValueChanged(ByVal sender As System.Object, ByVal e As
            System.EventArgs) Handles EarlyDate.ValueChanged
            NumberOfDays.Text = CStr(System.Math.Abs(CInt((EarlyDate.Value -
            LateDate.Value).Days)))
        End Sub

Private Sub LateDate_ValueChanged(ByVal sender As System.Object, ByVal e As
            System.EventArgs) Handles LateDate.ValueChanged
            NumberOfDays.Text = CStr(System.Math.Abs(CInt((EarlyDate.Value -
            LateDate.Value).Days)))
        End Sub
```

Notice that the same code line appears as the middle line in both private subs
(it is the bold line of code in both functions). Repeating this code line is *no
good,* because it violates the concept of reusing functionality. If you need to
change the functionality of this code line later on, you have to change the
same line in both places. Instead, you can put the repeated functional code
in one place in your program, give it a public name, and call it from the event
handler. To do this, you can build a procedure — just as in the class library in
Chapter 6 — and place it right in the code of the form.

Now when you want to do the date math, you can just call this function, and
it does the work. The following code shows the FindDateDiff function:

```
Public Sub FindDateDiff()
NumberOfDays.Text = CStr(System.Math.Abs(CInt((EarlyDate.Value -
            LateDate.Value).Days)))
End Sub
```

And the following code shows what the event handlers look like now that
they call the FindDateDiff function instead of repeating the code line.

```
Private Sub EarlyDate_ValueChanged(ByVal sender As System.Object, ByVal e As
            System.EventArgs) Handles EarlyDate.ValueChanged
            FindDateDiff()
End Sub

Private Sub LateDate_ValueChanged(ByVal sender As System.Object, ByVal e As
            System.EventArgs) Handles LateDate.ValueChanged
            FindDateDiff()
End Sub
```

When you place this new public subroutine within your Date Calculator form,
it is an example of encapsulated code (common code that appears in one
subroutine within a form for convenience). If you move the routine outside
the form, you can use it in another form only if you name the other form's
controls exactly the same as you named them in this application. That situation might not be possible, so making the function itself as abstract (that is,
independent of the controls) as possible is best.

Even with its limitations, I show you an example of code encapsulation because sometimes encapsulating is more important than reusing. Not every function needs to be abstracted to the *n*th degree. In fact, most of your code won't be in the form of abstract functions. Understanding when you need to reuse code and when it doesn't matter depends on your *business model* — that is, your program's overall purpose. For example, if a particular function is just maintenance code within the application itself — conversion from one local data format to another, for instance — it probably won't need to be reused outside the program.

To make a function appropriate for reuse by making it independent of specific names from the calling routine, you need to pass parameters to your function and accept returned values from it. In the Date Calculator application example, you accomplish this abstraction by:

- ✔ Passing the start date
- ✔ Passing the end date
- ✔ Accepting the returned interval (in days) as an integer

Effectively, you set the value of the `NumberOfDays.Text` text box equal to the return value of the `FindDateDiff` function by passing it the values of the two date pickers. I show this truly reusable function in Listing 12-1.

Listing 12-1: Abstracting Using a Function Rather than a Subroutine

```
Private Sub EarlyDate_ValueChanged(ByVal sender As System.Object, ByVal e As
            System.EventArgs) Handles EarlyDate.ValueChanged
NumberOfDays.Text = CStr(FindDateDiff(EarlyDate.Value, LateDate.Value))
End Sub

Private Sub LateDate_ValueChanged(ByVal sender As System.Object, ByVal e As
            System.EventArgs) Handles LateDate.ValueChanged
NumberOfDays.Text = CStr(FindDateDiff(EarlyDate.Value, LateDate.Value))
End Sub

Public Function FindDateDiff(ByVal startdate As Date, ByVal enddate As Date) As
            Integer
Dim difference As Integer
difference = (startdate - enddate).Days          '#1
Return difference
End Function
```

Notice the interesting element in the line numbered as 1. This line takes advantage of the property of the date calculation. That is, because `(start date - enddate)` is a subtraction of two dates, it returns an object of the `DateSpan` data type. An object of that type includes a `Days` property, which line #1 hooks on to. (To find out more about types and how they work, look at Chapter 9.)

Extending reusability with class files

For *real* reusability, you need to make the function part of a separate file called a *class file.* These class files are sort of in-project libraries and are handy when the code may be reused within a project, but the code is not likely to be used outside a project. A class file in a project is exactly the same kind of creature as a class file inside a DLL.

Follow these steps to set up and use a class file:

1. **With your program open in Visual Studio, make a new folder in your project.**

   I recommend that you store classes in a separate folder — with the clever name of Classes — inside your project. That way, your class files are easy to find.

2. **Right-click the Solution Explorer and choose Add➪Class to make a new class file. (See Figure 12-1.)**

3. **Type a name for your class file when prompted; make the name something appropriate for the kind of code it will be holding.**

   I named my new file DateMath.vb.

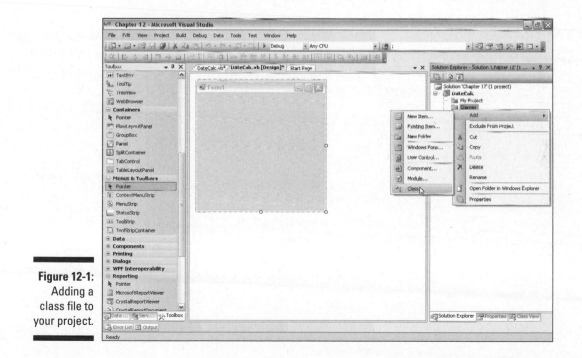

Figure 12-1: Adding a class file to your project.

4. **Copy and paste the reusable code (your function) from your application's form code into the class file.**

   My finished class file code looks like Listing 12-2.

Listing 12-2: The Function Code in a Class File

```
Public Class DateMath
 Public Function FindDateDiff(ByVal startdate As Date, ByVal enddate As Date) As
             Integer
 Dim difference As Integer
 difference = (startdate - enddate).Days
 Return difference
 End Function
End Class
```

When you create reusable functions and put them in class files, you naturally move the related code into a separate physical file in your project. In the Date Calculator example, taking the date-calculating function out of the `Date Calc` form code means that Visual Studio can no longer find the `FindDate Diff` method. You can tell as much because a blue squiggly line appears under the method name. The ability to call the date-calculating code is effectively lost because the method is no longer located in the same class that calls it.

Visual Basic gives you two ways to fix the problem. You get no real benefit by choosing one way of referencing over the other; it is just personal preference for how you want your code to look. You have these choices:

✔ **You can add a reference in your form** to the new class you created to hold your reusable functions. This process is similar to adding a reference to a new class library, as I describe in Chapter 6. Add the necessary code above the class name using the `Imports` statement, as I show in the following code:

```
Option Strict On
Option Explicit On
Imports DateCalc2008.DateMath
Public Class CalculatorMain
```

✔ **You can directly reference the function** by using the class name in front of the function name when calling the function, as demonstrated by `DateCalc2008.DateMath.FindDateDiff` in the following code:

```
Private Sub EarlyDate_ValueChanged(ByVal sender As System.Object, _
    ByVal e As System.EventArgs) Handles EarlyDate.ValueChanged
    Dim dateCalc as new DateCalc2008()
    NumberOfDays.Text = CStr(dateCalc.DateMath.FindDateDiff( _
    EarlyDate.Value, LateDate.Value))
End Sub
```

Public and Private stuff

The `Public` and `Private` keywords for class files and functions become especially important when you're creating reusable code. You have been using them all along as part of forms, but they take on a new significance when it comes to calling a function outside of the class in which it was declared.

A *Public* function can be seen and called by any program that references the class in which it resides. The `Imports` statement in the example in the nearby section "Extending reusability with class files" references the class, and then you can use all the `Public` statements within it. A *Private* class can only be seen and used by other functions within the same class. In the example in the "Extending reusability with class files" section, if `FindDateDiff` were `Private`, it would be invisible even if an `Imports` statement were used. `Friend` and `Protected` are other options, but they control access within *assemblies* (compiled blocks of code). `Public` and `Private` are the options you will see most often.

To directly reference a method in a class, the method must be `Shared`, or you must `Dim` a new instance of the class and reference the method by the new variable name. In the case where you are writing a class file that is mostly oriented toward sharing, marking the methods as `Shared` allows you to use them without instantiating an instance of the class. If the object represented by the class needs to be created first, though, you have to `Dim` a new instance of the class before calling the method. In that case, you use the variable name to refer to the method in question. To see a great example of `Shared` classes, check out `File` and `FileInfo` in the `System.IO` namespace, covered in Chapter 16.

Avoiding the Code-Complexity Trap

Complexity, that is, writing more code than is necessary to solve a programming quandary, is a problem for all applications, no matter what platform or language they are built with. Complexity causes problems, such as programs you can't maintain, and it also makes existing problems harder to find because it is difficult to follow the logic represented by the code.

As a developer, you need to balance complexity with common sense. Making code so sophisticated that you can never find errors is a particularly dangerous situation. Imagine a function that calls a function that calls a function that calls a function . . . you get the idea. You can lose yourself in the flow of the code very fast.

However, you can't put all the procedural code into one large file either. If your `button1.click` method has all the logic in it to handle an order, from billing to shipping, you will have a 1,000-line event handler. This isn't the way to go either.

You can employ two good programming practices that help you avoid complexity problems in your procedures:

✔ Prevent logic problems by protecting the parameters you pass to the functions in the procedures.

✔ Incorporate error handling to help you with procedural programming.

Protecting the values of parameters

When using a procedure, you have two ways to pass the parameters. You can pass a copy of the information held by the variable you use as the parameter, or you can pass the actual variable.

Determining how to pass your parameters harkens back to the programming languages that use pointers. For example, the C language made use of pointers to reference information expected to be in certain memory locations. You could pass a copy of information or a pointer to the actual information.

Ask yourself this question to decide how to handle passing parameters: Do you need your original data to be protected from the procedure you're calling, or are you expecting the called procedure to change your data? Answer this question and then choose the Visual Basic structure that gets you the result you want. Visual Basic handles passing parameters with the following keywords:

✔ `ByVal` refers to *By Value,* and using this keyword assures that a copy of the parameter's data (its value) is made before it's passed to the function. If the function changes the value of the parameter, that changed value is discarded at the end of the functional life of the parameter (which is at the end of the subroutine or function). In general, functions don't change the values that are passed to them, but if you want to be absolutely sure, you should protect those values by choosing to pass parameters `ByVal`. This is the default option.

✔ `ByRef` stands for *By Reference,* and this keyword sees to it that a reference to the original variable passes to the function as the parameter. The reference points to the actual location of the variable value, so i f the function changes the parameter, the variable in the host program changes as well. You may actually want the function to change the original values — for instance, a billing operation might always want to zero out a cumulative fees variable passed into a function. In this case, using `ByRef` allows the function to directly access the original variable and saves you a lot of code.

TIP

You may notice that if you don't type in the keyword yourself, Visual Basic sets the default parameter passing to ByVal for all functions and subroutines. Having ByVal as the default state is safer (because the variable's original value is preserved) and avoids the logic errors (such as accidentally overwriting a value that the calling code expects to be the same) that can result from using ByRef and that are difficult to find later.

Handling errors effectively in an abstract environment

Another consideration for limiting complexity in procedural programming relates to handling errors. I cover error handling using the Try-Catch block in Chapter 10. In this section, I talk about the details of determining how to deal with errors thrown in procedural programming.

The problem with errors in procedural code is one of abstraction (the same functional separation you are aiming for when you create a reusable class). If you create reusable code using class files and procedures, you can lose the ability to communicate with the user interface and thereby inform users when an error occurs. Figure 12-2 illustrates this concept.

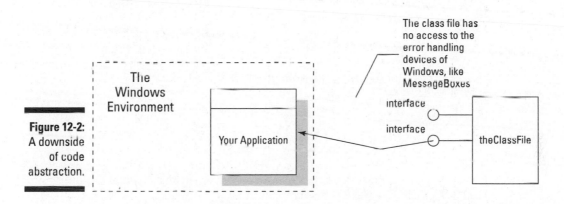

The class file has no access to the error handling devices of Windows, like MessageBoxes

Figure 12-2: A downside of code abstraction.

So what happens when an error occurs in the procedure that is abstracted from the application? You handle this situation by allowing exceptions to bubble up from the procedure to the user interface, rather than trying to handle them in the class file itself. For example, rather than handling a database conversion error in a reusable function with a Try-Catch statement, you should just allow the error to be thrown up to the source application.

Abstraction, therefore, has an impact beyond facilitating code sharing. When you move a procedure containing reusable code into an isolated environment (like a class file), you cannot assume that the program using the class file can pop up a message box if (and when) an exception occurs! You must make good decisions about when and how to deal with exceptions. Here are a few pointers:

- **Allow the majority of errors to bubble up to the code that calls the procedure.** Don't try to handle errors that you can let the system handle for you. When an error occurs that is covered by a system exception (such as the database being out of whack), the error will cause the procedure to stop executing and then pass execution back to the calling program. This automatic process is good enough to deal with most errors.

- **Organize your business logic to avoid exceptions in the class files.** Procedures that you design to be shareable need to be better than they have to be. In other words, your reusable functions and subroutines must be as infallible as possible. Do the little things that reflect careful programming practices — like making sure that your loops won't over-stretch their bounds or that your data won't be subject to type confusion. Check that the values your procedure accepts as parameters are what the code really needs so that you don't have to worry about conversion errors. Taking care of details like this makes reusable code much more useful.

- **When a business logic error occurs, inform the calling program by creating an error of your own.** This programming practice is called *throwing an error,* and it is unsurprisingly handled by the keyword `Throw`. For instance, suppose your procedure wants to make sure that the passed parameter called `startdate` is always earlier than the passed parameter called `enddate`. The following code shows how to throw an error after checking the two values:

```
Public Shared Function FindDateDiff(ByVal startdate As Date, _
ByVal enddate As Date) As Integer
 Dim difference As Integer
 If enddate > startdate Then
 Throw New ApplicationException("End Date cannot " + _
                           "be before Start Date")
 End If
 difference = (startdate - enddate).Days
 Return difference
 End Function
```

If the `startdate` is not earlier than the `enddate`, this code causes the execution of the procedure to stop, and control is returned to the calling program with the `ApplicationException` in tow. If your program wraps the call to the procedure in the Try-Catch block (which I discuss in Chapter 10), the program handles the exception. If not, Windows handles it for you!

Finding Other Ways to Reuse Code

Other ways to write reusable code are built into the Visual Studio environment. The `Server` controls (components such as text boxes and buttons) that you can use in Windows and Web Forms are built into the environment, and you can create your own reusable components. You also find a simpler control concept, a user control, in ASP.NET pages. And you can build easy-to-reuse page templates, such as master pages in ASP.NET, as well.

Creating custom controls

Server controls — such as the `TextBox` and `Button` controls that I show in many examples — are easily built using a special project type in Visual Studio. Although creating custom controls is a little beyond the scope of this book, follow these steps to create a simple custom control and make it available to your Windows Forms projects:

1. **Open Visual Studio and select a new Windows Forms Control Library project.**

   The editor opens with a workspace that looks much like the regular Windows Forms designer, but with just a gray area to work in. I name my example Sample Windows Control.

2. **Drag one or more controls from the Toolbox to the gray area, and resize the area to fit around them.**

   I drag three text boxes to the gray area in my project and arrange them as shown in Figure 12-3.

3. **Right-click the default `.vb` file in the Solution Explorer, and give your control a name you can remember.**

   I call my file `PhoneNumber.vb`.

4. **Choose Build⇨Build Solution from the main menu to compile the project.**

5. **Choose File⇨Add⇨New Project and select a new Windows Application project to add another project to the solution.**

   I call my new project Sample Control Test.

6. **Right-click the new project and choose Set as Start Up Project.**

7. **Right-click the new project again and choose Add Reference.**

   The dialog box shown in Figure 12-4 appears.

Figure 12-3:
The start of
a custom
control.

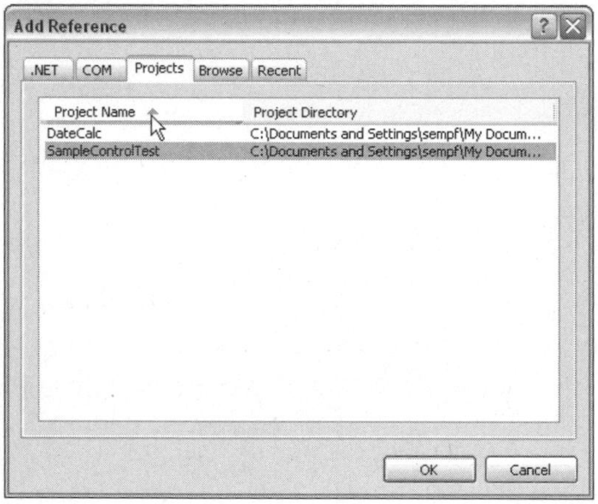

Figure 12-4:
Adding a
project
reference.

8. **Click the Projects tab, select the SampleControlTest project, and click the OK button.**

9. **Expand the Toolbox and note the addition of your new control.**

In my example, I see the `PhoneNumber` control. It should be in a new group above the All Windows Forms group.

10. Drag your new control onto the default form.

The new control appears on your form just as if it were any of the built-in controls.

How making custom controls helps you share code is obvious. If you define a common set of controls that have common logic, you can create custom controls and write the code for these controls just once. Your logic is protected by the compilation, and you can redistribute the customized controls within your organization. In short, making custom controls is a tremendous tool in terms of sharing code.

Adding user controls

Another great tool in the code-sharing arena is the ASP.NET user control. A *user control* is a simpler version of the custom control and is represented by a special file — an ASCX file — in the ASP.NET Web project.

Otherwise, a user control works and acts the same as a custom control. A user control

✔ Encapsulates other controls and the logic around them.

✔ Shows up as a separate object within the project.

✔ Is built in a separate design space.

If you open a Web project and right-click the project file in the Solution Explorer, you can see that one of the options is the Web User Control, as highlighted in Figure 12-5. Click the Web User Control icon to add a user control to your project.

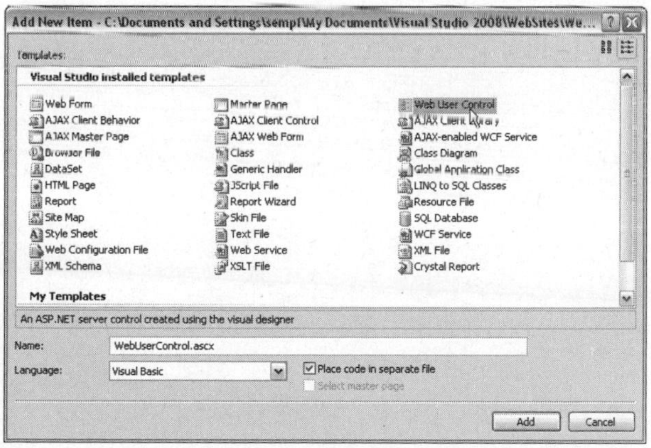

Figure 12-5: Selecting a Web User Control.

The process for developing a user control is just like the process for developing a Web Forms page. Drag controls to the screen and double-click to add code to the control. To add your new control to a Web page, just drag the ASCX file to the ASPX page in Design View.

You should keep in mind, though, that ASP.NET user controls are not as versatile as custom controls. User controls are not compiled into class files, but are built into the Web site itself. To reuse the user control code in another project, you need to copy the code from one project to the other. And when you add user controls to a page, they don't appear exactly as you designed them, but are represented by a placeholder.

Regardless of their shortcomings, user controls can be important parts of a Web project. Lots of Web-page elements are repeated — for example, navigation controls, footers and headers, and so on. All such elements make fantastic user controls.

Making master pages

Another ASP.NET feature, along the lines of a user control, is a master page. A *master page* is effectively a page template for Web sites, so it isn't shared code as much as it's a common framework for a project.

You add master pages to projects just as you add user controls. You can right-click the project file and select the Master Page icon to add one to a project. From that point, you edit a document that is just like a Microsoft Word template for Web pages.

The master page uses a construct called a *content placeholder* to determine the layout and placement for content of the ASPX pages. The `ContentPlaceHolder` construct allows you to structure where on the page the content from a content page is placed. The content control in the ASPX pages defines what content goes with each control. For instance, the following code shows a master page with two `ContentPlaceHolder` controls right next to one another in a table:

```
<%@ Master Language="VB" CompileWith="MasterPage.master.vb"
            AutoEventWireup="false" ClassName="MasterPage_master" %>

<!DOCTYPE html PUBLIC "-//W3C//DTD XHTML 1.1//EN"
            "http://www.w3.org/TR/xhtml11/DTD/xhtml11.dtd">

<html xmlns="http://www.w3.org/1999/xhtml" >
<head runat="server">
 <title>Untitled Page</title>
</head>
<body>
 <form id="form1" runat="server">
```

```
<table>
<tr>
<td>
<asp:ContentPlaceHolder id="ContentPlaceHolder1" runat="server">
</asp:ContentPlaceHolder>
</td>
<td>
<asp:ContentPlaceHolderid="ContentPlaceHolder2" runat="server">
</asp:ContentPlaceHolder>
</td>
</tr>
</table>
</form>
</body>
</html>
```

To run this master page with content, the content page must have

- ✔ A `Master` attribute in the `Page` directive.

- ✔ Two content controls in the page that have the content to be placed in the `ContentPlaceHolder1` and `ContentPlaceHolder2` controls in the master page.

Using a master page to control the layout prevents you from having to recode the HTML tags repeatedly from page to page. You can also accomplish this reusable structure with user controls, but the master pages are much more efficient.

Reusing Programs Outside of the Framework

I know of two reasons to think about reusing program functionality outside of the .NET Framework:

- ✔ You may have older programs — legacy code written before the .NET Framework existed — that have business logic you still want to use.

- ✔ You may need to work with parts of the Windows operating system that are not available in the .NET Framework.

At least 90 percent of programmers have legacy code to work with. While you can rewrite most of your legacy code into VB 2008, you won't always have the time or energy. The ability to directly implement the world of COM (the Component Object Model architecture used prior to .NET) in Visual Basic and the .NET Framework will significantly simplify your work environment.

Fortunately for VB 2008 programmers, working with COM objects is now easier than ever. Additionally, the Visual Basic developers had a very realistic view of the Windows platform. While Microsoft's developers are very focused on the .NET Framework, not every product sold by their third-party providers is .NET ready. Also, certain Windows elements (such as NT file properties) still don't have .NET objects associated with them.

I start my discussion about connecting to old code with implementing COM because that topic covers a lot of the legacy code reuse problems you will have to solve. Then I talk about getting down to the operating system's legacy operations. You may not connect to the old OS operations a lot, but some situations — like dealing with older hardware — still require that you know how.

Referencing the old Component Object Model

The Component Object Model (COM) is the library of code that allowed the development of DLL files before .NET existed. Nothing is wrong with COM per se, but .NET is much more appropriate for development in today's environment.

Nonetheless, at times you will need to write code that uses logic in old COM objects. Visual Basic 2008 provides a function, called `CreateObject`, that is built into the language. This function allows you to dimension an object and then assign it to an existing COM class if you know the reference to that class.

For example, to make a new Microsoft Word file, you could use the following code. The code simply defines a new object placeholder and assigns it to the `Word.Application` class, which is the old COM class for Microsoft Word functionality. The class exposes several methods, properties, and events, but this code uses the `Save` method and supplies the newly created object with a filename.

```
Public Sub MakeWordFile()
 Dim myWord as Object
 myWord = CType(CreateObject("Microsoft.Office.Interop.Word.Application"),
           WordApplication)
 myWord.Save("c:\NewFile.doc")
End Sub
```

Before you have access to any of this functionality, you need to reference the DLL file in your project. In this case, you click the COM tab in the Add Reference dialog box (refer to Figure 12-4). From this dialog box, you need to add a reference to the local version of Word. On my PC, it is Version 11, and the DLL is called Microsoft Word 11.0 Object Library.

When you use Visual Basic's `CreateObject` function and link to old COM classes, you may get some pushback from Visual Studio. In the Code View, Visual Studio may warn you that the Late Bound Resolution could cause errors. Such a warning appears because you didn't use Visual Studio to create the new object, and that means Visual Studio can't confirm that the `Save` method actually exists.

Calling methods in COM objects

If you don't need an actual instance of the object defined by a COM class, you can use the `CallByName` function to just run a method as defined by a class. For example, the following code shows how you could call the `Save` method in the preceding example without using an object:

```
CallByName(myWord, "Save", CallType.Method,
          "c:\NewFile.doc")
```

Using other programs with the Process class

By far, the best way to get information to another program from a VB 2008 program is the `Process` class. The `Process` class makes use of the file-extension mappings in Windows to determine what application to launch. A great example of this use involves the Google Search Tool. The Google Search Tool is a very simple Windows application that presents users with a text box and a button. It returns a URL based on the search term entered in the text box and lets Windows decide what application to launch to view the URL.

To build your own Google Search Tool, follow these steps:

1. **Open Visual Studio and start a new Windows Forms Application project.**

   Surprisingly enough, I name my application Google Search Tool.

2. **Right-click the project and choose Add a Reference.**

   The Add Reference dialog box appears.

3. **On the .Net tab, add a reference to the** `System.Web` **component.**

4. **Drag a text box and button from the Toolbox to the form.**

   My form looks like the one shown in Figure 12-6.

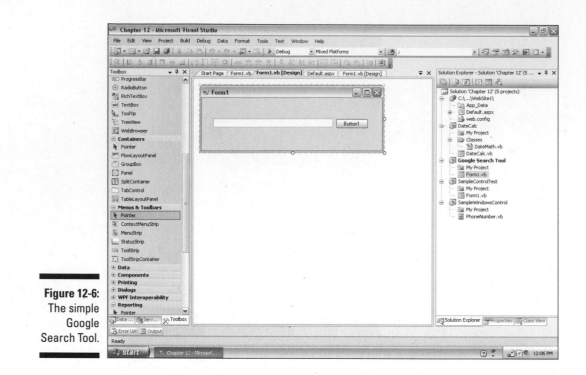

Figure 12-6:
The simple
Google
Search Tool.

5. **Double-click the button to get to the** `OnClick` **event handler and add the code to incorporate the outside program.**

   The code looks like the following:

```
Dim myProcess As New Process()
Dim searchString As String = _
        System.Web.HttpUtility.UrlEncode(TextBox1.Text)
Dim urlString As String = "http://www.google.com/search?q=" + searchString
myProcess.StartInfo.FileName = urlString
myProcess.Start()
```

6. **Click the Play button to run the application. Type a search term in the text box and click the button to cause your default browser to load.**

   Figure 12-7 shows my results. For this example, I use Mozilla Firefox rather than Internet Explorer, and the `Process` class still works great!

The code to include this outside application is surprisingly simple. The lines work as follows:

✔ Get the search term from the text box, and combine it with the search URL that Google provides to create a new variable called `urlString`:

```
Dim searchString As String =
        System.Web.HttpUtility.UrlEncode(TextBox1.Text
        )
```

```
Dim urlString As String =
       "http://www.google.com/search?q=" +
       searchString
```

✔ Set the new variable equal to the `StartInfo.FileName` property of the new `Process` object I created. If I had wanted a Word document instead of a URL, I could have provided a Word filename:

```
myProcess.StartInfo.FileName = urlString
```

✔ Call the `Start` method, and VB 2008 looks in the registry to see what application is set to handle a URL:

```
myProcess.Start()
```

Visual Basic then runs the app for me, sets the URL in the address bar, and away it goes!

Though I did not use it, the Windows Forms program created to incorporate the Google Search Tool now has control of the `browser` process it has spawned. I can review its progress, pause its execution, or end it from the program if I so desire. For a complete list of the functionality of the `Process` class, you can search for "Process Class" in the MSDN documentation.

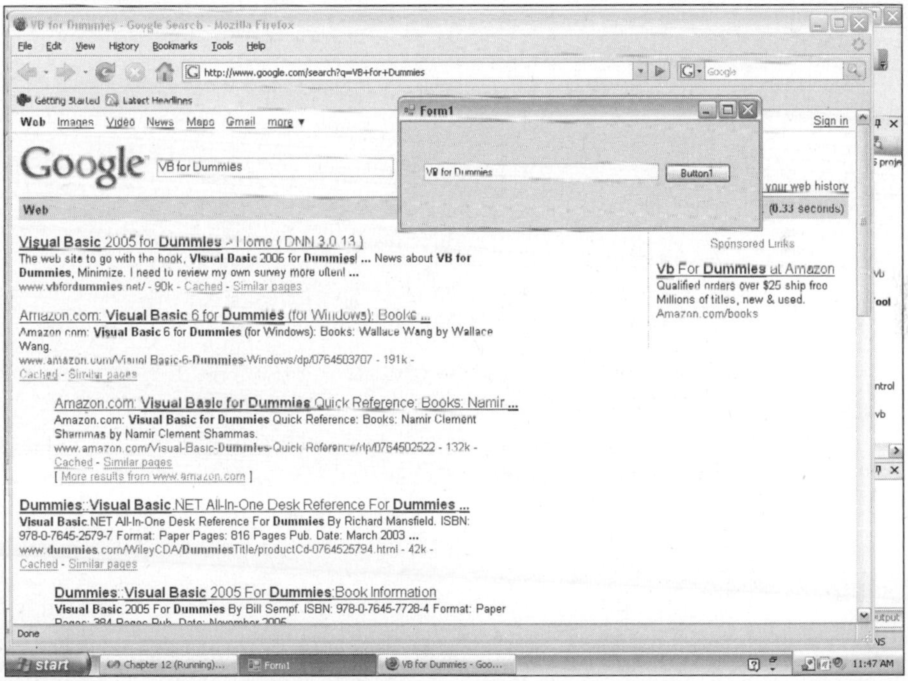

Figure 12-7:
The Process
class at
work
loading
a URL.

Accessing DOS: But Only as a Last Resort

DOS is dead. The operating system that many experienced programmers cut their teeth on in the PC world is simply emulated in newer operating systems such as Windows Vista systems and the even newer Windows Server systems that are in development as I write this book.

Nonetheless, you may want to use bits of DOS and older Windows applications in your programs, and VB 2008 supports that, too. For a number of reasons (such as the possibility of Microsoft removing the function in a later version of Windows), digging into the older operating systems is not something you want to do — unless you have no other choice. But it's nice to know that if you have to go that low, you can.

Running command-line programs with Shell

If you have done any systems administration work, you know that a lot of powerful and necessary applications are available only from the command line. Also, you can write a command-line application in Visual Studio by using the Console project type. To run such programs from your VB 2008 programs, you can use the `Shell` command.

The following code shows a very simple example that launches the Windows Calculator using its command name, `calc.exe`. I implemented this code by putting it in the `OnClick` handler of a button on a blank form.

```
Private Sub Button1_Click(ByVal sender As System.Object,_
          ByVal e As System.EventArgs) Handles
             Button1.Click
Dim CalcId As Integer
CalcId = Shell("C:\Windows\system32\calc.exe", _
             AppWinStyle.NormalFocus)
End Sub
```

The process ID returns to your program in the form of an integer (in this case, `CalcId`), and the program can refer to the application or process as long as that process remains running. As with the `Process` class, the process ID gives you the ability to hold up your application while the referenced process runs, check its progress, or kill it as you wish.

The `Shell` command takes a few parameters. The first is (obviously) the name of the process to be run, complete with the parameters the process might accept. The second parameter is the `AppWinStyle`, which is a collection that defines how the process will appear to the user. It includes the following:

- ✔ `Hide`: Doesn't show in the taskbar.

- ✔ `NormalFocus`: Shows normally, based on the system default.

- ✔ `MinimizedFocus`: Is minimized in the taskbar and has focus as though the user had clicked on it.

- ✔ `MaxamizedFocus`: Fills the screen and has focus.

- ✔ `NormalNofocus`: Shows normally with no focus.

- ✔ `MinimizedNoFocus`: Is minimized without having focus.

The third parameter of `Shell`, which I didn't use in my example, is a `Boolean` parameter that tells the program whether the calling program should wait for the process called to finish. The fourth, and final, parameter is a timeout value that tells the calling program when to let go of the reference.

Getting focus with AppActivate

No matter what tool you use to run a program from your VB 2008 application — whether it's a `Process` class, the `Shell` command, or the `Interop` function — you can give the program focus with `AppActivate`. The `AppActivate` function accepts a window name of a running program or a process ID, and gives focus to that application.

For example, running Calculator as shown in the following code initially sets the application to have no focus. The `AppActivate` line then gives the application focus using the process ID that was returned from the `Shell` command.

```
Private Sub Button1_Click(ByVal sender As System.Object, _
         ByVal e As System.EventArgs) Handles Button1.Click
Dim CalcId As Integer
CalcId = Shell("C:\Windows\system32\calc.exe", _
             AppWinStyle.MinimizedNoFocus)
AppActivate(CalcId)
End Sub
```

In the `Process` example from the section "Using other programs with the Process class," earlier in this chapter, you can give the browser focus if you know exactly what the window name will be. The following code demonstrates this:

```
Dim myProcess As New Process()
Dim searchString As String = System.Web.HttpUtility.UrlEncode(TextBox1.Text)
Dim urlString As String = "http://www.google.com/search?q=" + searchString
myProcess.StartInfo.FileName = urlString
myProcess.Start()
AppActivate("Google Search: Bill Sempf - Mozilla FireFox")
```

Using `AppActivate` would not be the best solution in many circumstances. In this example, if you aren't using Mozilla Firefox, this code will not work for you! You want to avoid using the Windows name string when the name varies based on the user. As it turns out, the `Process` object has a `ProcessId` parameter that gives you a much more flexible result.

Chapter 13

Making Arguments, Earning Returns

*V*isual Basic 2008 is still, at its heart, a very functional language. Much of the benefit from using VB revolves around calling functions and getting values back. Even with the movement toward more object- and service-oriented use of the language, you will always need to know how to call a function and get a return value — no matter what the higher cause happens to be.

The Visual Basic language is heavily based on designing, defining, and calling procedures, passing arguments, and getting return values that are useful to your program. Understanding how to make highly intricate functions and subroutines makes your programs run better and your code more readable.

In this chapter, I discuss advanced procedure design — sophisticated functions and subroutines. In Chapter 6, you design class files, and in Chapter 12, you make reusable code realistic. The information in this chapter gives you the last bit of detail that you need to make the best possible functional code you can.

This chapter covers the last few details of function design and creation that haven't been discussed in previous chapters. You find the following:

✔ An in-depth description of the parameters and return values of functions

✔ Procedures that accept different sets of values using overloading

✔ Tricks for calling and using classes

✔ An introduction to making flexible objects with generics

✔ A description of event handling

✔ A fun example of object timing that uses threading

Using Classes Effectively

Although I discuss class library design, programming, and testing in Chapters 6 and 8, in this chapter, I discuss the most effective ways to use classes. The logic contained in classes is important because you use it over and over. You can significantly improve overall reliability of your programming efforts if you follow a few of the suggestions I go over in the following sections.

For example, how you instantiate and destroy objects can have a distinct impact on your application's memory management. Understanding whether an expensive resource is being utilized is important. Finally, you should know about a few tricks of the trade that can make your code cleaner.

Making and destroying objects

Behind the scenes, when you make an object, you are taking information from the program file and storing it in the RAM of the machine. You have a lot more room on the hard drive than in RAM, so you should be cautious using your RAM.

Every Dim statement takes up more memory on the machine. Some things, such as graphics and network connections, take up more memory than others. Because of this fact, you must be cautious what you make and when you destroy it.

For the small programs I go over in this book, you don't need to worry about making and destroying objects in a timely fashion. Because the programs are so small, the memory management is negligible.

However, it's easy to create a program that would need to use tons of memory and where memory management would become important. For instance, imagine a program that looped through a large number of records in a file and started a mechanism to confirm them. At the end of the loop, that process will have one copy of the mechanism for every line of the file alive in memory!

.NET has something called *garbage collection* that gets rid of unused objects. It usually takes objects that were used in a method and destroys them after that method has run. If the method is particularly long, however, you might want to get rid of an object early. I show an example of this garbage collection in the following code. To get rid of an object early, you use a method that all objects inherit from the .NET Framework: Finalize.

```
'Get a new instance of the Date Calculator
Dim currentCalculator as new Calculator
'Get rid of it for good!
currentCalculator.Finalize()
```

Resource utilization

Another consideration in deciding when to destroy an object is what happens to the resources handled by the class you instantiated. I cover resources (such as network and database connections) in greater detail in Chapters 15 and 17. The resource may be locked by the object, and if you're depending on having that resource later, this lock could be a bad thing.

The following constraints should govern how you make and destroy objects. If you are in a tight resource situation, consider the following best practices:

- ✔ Use a `Dim` or `Private` statement to dimension the object right before you are ready to use it, rather than at the beginning of your code.

- ✔ When you are through with the object, call its `Finalize` method.

Keep in mind that using `Finalize` is for specific situations. I try to implement Resource Utilization Management when I am having a problem with a resource, or I am working with objects like networks, files, or databases. Generally speaking:

- ✔ The garbage collector will run after every method signature.

- ✔ Most classes in .NET are very lightweight, and the garbage collector will handle them just fine.

With and Using

When working with objects, don't type them so often. Really — take a look at the following code! The `With` keyword tells VB that the next few lines of code are to be used "With" a given object — it's pretty cool.

```
With myArray
      .Add(1)
      .Add(3)
      .Sort()
End With
```

Like `With`, `Using` defines a new resource that should be used as part of the code inside the block and then discarded. The MSDN documentation has a great example using a `Font` in the `Drawing` classes, which I show here:

```
Public Sub makeBig(ByVal myControl As Control)
Using myFont As New System.Drawing.Font("Garamond", 18.0F, FontStyle.Normal)
        myControl.Font = myFont
        myControl.Text = "Big Garamond Title!!"
End Using
End Sub
```

Using Event Handlers

Event handlers are methods that automatically run when an event occurs that the .NET Framework knows about. The most obvious example is a button click — when the user clicks a button, the framework knows it as an `OnClick` event. It looks in the code for that screen for a method designed for that button's `OnClick` event. That method is an event handler. An example follows:

```
Private Sub Button1_MouseEnter(ByVal sender As Object,
        ByVal e As System.EventArgs) Handles
        Button1.MouseEnter
End Sub
```

Two qualities designate an event handler:

- ✔ **The `Handles` statement:** The `Handles` statement tells the framework that this method in particular is designed to deal with a specific event for a specific object.

- ✔ **Special parameter types that event handlers require:** These are the `Sender` and the `Event` arguments. The `Sender` represents a reference to the object that sent the event, and the `Event` arguments are a custom collection of properties that relate to the request — like the position of the mouse on a click or the exact time of a network event.

To support an event handler, the event must be exposed by an object. Using Visual Studio, you can see what events are exposed by an object in Design View by using the Properties window and by using IntelliSense. The following sections look at both of them.

Event handling using the Properties window

By far the easiest way to work with event handlers is by using the Design View. The Properties window, which I go over in Chapter 2, has a special panel designed for working with events.

To get started, try this little sample:

1. **Open Visual Studio 2008 and create a new Visual Basic Windows Application project by choosing File⇨New Project.**

2. **In the Form1 designer, add a button and a timer.**

   The Timer control is under the Components tab in the Toolbox.

3. **Select the button, and then open the Properties window.**

4. **Click the Events button, shown in the margin.**

5. **Note the events available for use.**

   Figure 13-1 shows what can happen to a button in the user environment. Do you want code to run when the user hovers the mouse cursor over your button, rather than when it is clicked? If so, use the MouseEnter event. Do you want code to run when the user drags something over the button? Use the DragDrop event. The Events panel is shown in Figure 13-1.

6. **To see how this can be used, double-click in the property area to the right of the MouseEnter event.**

   Visual Studio will automatically generate an event handler for you and send you to Code View. The event will probably be called Button1_ MouseEnter. Notice the Handles statement? It tells the .NET Framework that you want this method to handle any instance of that event. Here's an example of an event handler for the MouseEnter event:

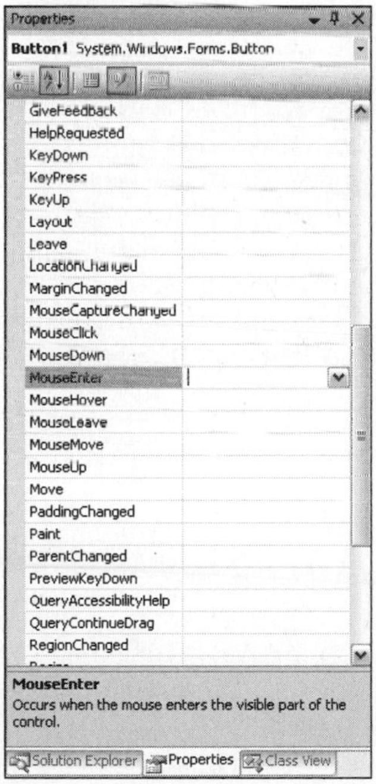

Figure 13-1:
The Events panel.

Properties

Button1 System.Windows.Forms.Button

GiveFeedback
HelpRequested
KeyDown
KeyPress
KeyUp
Layout
Leave
LocationChanged
MarginChanged
MouseCaptureChanged
MouseClick
MouseDown
MouseEnter
MouseHover
MouseLeave
MouseMove
MouseUp
Move
PaddingChanged
Paint
ParentChanged
PreviewKeyDown
QueryAccessibilityHelp
QueryContinueDrag
RegionChanged

MouseEnter
Occurs when the mouse enters the visible part of the control.

Solution Explorer   Properties   Class View

```
Private Sub Button1_MouseEnter(ByVal sender As Object,
        ByVal e As System.EventArgs) Handles
        Button1.MouseEnter
End Sub
```

Event handling using IntelliSense

The second way to create methods for event handlers is using IntelliSense and the Code View. While in the Code View, you can use the selectors at the top of the screen to pick event handlers! For instance, pick the timer in the drop-down list at the top of the code window, on the left side, as shown in Figure 13-2. The right-hand drop-down list changes to show all the events of the timer that are available.

Now that right-hand drop-down list has all the events that would show in the Events panel. Just pick one (as shown in Figure 13-3) to generate an event handler for it.

If you aren't sure what the event is all about, generate the handler, highlight the name of the event in the Handles statement, and press F1 for help. You can always delete the method without penalty.

Relaxed event handlers

It's clear that event handlers are just subroutines. Just like any other subroutine, you might or might not need input parameters. Fact is, if you are adding the date in one datetimepicker with the date in another datetimepicker, you might just not need any input parameters.

Until now, the compiler has just required that you include those input parameters: the sender and the event arguments. Now, with *partial classes,* they aren't really necessary, and you don't have to put them in. If you get a default handler, by double-clicking a control for instance, you will get the parameters by default. If you are just typing code, you don't need them. For instance:

```
Private Sub Button1_MouseEnter() Handles Button1.MouseEnter
    'Functional code here
End Sub
```

Where this really helps you is when you are just creating an event for something at the code level, and you are using IntelliSense to help you along. Sometimes you just want to type **Private Sub NewFunction Handles** and see what IntelliSense will make available to solve a certain problem. Before this, you needed to figure out the formatting of the input parameters. Now, you don't.

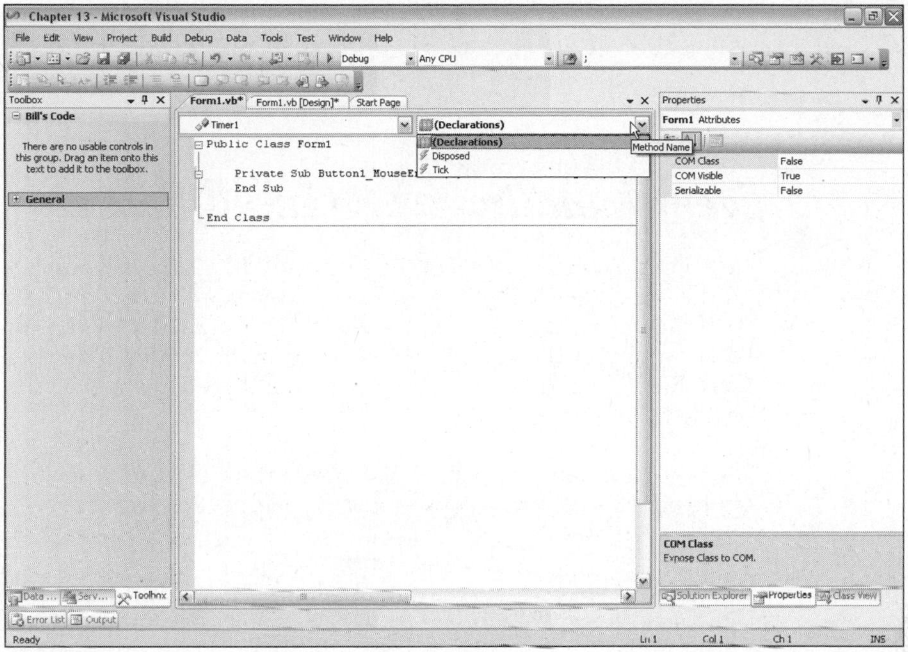

Figure 13-2:
Picking an
object in
Code View.

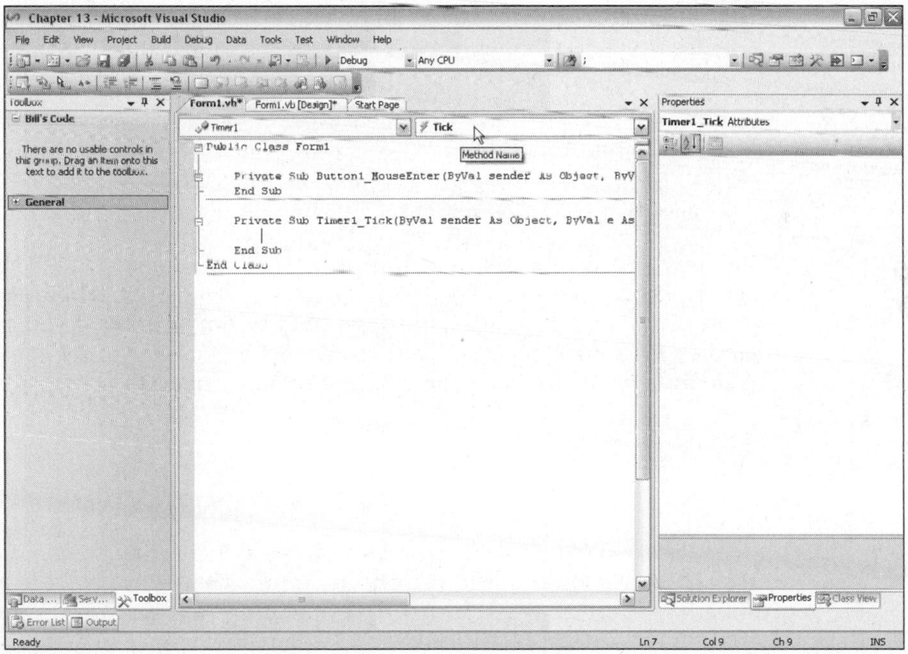

Figure 13-3:
Picking
an event.

Making Sensible Procedures with Overloading

Overloading is an organizational feature that allows a variety of parameter counts and types to be used in one logical procedure. For instance, you could have a method that adds two numbers or three numbers. When you are using the procedure, it seems to work like one function that takes two or three numbers. When you are writing the procedure, though, it is actually two functions.

Although overloading doesn't do anything you can't do by coding multiple procedures, you can use it to make your code make more sense.

Reusing your procedure names

Let me show you an example by reusing a procedure that you have already written with overloading. Take the previously mentioned specification — an add function that can add two or three numbers. You can imagine the function in VB; it would look like the following:

```
Public Function add(ByVal numberOne As Integer, ByVal
        numberTwo As Integer) As Integer
    Return numberOne + numberTwo
End Function
```

With the requirement in the introduction, you will need to create an add procedure that accepts three integers. You could make a whole new function, but wouldn't you rather just use the add name again, with the new method signature? As you can see in the following code, with overloading you can:

```
Public Function add(ByVal numberOne As Integer, ByVal
        numberTwo As Integer, ByVal numberThree As
        Integer) As Integer
    Return numberOne + numberTwo + numberThree
End Function
```

If you are experienced in VB.NET 1.0 or 1.1, you will notice that I didn't use the Overloads keyword. It is no longer required unless you are overloading a built-in function.

What does this do for you in the development environment? Primarily, it makes IntelliSense make a lot more . . . sense. I show this in Figure 13-4.

If you use IntelliSense, you can see the two add methods shown as one method. This has no real impact on functionality — it is just a convenience — but boy does it help your code make a lot more sense!

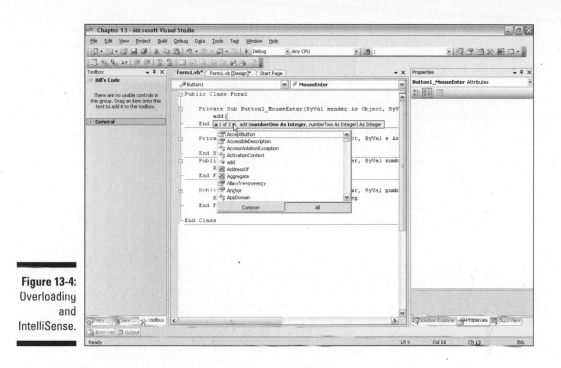

Figure 13-4:
Overloading
and
IntelliSense.

Changing built-in functions with operator overloading

Overloading isn't limited to methods you have written yourself. You can overload built-in methods and operators, too! As I discuss in Chapter 9, operators are mostly math symbols, with a few Boolean logic bits thrown in. Operators are shortcuts for longer math expressions.

For instance, instead of the add method shown in the preceding section, you can just write answer = numberOne + numberTwo + numberThree. It's much easier to create something like that.

If you want the add function to do something different, such as warn people if they are adding a negative number to a positive number, you could write a function to do this, or you could overload the + operator. The following code shows an example of this:

```
Public Shared Operator + (ByVal numberOne as Integer,
         ByVal numberTwo as Integer) as Integer
   If (numberOne < 0) Or (numberTwo < 0) Then
        MessageBox.Show("You are adding a negative
           number!")
   End If
End Operator
```

When you do this, the add operator works as originally designed, but it has this added functionality that you have placed on it — and only when you add two integers.

This is new functionality in VB 2008, though it has been available in other Microsoft languages for a while. Overloading might seem to be a theoretical programming concept, but in general it really does have a big place in writing clear, concise code. See what I mean in the next section.

Designing for overloading

Even though overloading doesn't have a direct impact on functionality, it can have a big impact on how you think about software. When you are writing Windows or Web Forms, overloading doesn't have a big impact, but when you are writing libraries of classes or a DLL file, it is very significant.

For the ultimate example, look at the .NET Framework itself. Remember arrays, those lists of things one can keep in memory? You sort a few in Part II. Anyway, that Sort subroutine has 18 different versions, each one accepting a slightly different set of parameters based on the needs of the programmer.

Each of those versions of the Sort subroutine is coded separately and looks like different subroutines in the source code of the .NET Framework. But to you, the user of the framework, there is just one method, Sort, and it just happens to take exactly the parameters you need!

Without overloading, the Array class would have 18 Sort subroutines, rather than just one. And when you were coding for an array, you would need to remember just the particular Sort subroutine you wanted or dig through all 18 in IntelliSense or the documentation.

Twenty-four methods are already part of the Array class. With all the overloads, my rough count shows that there would be 107 methods — functions and subroutines — in the Array class. That's over four times as many. Now, 220,000 methods, properties, and events exist in the .NET Framework, so without overloading, almost a million would exist if the ratio held. That's significant!

Note that you can overload too much. If you find yourself overloading a method 250 times to deal with a lot of parameters, you might want to check into a parameter array. These arrays allow you to pass in a variable quantity of parameters.

So overloads are really a design issue. When you are building a class library, think about how the methods are named and whether your patterns make sense. Have another programmer look over them. Compare it to what has already been done in the .NET Framework. Then see whether overloading can help you design better classes.

Optional parameters

Using optional parameters is another way to structure procedure naming, but rarely does it have benefits over overloading. Since early versions of Visual Basic, optional parameters have been available for use when writing subroutines or functions. In fact, Visual Basic is the only contemporary language that allows optional parameters.

Optional parameters are used by including parameters at the end of the method signature that are not required for the method to run. For instance, I could implement optional parameters in my add method, as shown in the following code:

```
Public Function add(ByVal numberOne As Integer, ByVal
        numberTwo As Integer, Optional ByVal
        numberThree = 0) As Integer
    Dim result as Integer
    If numberThree > 0 then
        result = numberOne + numberTwo + numberThree
    Else
        result = numberOne + numberTwo
    End If
    Return result
End Function
```

The differences between optional parameters and overloaded procedures are pretty clear:

✔ You find a third parameter called numberThree, which has an Optional keyword.

✔ The optional parameter has a default value.

✔ I had to include logic in the code to handle the possibility that the optional parameter was left as the default value.

Because of the rules of addition, I could have just used the optional parameter no matter what — it would have either been a number or 0, right? Adding anything to 0 returns the original value. But that is specific to this example. If this were a divide method, that wouldn't be the case.

Generally, use overloading rather than optional parameters. Overloading makes a lot more sense to the end programmer using the method.

Flexible Objects with Generics

Generics are exactly what they sound like — objects that accept their own type as a parameter. In Chapters 6, 9, and 12, I mention that properties of objects are of certain types, such as strings or integers. With generics, you can make an object that holds items of a generic type so that you can define it when you use it, rather than when you code it.

Confused? Don't be. The keyword you want to remember is Of. Of is your best friend. When you build a new generic class, it should be declared as Of a certain type. Then a list within that object can be a list of anything you need the object to be at code time. At runtime, then, the object can be declared to be Of a type, like Integers or Apples, to make sure that it gets the right types of values.

Building generics

I have a very simple example in the following code. The Staff object is a list of people. You may want to hold the names in the list, or their IDs, or even Person objects if you were to create one. You might not know when you build the Staff object, so you make it generic, as follows:

```
'First, declare the object with the generic type.
'The name can be anything, I just invented the staffType
Public Class Staff(Of staffType)
   'You need a private array to hold your list of ten
         People
   Private peopleArray(10) as staffType
   'The Add method will add one of whatever you have
   'instantiated the object as to the collection.
   Public Sub Add(ByVal person as staffType)
     peopleArray.SetValue(person, peopleArray.Length + 1)
   End Sub
End Class
```

So now when you go to use the Staff object, you have to declare what kind of things you will be keeping in it. This is shown in the following code:

```
'This could hold a list of names
Dim myStaffofStrings as New Staff(Of String)

'This could hold a list of IDs
Dim myStaffOfIntegers as New Staff(of Integer)

'Or even a list of People for a previously coded Person
         object
Dim myStaffOfPeople as New Staff(Of Person)
```

What you have created here is a generic `Staff` list capable of holding whatever you want to be in it when you use it. When you declare what you are going to put in it, it holds you to it. In Figure 13-5, you can see that when I declared the `Staff` object as holding `Integers`, it even showed up in IntelliSense.

Designing for generics

Perhaps you're wondering what the point is, and I can understand that. Basically, you are preventing having to write classes twice. If `Staff` can be a collection of names or ID numbers, you would have to write it twice (without generics) and name it two different things. With generics, that is no longer necessary.

From a design perspective, this is just like overloading. Overloading prevents you from having to write two methods to handle two different parameter types. Generics prevent you from having to write two different classes to hold collections of two different kinds of types.

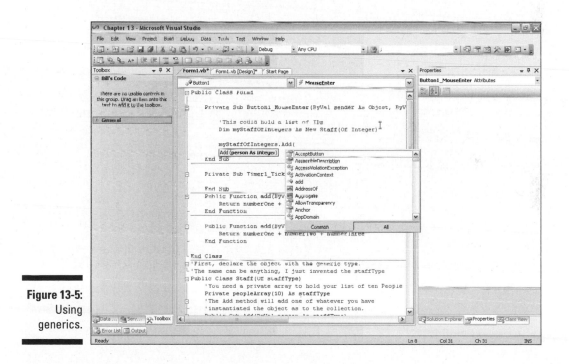

Figure 13-5:
Using
generics.

If you think of classes as molds and objects as the items that come out of those molds, you can think of generics as a way to modify the mold on the fly. It is another tool in your toolkit, and it isn't a requirement for class design. When you have a problem that can only be solved by using generics, though, you will know about it.

Controlling Objects with Threading

I show you a lot about building and using objects, but not much about their feeding and care. Generally, the .NET Framework takes care of the objects for you, but at times, you need to take control. That's when you need to know about threading.

Designing for threading

From a design perspective, threading is very simple. If you have a very time-consuming operation, you may need to put it on the back burner and return control to the user. Have you ever done something in Word and had the hourglass show up? That's an example of a blocking operation. The whole application had to wait for that operation to complete before returning control to the user.

If the operation is such that the application doesn't have to wait, you as the programmer can run that operation on a separate thread, running parallel to the application as a whole, and leave the user's control of the application on the original thread. (I demonstrate this concept in Figure 13-6.) The user might not even know that another process is running!

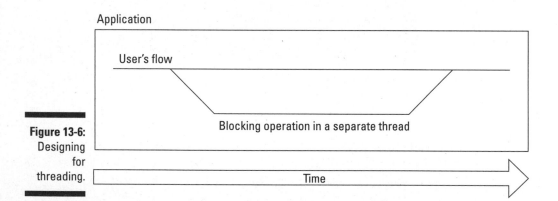

Figure 13-6: Designing for threading.

Lots of applications that you use every day use separate threading. Word uses it when you spell-check or print. Outlook uses it when it sends or receives e-mail. Excel uses it while calculating values in cells. All of these things go on while you are still typing away, for the most part. The number of simultaneous threads is only limited by the amount of memory in the machine.

The Office examples are good ones because they show the most-often-used reason for implementing threading — access to a resource. Network connections, dictionaries, and databases might only accept one connection at a time. If you want to let the user continue using the program while the application is processing, you need to use threading.

Implementing threading

To get an idea of how a blocking operation works in and out of a thread, try this simple example using a timer to emulate a troublesome operation:

1. **Start Visual Studio and create a new Windows Application project in Visual Basic.**

   I called mine ThreadingExample. You can find it on this book's companion Web site at www.vbfordummies.net.

2. **Add two buttons, called** StartThread **and** TestLocking, **to the form.**

3. **Change the text of** StartThread **to "Start The Timer."**

4. **Change the text of** TestLocking **to "Test The Lock."**

   Figure 13-7 shows an example of how the form should look.

5. **Double-click the Start the Timer button to launch the Code View and get the** OnClick **event handler.**

6. **Add an** imports **statement to the top of the code —** Imports System.Threading.

   This will make available the new Timer methods to allow the timer to run in a separate thread.

7. **Add the following code to the** StartThread_Click **event handler:**

```
Dim NetworkEmulator As New Timer(New _
        TimerCallback(AddressOf FakeNetworkCall), _
        Nothing, 0, 4000)
```

8. **Add the following code to the class to generate the** FakeNetworkCall **that you are emulating with the timer:**

```
Public Sub FakeNetworkCall(ByVal state As Object)
    MessageBox.Show("This is a network call!!")
End Sub
```

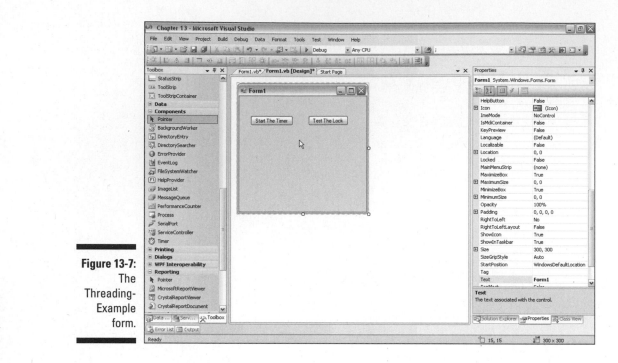

This will pop up a message box every four seconds — not usually recommended.

9. **Add the following code in the Code View to make an event handler for the click event of the** `TestLocking` **button:**

```
Dim TestNumber As Integer = 0
Private Sub TestLocking_Click(ByVal sender As
      System.Object, ByVal e As System.EventArgs)
      Handles TestLocking.Click
   TestNumber = TestNumber + 1
   Me.Text = Me.Text + TestNumber.ToString
End Sub
```

When you run this code, you will find that nothing happens until you click the Start the Timer button. Then, every four seconds, you will get a dialog box with the test message inside. Try and keep up with them. Every now and again, click the Test the Lock button. The counter should increment in the name of the form. You can see my crazy test in Figure 13-8.

What does this program prove? It shows that an application can run two things at the same time — for real. At the same time, the program was counting to 4,000 over and over, and it was still allowing you to work with the form.

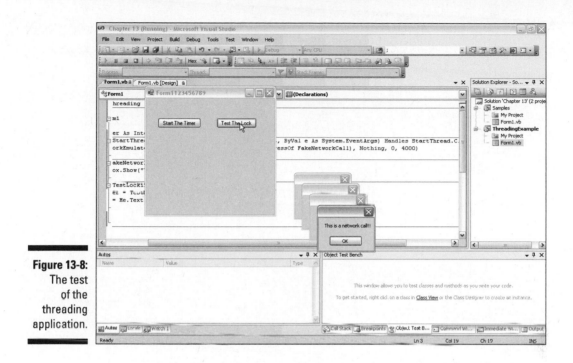

Figure 13-8:
The test
of the
threading
application.

This was all due to the `TimerCallBack` object, which is a thread encapsulation. You told the .NET Framework, "Hey, launch a thread that does a timer every four seconds and calls this method." It works pretty well. There are other things that threading will do for you, too, including the following:

- Many network calls have an asynchronous set of methods, which enable threading.

- Priority is built in, so when you have several threads, you can say which thread is the most important.

- File reading and writing can be automatically threaded.

- You can define a block of code as threaded.

All of this is in the MSDN documentation, of course. Just search for "threading," and start with About Threading. If you are writing large-scale Windows applications that do more than read from and write to a database, you will be interested — I promise!

Part IV
Digging into the Framework

The 5th Wave — By Rich Tennant

FREELANCER NED WILLIS CONSULTS WITH A MEMBER OF HIS TECHNICAL STAFF

"...and that's pretty much all there is to creating a dynamic array."

In this part . . .

The .NET Framework is the backbone of Visual Basic 2008. It provides access to databases, graphics, security, files, and just about everything that your program might want to use. In this part, you use the tools that do that work for you, and, trust me, you'll be amazed at how that framework makes some very difficult features seem very, very easy.

Chapter 14

Writing Secure Code

● ●

● ●

Security is a big topic. Ignoring for a moment all the buzzwords surrounding security, I'm sure you realize that you need to protect your application from being used by people who shouldn't be using it. You also know that you need to prevent your application from being used for things it shouldn't be used for.

At the beginning of the electronic age, security was usually performed by obfuscation. If you had an application that you didn't want people peeking at, you just hid it, and no one would know where to find it. Thus, it would be secure. (Remember the movie *War Games*? The military just assumed that no one would find the phone number to connect to their mainframes — but Matthew Broderick's character did.)

That obviously doesn't cut it anymore, and now you need to consider security as an integral requirement of every single system that you write. Your application might not have sensitive data in it, but can it be used to get to other information on the machine? Can it be used to gain access to a network that it shouldn't? The answers to these questions matter.

The two main parts to security are authentication and authorization. *Authentication* is the process of making sure that a user is authentic — that is, that the user is who he or she claims to be. The most common method of authentication is to require the use of a username and password, though other ways exist, such as thumbprint scans. *Authorization* is the act of making sure that a user has the authority to do what he or she asks to do. File permissions are a good example of this — users can't delete system-only files, for instance.

The silent partner of security is making sure that your system can't be fooled into believing a user is authentic and/or authorized. Because of this requirement, there is more to security than just inserting username and password text boxes in your program. In this chapter, I tell you what tools are available in the .NET Framework to help you make sure that your applications are secure.

Designing Secure Software

Software security is a fair amount of work to design accurately. If you break the process into pieces, you find that it is a lot more reasonable to accomplish. The Patterns and Practices team (a group of software architects at Microsoft who devise programming best practices) has created a systematic approach to designing secure programs that I think you will find very straightforward, so I describe it in the following sections.

Determining what to protect

Different applications have different artifacts that need protection, but all applications have something that needs protection. If you have a database in your application, that is the most important item to protect. If your application is a server-based application, the server should rate pretty high when you're determining what to protect.

Even if your program is just a little single-user application, the software should do no wrong — an outsider shouldn't be able to use the application to break into the user's computer.

Documenting the components of the program

If you think this section's title sounds similar to the "documentation" part of the design process described in Chapter 3, you're right. A lot of threat-modeling is just understanding how the application works and describing it well.

First, describe what the application does. This description becomes a functional overview. If you follow the steps laid out in Chapter 3, the use cases, requirements, or user stories document (depending on your personal methodology) should give you a good starting point.

Next, describe how the application gets all of that stuff done at the highest level. A Software Architecture Overview (SAO) diagram is a great way to do this. This diagram shows which machines and services do what in your software.

If you happen to be using Visual Studio Team System, building a diagram in the Enterprise Architect version is the ultimate SAO diagram and is a good model.

Sometimes the SAO is a very simple diagram — if you have a stand-alone Windows Forms program like a game, that's all there is! A stand-alone program has no network connection and no communication between software parts. Therefore, the software architecture is just the one machine.

Decomposing the components into functions

After you have a document that says what the software is doing and how, you need to break out the individual functional pieces of the software. If you have set up your software in a component fashion, the classes and methods show the functional decomposition. It's really simpler than it sounds.

The end result of breaking the software into individual pieces is having a pretty decent matrix of what components need to be protected, what parts of the software interact with each component, what parts of the network and hardware system interact with each component, and what functions of the software do what with each component.

Identifying potential threats in those functions

After you have the list of components that you need to protect, you get to do the tough part: Put two and two together. Identifying threats is the process that gets the security consultants the big bucks, and it is almost totally a factor of experience.

For instance, if your application connects to a database, you would have to imagine that the connection could potentially be intercepted by a third party. If you use a file to store sensitive information, it is theoretically possible that the file could be compromised.

To create a threat model, you need to categorize the potential threats to your software. An easy way to remember the different categories of threats is as the acronym STRIDE:

- **Spoofing identity:** Users pretending to be someone they are not.
- **Tampering with data or files:** Users editing something that shouldn't be edited.

- ✔ *Repudiation of action:* Users having the opportunity to say they didn't do something that they actually did.

- ✔ *Information disclosure:* Users seeing something that shouldn't be seen.

- ✔ *Denial of service:* Users preventing legitimate users from accessing the system when they need to.

- ✔ *Elevation of privilege:* Users getting access to something that they shouldn't have access to.

All these threats must be documented in an outline under the functions that expose the threat. This strategy not only gives you a good, discrete list of threats, but it also focuses your security hardening on those parts of the application that pose the greatest security risk.

Rating the risk

The final step in the process is to rate the risks. Microsoft uses the DREAD model to assess risk to its applications. DREAD is an acronym that defines five key attributes used to measure each vulnerability:

- ✔ *Damage potential:* The dollar cost to the company for a breach.

- ✔ *Reproducibility:* Are there special conditions to the breach that could make it harder or easier to find?

- ✔ *Exploitability:* How far into a corporate system could a hacker get?

- ✔ *Affected users:* Who is affected? How many users?

- ✔ *Discoverability:* How easy is it to find the potential breach?

You can research the DREAD model at `http://msdn.microsoft.com /security`, or just position your threat model to consider those attributes. The key is to determine what threats are most likely to cause problems and to mitigate them as best you can.

Building Secure Windows Forms Applications

The framework lives in a tightly controlled sandbox when running on a client computer. Because of the realities of this sandbox, the configuration of security policy for your application becomes very important.

The first place you need to look for security in writing Windows Forms is in the world of authentication and authorization. *Authentication* is confirming the identity of a user, and *authorization* is determining what he or she can and can't do within an application.

When you are threat modeling, you can easily consider all the possible authentication and authorization threats using the STRIDE acronym. (See the earlier section "Identifying potential threats in those functions" for more about STRIDE.)

Authentication using Windows logon

To be straightforward, I have to say that the best way for an application to authorize a user is to make use of the Windows logon. A whole host of arguments exist for this and other strategies, but it all comes down to simplicity: Simple things are more secure.

For much of the software developed with Visual Studio, the application will be used in an office by users who have different roles in the company; for example, some of those users might be in the Sales or Accounting departments. In many environments, the most privileged users are managers or administrators — yet another set of roles. In most offices, each employee has his or her own user account, and each user is assigned to the Windows NT groups that are appropriate for the roles he or she plays in the company.

Using Windows security only works if the Windows environment is set up correctly. You can't effectively build a secure application in a workspace with a bunch of Windows XP machines where everyone logs on as the Administrator, because you can't tell who is in what role.

Building a Windows Forms application to take advantage of Windows security is pretty straightforward. The goal is to check to see who is logged on (authentication) and then check that user's role (authorization).

The following steps show you how to create an application that protects the menu system for each user by showing and hiding buttons:

1. **Start a new Windows Application project by choosing File⇨New Project, and give your new project a descriptive name.**

   For example, I named my project *Windows Security*.

2. **Add three buttons to your form — one for Sales Menu, one for Accounting Menu, and one for Management Menu.**

   My example is shown in Figure 14-1.

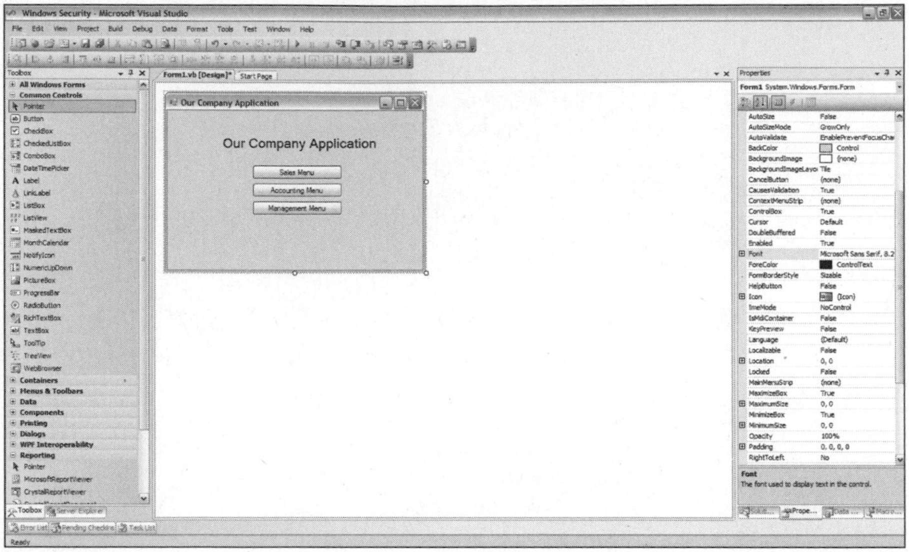

Figure 14-1:
The
example
Windows
Security
application.

3. **Set all the buttons' visible properties to** `False` **so that they are not seen on the form by default.**

4. **Double-click the form to get to the** `Form1_Load` **event handler.**

5. **Above the** `Class` **statement, import the** `System.Security. Principal` **namespace, as follows:**

```
Imports System.Security.Principal
```

6. **In the** `Class` **statement, dimension a new** `Identity` **object that represents the current user with the** `GetCurrent` **method of the** `WindowsIdentity` **object by adding the following code:**

```
Dim myIdentity As WindowsIdentity =
      WindowsIdentity.GetCurrent
```

7. **Get a reference to this identity with the** `WindowsPrincipal` **class, as follows:**

```
Dim myPrincipal As WindowsPrincipal = New
      WindowsPrincipal(myIdentity)
```

8. **Finally, in the** `Form1_Load` **subroutine, run a little If-Then statement to determine which button to show. All the code is shown in Listing 14-1.**

Listing 14-1: The Windows Security Application's Code

```
Public Class Form1
    Dim myIdentity As System.Security.Principal.WindowsIdentity =
            System.Security.Principal.WindowsIdentity.GetCurrent
```

```
      Dim myPrincipal As WindowsPrincipal = New
              System.Security.Principal.WindowsPrincipal (myIdentity)
      Private Sub Form1_Load(ByVal sender As System.Object, ByVal e As
              System.EventArgs) Handles MyBase.Load
         If myPrincipal.IsInRole("Accounting") Then
             AccountingButton.Visible = True
         ElseIf myPrincipal.IsInRole("Sales") Then
             SalesButton.Visible = True
         ElseIf myPrincipal.IsInRole("Management") Then
             ManagementButton.Visible = True
         End If
      End Sub
End Class
```

To successfully run this code, you must have an environment that has Accounting, Sales, and Management NT user groups.

In some cases, you don't need this kind of diversification of roles. Sometimes you just need to know whether the user is in a standard role. System. Security provides that, too. Using the WindowsBuiltInRole enumerator, you can describe actions that should take place when, for example, the Administrator is logged on:

```
If myPrincipal.IsInRole(WindowsBuiltInRole.Administrator) Then
      'Do something
End if
```

Encrypting information

Encryption is — at the core — an insanely sophisticated process. Five namespaces are devoted just to different algorithms. (Because encryption is so complex, I'm not going to get into its details in this book.)

Nonetheless, you must understand one cryptographic element for a key element of security — encrypting files. When you work with a file in a Windows Forms application, you run the risk of someone just loading it in a text editor and looking at it, unless you have encrypted the program.

DES (Data Encryption Standard) is a common encryption scheme that is implemented simply in .NET. It is not the strongest encryption in these days of 64-bit desktop machines, but it is strong enough to encrypt the data files for a Windows application. You can find the methods to encrypt for DES in the DESCryptoServiceProvider in the System.Security.Cryptography namespace.

Deployment security

If you are deploying your application using ClickOnce, you need to define the access to the PC that the application will request. ClickOnce is a server–based deployment strategy that allows users to run Windows Forms applications from a Web browser or file share. This is accomplished with the Security tab in the My Project configuration file, as shown in Figure 14-2.

Getting to the My Project configuration file is fairly straightforward. Follow these steps:

1. **From an open project, go the Solution Explorer by pressing Ctrl+Alt+L.**

2. **Double-click the My Project file.**

3. **Click the Security tab.**

Here, you can define the features that your application uses so that the user installing it will receive a warning at installation rather than a security error when running the application.

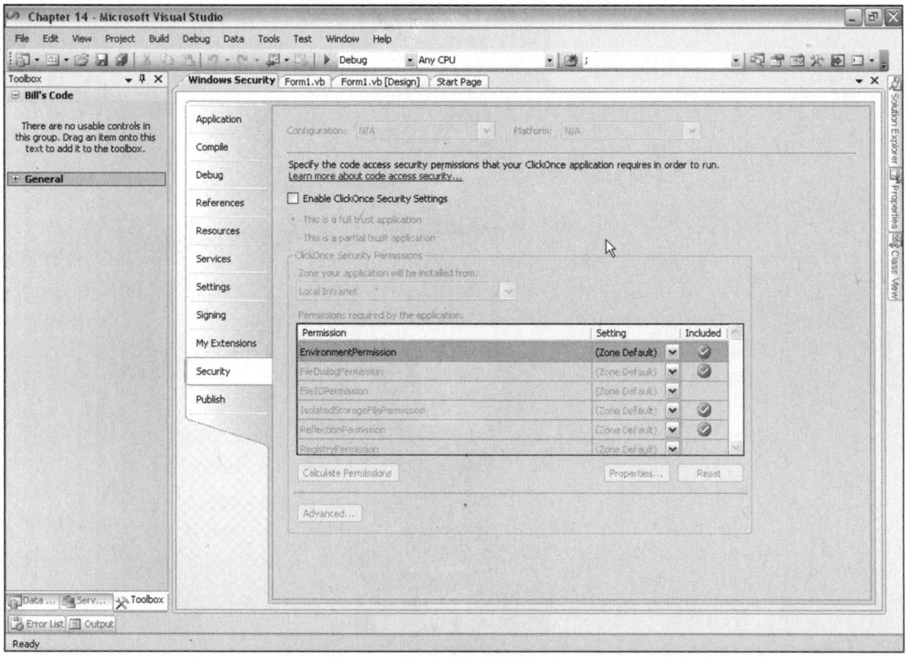

Figure 14-2: The Security tab of the My Project configuration file.

Building Secure Web Forms Applications

Web Forms applications are disconnected, loosely coupled programs that expose a server to potential attacks through the exposed ports used by the applications. By *loosely coupled*, I mean that they have a transact-and-wait relationship with the server.

Because of this coupling, building for security becomes more important than ever with a Web Forms application. A side effect of this is that your application can become less functional due to security considerations.

When building Web-based applications, you spend less of your time worrying about authentication (especially if your application is made publicly available) and more time worrying about crackers. Because you are making a server — usually something you would keep private — available to the public, your programs are subject to a whole new set of rules for security.

The key to protecting a public server is honesty. You have to be honest with yourself about the weaknesses of the system. Don't think, "Well, a cracker could figure out the password by doing XYZ, but no one would ever do that." Trust me; someone will figure it out.

The two main types of attacks you should be concerned about for a Web Forms application are SQL Injection attacks and script exploits.

SQL Injection attacks

A *SQL Injection attack* occurs when a hacker enters a line of SQL code into an input field used to query a database in a form on a Web page (such as the Username and Password text boxes in a logon form). This malicious SQL code is written to cause the database to act in an unexpected way or to allow the hacker to gain access to, alter, or damage the database.

Understanding SQL Injection

The best way to understand how a hacker uses an SQL Injection is to see an example. For instance, a Web page has code in place that accepts a Product ID from the user in a text box and returns product details based on the Product ID the user entered. The code on the server might look like this:

```
'Get productId from user
Dim productId As String = TextBox1.Text
'Get information from the database.
Dim selectString As String = "SELECT * FROM Items WHERE
          ProductId = '" & productId & "';"
Dim cmd As SqlCommand = New SqlCommand(selectString, conn)
conn.Open()
Dim myReader As SqlDataReader = cmd.ExecuteReader()
' Process results.
myReader.Close()
conn.Close()
```

Normally, a user would enter the appropriate information into the text box. But a cracker attempting an SQL Injection attack would enter the following string into textBox1:

```
"FOOBAR';DELETE FROM Items;--"
```

The SQL code that would be run by your code would look like this:

```
SELECT * FROM Items WHERE ProductID = 'FOOBAR';DELETE FROM
          Items;--'
```

The SQL server executes some code you didn't expect; in this case, the code deleted everything in the Items table.

The easiest way to prevent SQL Injection is to never use string concatenation to generate SQL. Use a stored procedure and SQL parameters. You can read more about that in Chapter 15.

Script exploits

A *script exploit* is a security flaw that takes advantage of the JavaScript engine in a user's Web browser. Script exploits take advantage of one of the more common features of public Web Forms applications — enabling interaction among users. For instance, a Web Forms application may enable a user to post a comment that other users of the site can view, or it may allow a user to fill out an online profile.

Understanding script exploits

If a malicious user were to put some script code in his or her profile or comment, that hacker could take over the browser of the next user who came to the site. Several outcomes are possible, and none of them are good.

For instance, the cookies collection is available to JavaScript when a user comes to your site. A malicious user would put some script code in his or her profile that could copy the cookie for your site to a remote server. This could give the malicious user access to the current user's session because the session identifier is stored as a cookie. The malicious user would then be able to spoof the current user's identity.

Preventing script exploits

Fortunately, ASP.NET prevents users from typing most script code into a form field and posting it to the server. Try it with a basic Web Forms project by following these steps (you will get the error shown in Figure 14-3):

1. **Create a new Web Forms project.**

2. **Add a text box and a button to the default page.**

3. **Run the project.**

4. **Type** <script>msgbox()</script> **into the text box.**

5. **Click the button.**

Additionally, you can use the Server.HTMLEncode method to encode anything that the Web Forms application sends to the screen — this will make script code appear in real text rather than in actual HTML.

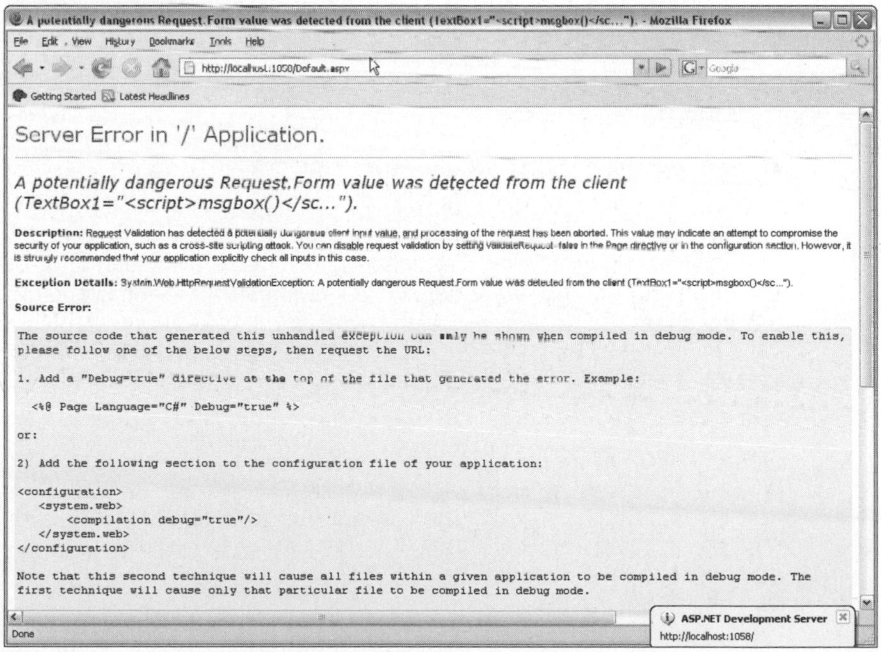

Figure 14-3: Script exploits are blocked by default.

Best practices for securing your Web Forms applications

Aside from making sure that your Web Forms application will prevent SQL Injection attacks and script exploits, you should keep in mind some good practices for securing your Web applications.

The following list outlines some of the most important practices for securing your Web applications:

- Keep your IIS box up to date.
- Back up everything.
- Avoid using a `Querystring` variable.
- Don't leave HTML comments in place. Any user can view the HTML code and see your comments by choosing View⇨Source in a browser.
- Don't depend on client-side validation for security — it can be faked.
- Use strong passwords.
- Don't assume what the user sent you came from your form and is safe. It is easy to fake a form post.
- Make sure that error messages don't give the user any information about your application. E-mail yourself the error messages instead of displaying them to the user.
- Use Secure Sockets Layer.
- Don't store anything useful in a cookie.
- Close all unused ports on your Web server.
- Turn off SMTP on IIS unless you need it.
- Run a virus checker if you allow uploads.
- Do not run your application as Administrator.
- Use temporary cookies, if possible, by setting the expiration date to a past date. The cookie will only stay alive for the length of the session.
- Put a size limit on file uploads. You can do this in the `Web.Config` file, as follows:

```
<configuration>
    <system.web>
        <httpRuntime maxRequestLength="4096" />
    </system.web>
</configuration>
```

- Remember that the `ViewState` of Web Forms is easily viewable.

Using System.Security

While much of the security tools are built into the classes that use them, some classes defy description or classification. For that reason, System.Security is the holding pot for stuff that doesn't fit anywhere else.

The more common namespaces for System.Security are described in Table 14-1. I show how to use the Security.Principal namespace in the earlier section "Authentication using Windows logon."

Table 14-1	Headings and Rules	
Namespace	*Description*	*Common Classes*
Security	Serves as the base class for security	CodeAccessPermission, SecureString
AccessControl	Hosts more sophisticated control for authorization	AccessRule, AuditRule
Authorization	Contains enumerations that describe the security of an application	CipherAlgorithmType
Cryptography	Contains several namespaces that help with encryption	CryptoConfig, DESCryptoService Provider
Permissions	Controls access to resources	PrincipalPermission, SecurityPermission
Policy	Defends repudiation with classes for evidence	Evidence, Site, Url
Principal	Defines the object that represents the current user context	WindowsIdentity, WindowsPrincipal

Chapter 15

Accessing Data

*N*ot to predispose you to the contents of this chapter, but you will proba-
bly find that data access is the most important part of your use of the
.NET Framework. You're likely to use the various features of the `System.
Data` namespace more than any other namespace.

Unquestionably, one of the most common uses of Visual Basic is the creation of business applications. Business applications are about data. This
is the black and white of development with Visual Basic 2008. While understanding a little of everything is important, complete understanding of the
`System.Data` namespace is very important when you're building business
applications.

You can look at the data tools in VB 2008 in three ways:

✔ **Database connectivity:** Getting information out of and into a database is
a primary part of the `System.Data` namespace.

✔ **Holding data in containers within your programs:** The `DataSet`, `Data
View`, and `DataTable` containers are useful mechanisms for holding
data. If you are a Visual Basic 6 or an ASP programmer, you remember
Recordsets, which have been replaced by the new constructs.

The Language Integrated Query now lets you get the data out of the data
containers using Structured Query Language (SQL) instead of complicated object language.

✔ **Integration with data controls:** The System.Web and System.Windows namespaces function to integrate with the data controls. Data control integration uses database connectivity and data containers extensively. This makes data controls a great target for your reading in this chapter.

Getting to Know System.Data

Data in .NET is different from data in any other Microsoft platform you have used before. Microsoft has and continues to change the way data is manipulated in the .NET Framework. ADO.NET, whose implementation is contained in the new data library System.Data, provides yet another new way to think about data from a development perspective:

✔ **Disconnected:** After you get data from a data source, your program is no longer connected to that data source. You have a copy of the data. This cures one problem and causes another:

- You no longer have a row-locking problem. Because you have a copy of the data, you don't have to constrain the database from making changes.

- You have the *last in wins* problem. If two instances of a program get the same data, and they both update it, the last one back to the database overwrites the changes made by the first program.

✔ **XML driven:** The data copy that is collected from the data source is actually XML under the hood. It might be moved around in a custom format when Microsoft deems it necessary for performance, but it is just XML either way, making movement between platforms, applications, or databases much easier.

✔ **Database-generic containers:** The containers don't depend on the type of the database — they can be used to store data from anywhere.

✔ **Database-specific adapters:** Connections to the database are specific to the database platform, so if you want to connect to a specific database, you need the components that work with that database.

The process for getting data has changed a little, too. You used to have a connection and a command, which returned a Recordset. Now, you have an adapter, which uses a connection and a command to fill a DataSet container. What has changed is the way that the user interface helps you get the job done.

`System.Data` has the classes to help you connect to a lot of different databases and other types of data. These classes are broken up into the namespaces shown in Table 15-1.

Table 15-1	The System.Data Namespaces	
Namespace	*Purpose*	*Most Used Classes*
`System.Data`	Classes common to all of ADO.NET	The containers `DataSet`, `DataView`, `DataTable`, `DataRow`
`System.Data. Common`	Utility classes used by database-specific classes	`DbCommand`, `DbConnection`
`System.Data. ODBC`	Classes for connections to ODBC databases such as dBASE	`OdbcCommand`, `OdbcAdapter`
`System.Data. OleDb`	Classes for connections to OleDb databases such as Access	`OleDbCommand`, `OleDbAdapter`
`System.Data. OracleClient`	Classes for connections to Oracle	`OracleCommand`, `OracleAdapter`
`System.Data. SqlClient`	Classes for connections to Microsoft SQL Server	`SqlCommand`, `SqlDataAdapter`
`System.Data. SqlTypes`	For referencing the native types common to SQL Server	`SqlDateTime`

Though there is a lot to the `System.Data` namespace and related tools, I focus on the way Visual Studio implements these tools. In previous versions of the development software of all makes and models, the visual tools just made things harder because of the black box problem.

The *black box problem* is that of having a development environment do things for you over which you have no control. Sometimes, it's nice to have things done for you, but when the development environment doesn't build things exactly how you need them, it ends up generating code that isn't very useful.

Fortunately, that isn't the case anymore. Visual Studio now generates completely open and sensible VB code when you use the visual data tools. I think you will be pleased with the results.

How the Data Classes Fit into the Framework

The data classes are all about information storage. In Chapter 13, I talk about collections, which are for storage of information while an application is running. Hashtables are another example of storing information. *Collections* hold lists of objects, and *hashtables* hold name and value pairs.

The data containers hold data in larger amounts and help you manipulate that data. The data containers include the following:

- ✔ `DataSet`: Kind of the granddaddy of them all, the `DataSet` container is an in-memory representation of an entire database.

- ✔ `DataTable`: A single table of data stored in memory, the `DataTable` container is the closest thing you can find to a Recordset, if you are a VB 6 programmer and are looking. `DataSet` containers are made up of `DataTable` containers.

- ✔ `DataRow`: Unsurprisingly, this is a row in a `DataTable` container.

- ✔ `DataView`: A copy of a `DataTable` that can be used to sort and filter data for viewing purposes.

- ✔ `DataReader`: A read-only, forward-only stream of data that is used for one-time processes such as filling list boxes. Usually called a *fire hose*.

Getting to Your Data

Everything in the `System.Data` namespace revolves around getting data from a database, such as Microsoft SQL Server, and filling these data containers. You can get to this data manually. Generally speaking, the process goes in stages that look something like this:

1. You create an adapter.

2. You tell the adapter how to get information from the database (the connection).

3. The adapter connects to the database.

4. You tell the adapter what information to get from the database (the command).

5. The adapter fills the `DataSet` container with data.

6. The connection between the adapter and the database is closed.

7. You now have a disconnected copy of the data in your program.

Not to put too fine a point on it, but you shouldn't have to go through that process. Visual Studio does a lot of the data management for you if you let it, and I recommend that you do.

Using the System.Data Namespace

The System.Data namespace is another namespace that gets mixed up between the code world and the visual tools world. Though it is more of a relationship between the form controls and the Data namespace, it often seems like the data lives right inside the controls, especially when you're dealing with Visual Basic.

In the following sections, you deal primarily with the visual tools, which are as much a part of the Visual Basic experience as the code. First, I go over connecting to data sources, and then I show you how to write a quick application using one of those connections. Finally, I go over a little of the code side.

Connecting to a data source

There is more to connecting to a database than establishing a simple connection to Microsoft Access. Visual Basic developers have to connect to mainframes, text files, unusual databases, Web services, and other programs. All of these disparate systems get integrated into windows and Web screens, with update, add, and delete functionality to boot.

Getting to these data sources mostly depends on the Adapter classes of the individualized database namespaces. Oracle has its own, as does SQL Server. Databases that are ODBC (Open Database Connectivity) compliant (such as Microsoft Access) have their own Adapter classes, and the newer OLEDB (Object Linking and Embedding Database) protocol has one, too.

Fortunately, a wizard handles most of this. The Data Source Configuration Wizard is accessible from the Data Sources panel, where you spend much of your time when working with data. To get started with the Data Source Configuration Wizard, follow these steps:

1. **Start a new Windows Application project by choosing File⇨New Project. Select a Visual Basic Windows Application and give it an appropriate name.**

   For this example, I named the Windows Application project Accessing Data.

2. **To open the Data Sources panel, choose Data⇨Show Data Sources, or press Shift+Alt+D.**

   It should tell you that you have no data sources, as shown in Figure 15-1.

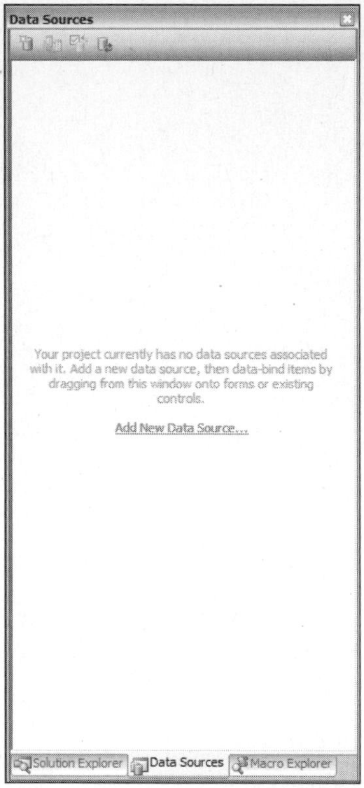

Figure 15-1:
The Data
Sources
panel.

3. **Click the Add New Data Source link in the Data Sources panel.**

   This brings up the Data Source Configuration Wizard. The wizard has a variety of data source types that you can choose from. The most interesting of these is the Object source, which gives you access to an object in an assembly to bind your controls to.

   Click the Object source type to see the options there, as shown in Figure 15-2, and click the Previous button to go back to the previous screen.

   You can pick a Web service to connect to a function on another computer. I cover Web service creation and consumption in Chapter 7, but this functionality sets you up to have a data source along with the Web service reference. It's pretty cool. I selected the USZipSoap from WebServiceX as an example in Figure 15-3.

   When you are done looking around, click the Cancel button to come back.

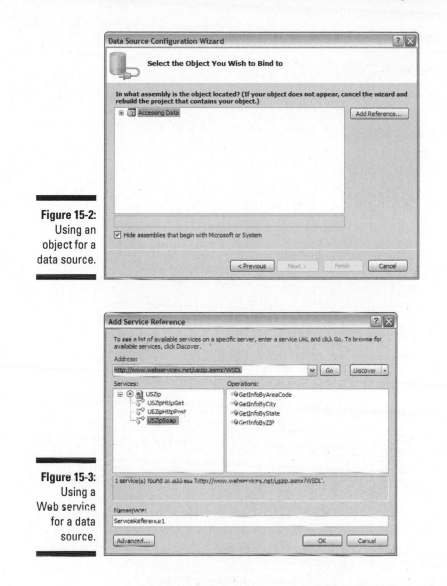

Figure 15-2:
Using an object for a data source.

Figure 15-3:
Using a Web service for a data source.

4. **Click the Database data source type to be taken to the Choose Your Data Connection screen, as shown in Figure 15-4.**

   The most common point of access is a database.

5. **If you have an existing data connection, it appears in the drop-down list. Otherwise, you need to click the New Connection button to open the Add Connection dialog box, as shown in Figure 15-5.**

   For this example, I click the New Connection button and select Northwind, the Microsoft sample database.

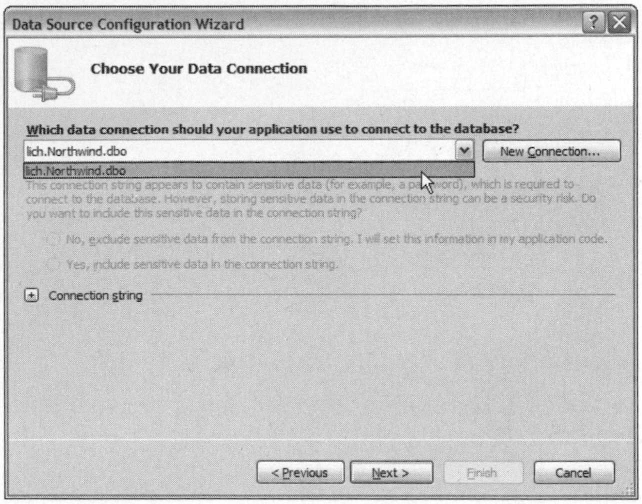

Figure 15-4:
Choosing
your data
connection.

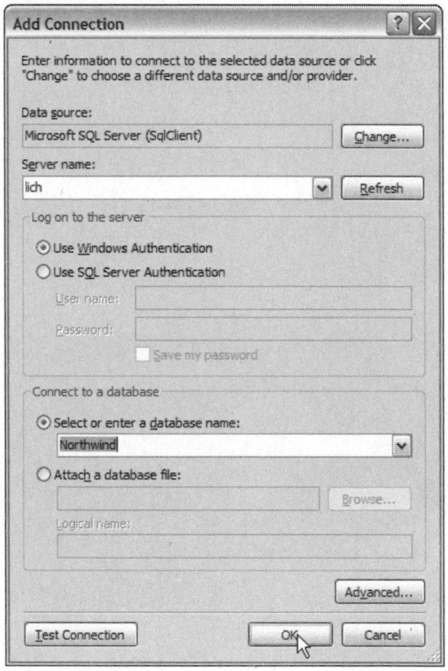

Figure 15-5:
The Add
Connection
dialog box.

The Add Connection dialog box assumes that you are going to connect to an SQL server. If that isn't the case, click the Change button to select a different database from the Change Data Source dialog box, as shown in Figure 15-6. For this example, I chose Microsoft SQL Server and clicked the OK button.

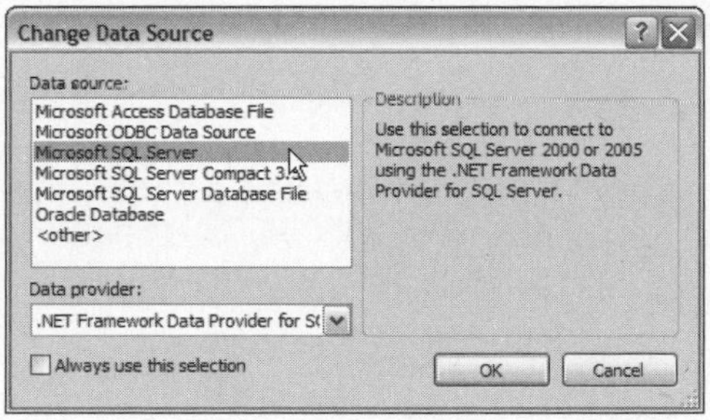

Figure 15-6:
The Change
Data Source
dialog box.

6. **Select a server from the Server Name drop-down list.**

7. **Select the Northwind database from the Select or Enter a Database
   Name drop-down list.**

8. **Click the OK button.**

   You go back to the Choose Your Data Connection screen.

9. **Click the Next button to save the connection string to the application
   configuration file.**

10. **Accept the defaults by clicking the Next button.**

    You go the Choose Your Database Objects screen. Here you can choose
    the tables, views, or stored procedures that you want to use.

11. **Under Tables, select Orders and Order Details (as shown in Figure
    15-7), and click the Finish button.**

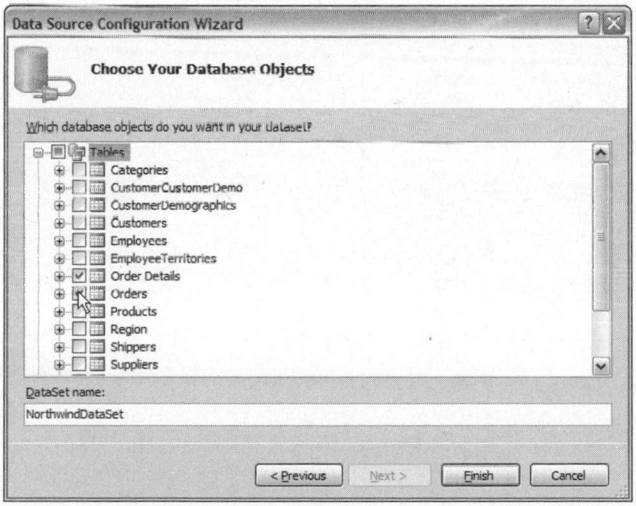

Figure 15-7:
Selecting
your data
objects.

You're done! If you look at the Data Sources panel, you find that the new data connection was added, as shown in Figure 15-8.

Note that the Data Sources panel has the Orders tables, and the Data Connections panel has all the tables. This is because the `DataSet` container that you built in the wizard just has the Orders table and related tables in it. The Data Connections panel shows everything in the database.

By following the preceding steps, you create two significant entities in Visual Studio:

✔ You create a connection to the database, shown in the Database Explorer. You find that it sticks around — it is specific to this installation of Visual Studio.

✔ You also create a project data source that is specific to this project, and it won't be there if you start another project.

Both of them are important, and they provide different functionality. In this chapter, I focus on the project-specific data source displayed in the Data Sources panel.

Working with the visual tools

The RAD data tools for Visual Basic are a massive improvement over what has previously been provided by Microsoft. The RAD data tools in Visual Basic 2008 are usable, do what you need, and actually write decent code for you.

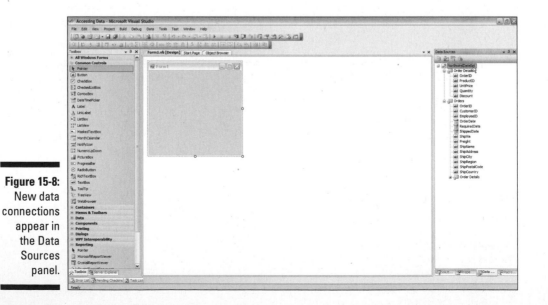

Figure 15-8:
New data connections appear in the Data Sources panel.

You need to know that I would *never, ever* show this kind of black magic if it was not a best practice. In the past, tools that did something that you couldn't see often did their job poorly. Using the tools, in the long run, actually made your program worse. The new tools, though, are a pretty good way to build software. People may tell you that I am wrong, but it really isn't bad. Try it!

If you click a table in the Data Sources panel, a drop-down arrow appears. Select it and you see something very interesting, as shown in Figure 15-9. A drop-down list appears that enables you to choose how that table is integrated into Windows Forms.

Change the Orders table to a Details view. It is used to create a detail type form — one that easily allows the user to view and change data. Then drag the table to the form, and the Details view is created for you, as shown in Figure 15-10.

A whole lot of things happened when you dropped the table on your form:

✔ The fields and field names were added.

✔ The fields are in the most appropriate format — note that the Order Date is a date chooser.

✔ The field name is a label.

✔ Visual Studio automatically adds a space where the case changes.

Note that each field gets a Smart Tag that allows you to specify a query for the values in the text box. You can also preset the control that is used by changing the values in the Data Sources panel, as shown in Figure 15-10.

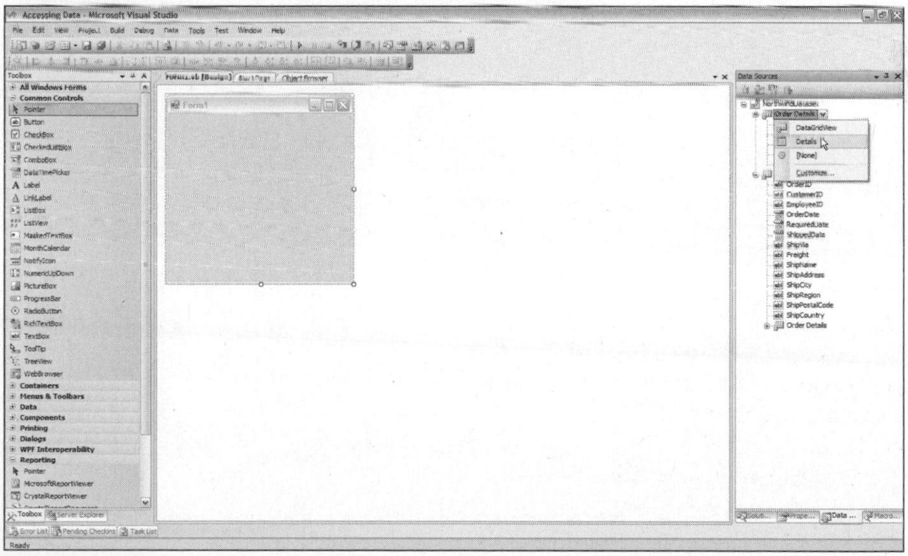

Figure 15-9:
Table
Options
drop-down
list.

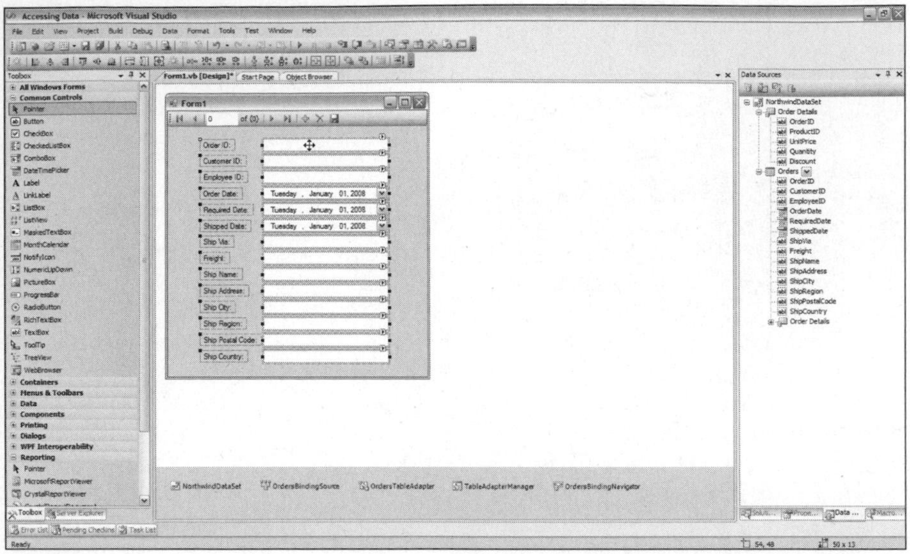

Figure 15-10:
Creating an
Orders
Detail data
form.

Also, a VCR Bar (technically called the `BindingNavigator`) is added to the top of the page. When you run the application, you can use the VCR Bar to cycle among the records in the table.

Finally, five completely code-based objects are added in the Component Tray at the bottom of the page: the `DataSet` called `NorthwindDataSet`, the `BindingSource` called `OrdersBindingSource`, the `TableAdapter` called `OrdersTableAdapter`, the `TableAdapterManager` and the `BindingNavigator` called `OrdersBindingNavigator` objects.

Click the Play button and you can easily see the VCR Bar work. You can walk through the items in the database with no problems, as shown in Figure 15-11. It's just like working in Access or FoxPro, but with enterprise quality!

It gets better. Follow these steps to create a child table interface:

1. **Open the Order table in the Data Sources panel by clicking the plus sign next to the table.**

2. **Scroll down until you see the Order Details table nested in the Orders table.**

3. **Drag that instance of the table over to the form and place it under the Orders fields that you placed on the form earlier in this section (refer to Figure 15-10).**

4. **Click the Play button to run the example, as shown in Figure 15-12.**

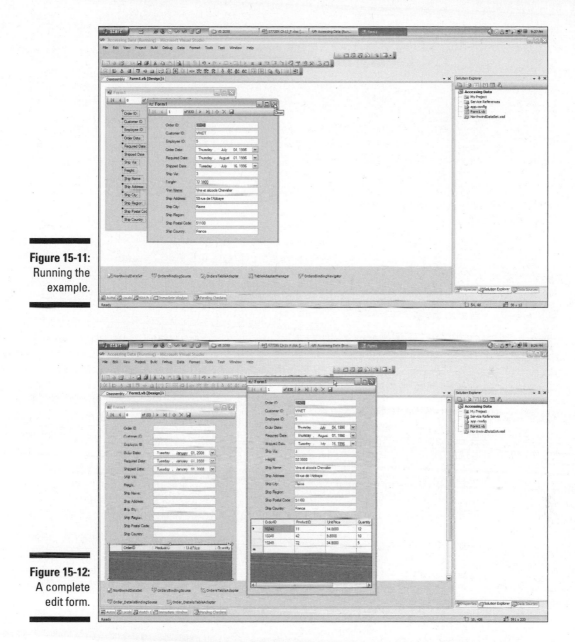

Figure 15-11:
Running the
example.

Figure 15-12:
A complete
edit form.

You have a running, easy-to-use parent/child form, with orders and order details. Creating this form would have required you to write 100 lines of code, even in previous versions of VB. With the ability to choose an assembly for a data source that Visual Basic 2008 grants you, the form is even enterprise ready. It's pretty slick stuff.

Writing data code

In most enterprise development environments, you won't be using the visual tools to build data access software. Generally, an infrastructure is already in place.

The reason for this is that often enterprise software has very specific requirements, and the easiest way to manage those specifications is with unique and customized code. In short, some organizations don't want things done the way Microsoft does them.

Output of the visual tools

The reason that the visual tools are often not used in enterprise environments is that the code the tools put out is rather sophisticated. If you switch to Code View, right-click an instance of an object (such as the `CustomersTableAdapter` object), and select Go to Definition, you go to the code behind the designer. I count 212 lines of code in that file — much of it going to defining the data objects being used, as shown in the following code:

```
'NorthwindDataSet
Me.NorthwindDataSet.DataSetName = "NorthwindDataSet"
'CustomersBindingSource
Me.CustomersBindingSource.DataMember = "Customers"
Me.CustomersBindingSource.DataSource = Me.NorthwindDataSet
'CustomersTableAdapter
Me.CustomersTableAdapter.ClearBeforeFill = True
'CustomersBindingNavigator
Me.CustomersBindingNavigator.AddNewItem = Me.bindingNavigatorAddNewItem
Me.CustomersBindingNavigator.BindingSource = Me.CustomersBindingSource
Me.CustomersBindingNavigator.CountItem = Me.bindingNavigatorCountItem
Me.CustomersBindingNavigator.CountItemFormat = "of {0}"
Me.CustomersBindingNavigator.DeleteItem = Me.bindingNavigatorDeleteItem
Me.CustomersBindingNavigator.Items.AddRange(New
            System.Windows.Forms.ToolStripItem()
            {Me.bindingNavigatorMoveFirstItem,
            Me.bindingNavigatorMovePreviousItem, Me.bindingNavigatorSeparator,
            Me.bindingNavigatorPositionItem, Me.bindingNavigatorCountItem,
            Me.bindingNavigatorSeparator1, Me.bindingNavigatorMoveNextItem,
            Me.bindingNavigatorMoveLastItem, Me.bindingNavigatorSeparator2,
            Me.bindingNavigatorAddNewItem, Me.bindingNavigatorDeleteItem,
            Me.bindingNavigatorSaveItem})
Me.CustomersBindingNavigator.Location = New System.Drawing.Point(0, 0)
Me.CustomersBindingNavigator.MoveFirstItem = Me.bindingNavigatorMoveFirstItem
Me.CustomersBindingNavigator.MoveLastItem = Me.bindingNavigatorMoveLastItem
Me.CustomersBindingNavigator.MoveNextItem = Me.bindingNavigatorMoveNextItem
Me.CustomersBindingNavigator.MovePreviousItem =
            Me.bindingNavigatorMovePreviousItem
Me.CustomersBindingNavigator.Name = "CustomersBindingNavigator"
Me.CustomersBindingNavigator.PositionItem = Me.bindingNavigatorPositionItem
```

```
Me.CustomersBindingNavigator.Size = New System.Drawing.Size(292, 25)
Me.CustomersBindingNavigator.TabIndex = 0
Me.CustomersBindingNavigator.Text = "BindingNavigator1"
'bindingNavigatorMoveFirstItem
Me.bindingNavigatorMoveFirstItem.DisplayStyle =
            System.Windows.Forms.ToolStripItemDisplayStyle.Image
Me.bindingNavigatorMoveFirstItem.Image =
            CType(resources.GetObject("bindingNavigatorMoveFirstItem.Image"),
            System.Drawing.Image)
Me.bindingNavigatorMoveFirstItem.Name = "bindingNavigatorMoveFirstItem"
Me.bindingNavigatorMoveFirstItem.Text = "Move first"
```

Nothing is wrong with this code, but it is purposely very generic to support anything that anyone might want to do with it. Enterprise customers often want to make sure that everything is done the same way. For this reason, they often define a specific data code format and expect their software developers to use that, rather than the visual tools.

Basic data code

The code of the sample project is pretty simple:

```
Private Sub Form1_Load(ByVal sender As System.Object, ByVal e As
            System.EventArgs) Handles MyBase.Load
'TODO: This line of code loads data into the 'NorthwindDataSet.Customers' table.
            You can move, or remove it, as needed.
Me.CustomersTableAdapter.Fill(Me.NorthwindDataSet.Customers)
End Sub


Private Sub bindingNavigatorSaveItem_Click(ByVal sender As System.Object, ByVal
            e As System.EventArgs) Handles bindingNavigatorSaveItem.Click
If Me.Validate Then
    Me.CustomersBindingSource.EndEdit()
    Me.CustomersTableAdapter.Update(Me.NorthwindDataSet.Customers)
Else
    System.Windows.Forms.MessageBox.Show(Me, "Validation errors occurred.",
            "Save", System.Windows.Forms.MessageBoxButtons.OK,
            System.Windows.Forms.MessageBoxIcon.Warning)
End If
End Sub
```

While this is fairly straightforward, it obviously isn't everything you need. The rest of the code is in the file that generates the visual form itself, supporting the visual components.

This becomes useful especially when you want to build a Web service or a class library — though it should be noted that you can still use the visual tools in those project types.

A time may come when you want to connect to a database without using the visual tools. I discuss the steps in the earlier section "How the Data Classes Fit into the Framework," and here I show the code to go with it:

```
Dim myConnection As New SqlConnection
myConnection.ConnectionString =
              "server=(local);database=Northwind;Trusted_Connection=True"
Dim myAdapter As SqlDataAdapter
myAdapter = New SqlDataAdapter("SELECT * FROM Customers", myConnection)
Dim myDataSet As New DataSet
myConnection.Open()
myAdapter.Fill(myDataSet)
myConnection.Close()
```

After running this code, you would have the Customer's table in a `DataSet` container, just as you did in the visual tools in the earlier section "How the Data Classes Fit into the Framework." To access the information, you would set the value of a text box to the value of a cell in the `DataSet` container, like this:

```
TextBox1.Text = myDataSet.Tables(0).Rows(0)("CustomerName")
```

To change to the next record, you would need to write code that changes the `Rows(0)` to `Rows(1)` in the next example. As you can see, it would be a fair amount of code.

That's why few people use the basic data code to get the databases. Either you use the visual tools, or you use a data broker of some sort.

Using data brokers

A *data broker* is a block of code that makes data access simpler. Basically, it puts all the complicated piping of the database connection in a class file so you can call — from one place — the code that's common to all your database access.

The Patterns and Practices team at Microsoft (`http://msdn.microsoft.com/practices`) created a broker called the Enterprise Library Data Access Application Block that does exactly this. It is designed for use by the large enterprises I mention throughout this chapter, but the broker is excellent for use in stand-alone applications as well, especially if you find that the visual tools don't do the trick for some reason.

With the Enterprise Library Data Access Application Block data broker, you only need to be concerned about the most customized parts of the data access process, specifically these three general steps:

1. Create the database object.

2. Supply the parameters for the command, if they are needed.

3. Call the appropriate method.

These steps can be executed in one line of code that looks something like this:

```
myDataSet = DatabaseFactory.CreateDatabase("Northwind").ExecuteDataSet("SELECT *
            FROM Customers");
```

These steps assume that you have the Enterprise library already installed, referenced, and configured. You can find the Enterprise library at http://msdn.microsoft.com/practices/default.aspx?pull=/ library/en-us/dnpag2/html/entlib.asp, or you can get it from this book's companion Web site at www.vbfordummies.net.

Using LINQ

LINQ is a set of classes in the .NET Framework designed to help you with data manipulation — just like some of the classes in System.Data. It is more or less a new way to handle data in .NET, rather than the ADO.NET methods of DataSets. The goal is to make relational databases, like those found in Microsoft Access and SQL Server, look more like the classes discussed in Chapter 6.

LINQ is a very large topic. Even the introductory article on it in the MSDN is 50 printed pages. While a full discussion is beyond the scope of this book, here's a brief introduction.

In the example in this section, you get the Order information from NorthWind. Using LINQ, first you would define what you're going to get from the table using a class, just the way we did with the DateCalculator in Chapter 6. Adding a few modifiers makes the class data-aware so we can query the information with LINQ. Use the following steps to get started with a basic LINQ project:

1. **Add a reference to** System.Data.Linq, **using the Add Reference panel (as shown in Figure 15-13).**

2. **Add a few** Imports **statements to the code that will have the LINQ statements:**

   ```
   Imports System.Data.Linq
   Imports System.Data.Linq.Mapping
   ```

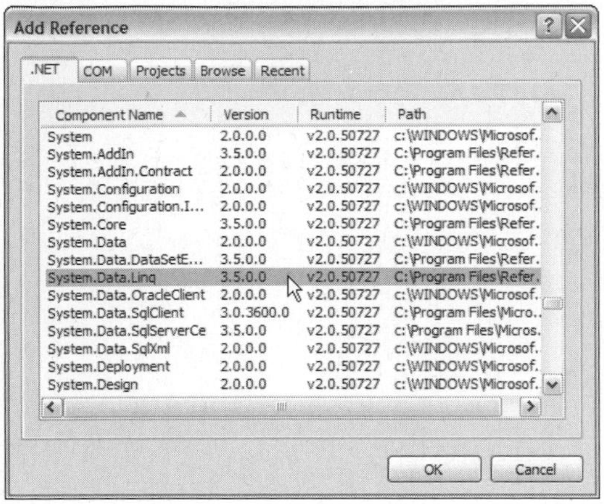

Figure 15-13:
Adding a
reference to
System.
Data.Linq.

3. **Make a class in your project that references the** `Table` **attribute, as shown in the following code:**

```
<Table(Name:="Orders")> _
Public Class Orders
    <Column()> _
    Public OrderDate As DateTime
    <Column()> _
    Public ShipName As String
End Class
```

4. **Generate a way to get data out of the database using a** `DataContext` **object, as shown here:**

```
Dim currentContext As DataContext = New _
DataContext("server=(local);database=Northwind;Trusted_Connection=True")
Dim myOrders As Table(Of Orders) = currentContext.GetTable(Of Orders)()
```

5. **Now you have a collection drawn from a database.**

If you wanted to loop through them, you could put a `For Each` order in `latestOrders` and process them that way.

As you can see, LINQ is another way of handling data. If you are building large-scale systems, LINQ makes a lot of sense. For smallish Windows applications, LINQ is not a lot better than ADO.NET.

For more information, check out LINQ to SQL: .NET Language Integrated Query for Relational Data, at `http://msdn2.microsoft.com/en-us/library/bb425822.aspx`. The VB code in the article has a few bugs, but the principles discussed are sound.

Chapter 16

Working with the File System

Storing information in files is one of the most common tasks of a computer program, and Visual Basic makes it simpler to perform those tasks in the 2008 version. Visual Basic is not known as a strong file-handling language. With the addition of the .NET Framework, though, a surprising number of file-handling tools are available for your use.

In this chapter, I show you how to work with the directories and files on your computer. The `System.IO` namespace and its classes, along with the `My.Computer.FileInfo` class, contain the tools you need to read directories, parse files, save information to files, get file information, and more.

I also describe the controls that Visual Studio provides for manipulating files in Windows Forms applications. The `OpenFileDialog`, `SaveFileDialog`, and `FolderBrowserDialog` speed development of programs that manage files. The `FileSystemWatcher` component makes it easier to maintain communication between an application and its files.

The key to working with files in .NET is getting familiar with them. While it requires some effort to design in a file format or to figure out an existing format, I recommend that you use files when you need files. The controls in Visual Basic 2008 make using files much more straightforward than ever before.

Getting to Know System.IO

`System.IO` has two categories of classes and a set of components that you want to become familiar with: the stream classes, the file and directory classes, and the `Dialog` controls.

Stream classes allow you to handle the contents of files as a sequence of characters. Table 16-1 describes some of the common stream classes available in Visual Basic.

Table 16-1	Stream Classes in System.IO
Classes	**Description**
BinaryReader, BinaryWriter	Used to read and write nontext files, such as images, in a stream
FileStream	Can be used to make any file into a stream
TextReader, TextWriter	Specifically used for reading and writing text to streams

Streams are tricky tools, and I don't cover them much here. They are mostly used for movement of information in various states of connection, and, while this is important, it is beyond the scope of this book. I instead focus on the file and directory tools in System.IO, which you are much more likely to need on a daily basis.

The file and directory maintenance classes are partially *shared,* meaning that you don't need to get a copy to use them because they are always available. You can also use the instance implementations, which accept the path to the file or directory in question as a parameter. The file management classes are shown in Table 16-2.

Table 16-2	File Management Classes in System.IO
Classes	**Description**
Directory, DirectoryInfo	Shared and instance tools for maintaining directories
DriveInfo	Helps with maintaining a drive (such as a hard drive or a virtual drive)
File, FileInfo	Shared and instance tools for maintaining files
FileSystem Watcher	A really cool class that keeps an eye on the file system and raises events when specific things happen
Path	Helps to maintain UNC paths to files and so on

The File Management classes in System.IO replace the old FileSystemObject in VB 6 and VBScript.

The classes that end in `Info` are *instance classes,* meaning that you need to dimension them before you use them and give them a path to start out with. This is handy when you are doing a lot of operations on a single file or directory. The classes without `Info` at the end are *shared,* meaning that you can use them whenever you want, like a digital toolbox. The shared classes are great for a quick change to a file or directory.

You get the most use out of the `File` and `Directory` classes. For instance, both classes support an `Exists` method, which accepts a path and returns a Boolean value that shows whether that file or directory exists — very simple, useful, and something you just can't live without.

The third important category of tools that the `System.IO` classes provide isn't really made up of classes — it is made up of controls. What used to be called the `CommonDialog` control is now a set of controls, among those generically categorized as `Dialogs`.

These controls make a lot of use of the `File` and `Directory` classes, and they make it a lot easier for you to give the users control over the files that relate to the application. You have seen these `Dialog` controls in other programs (such as Microsoft Office programs). Table 16-3 describes the `Dialog` controls available in Visual Basic.

Table 16-3	The Dialog Controls
Class	*Description*
`FolderBrowserDialog`	Shows a dialog box that enables the user to browse for and choose a directory
`OpenFileDialog`	Shows an Open dialog box that allows the user to select a file from the local file system
`SaveFileDialog`	Shows a Save dialog box that enables the user to save a file to the local file system

Using the System.IO Namespace

Some of the applications you write will require a lot of file access. Some applications need practically no file access. No matter what, being able to quickly set up an application to get to a file, move it, copy it, read it, or delete it is an important part of day-to-day programming.

The following sections provide a series of the most common tasks that your programs need to perform with files and describe how `System.IO` and the related tools in the VB language make handling files easy.

Saving files to a Web server

The classes described in Table 16-3 are Windows Forms controls. Web applications that need to work with files are subject to the whims of the browser and are stuck using HTTP Upload.

HTTP Upload gives you access to a few controls, namely the `FileUpload` control. The `FileUpload` control allows the user to select a file on his or her local file system to upload to the server. Remember, the Web is disconnected, so the files that the user sees in the browser are on his or her machine.

After the file is uploaded on the server, the `File` and `Directory` classes are used to

save the file on the server. For instance, the following code might be used to handle a file uploaded with the `FileUpload` control:

```
myPath = "C:\files\"
Dim fileName As String =
      FileUpload1.FileName
myPath += fileName
FileUpload1.SaveAs(myPath)
```

Behind the scenes, this code uses a `Stream Writer` to save the file, which is part of the `System.IO` class. You see this a lot, and are shielded from it a lot, throughout the .NET Framework.

All the following examples — where appropriate — use a text file in the `C:\` directory called `inputFile.txt` and write to a text file called `outputFile.txt`.

Opening a file

You have a few ways to open a file in Visual Basic, but there is only one good way to have the user select a file to open — the `OpenFileDialog` control. The `OpenFileDialog` control is a Component Tray control — it doesn't go right on a form, but you call it from another firm object, such as a button.

Start a new Windows Application project by choosing File➪New Project. Name your new Windows application something appropriate; I used the name File Management for this example. When you have a new Windows Application project ready, follow these steps to use the `OpenFileDialog` control to enable the user to open a file:

1. **Drag an** `OpenFileDialog` **control from the Toolbox into the form.**

   The `OpenFileDialog` component is in the Dialogs portion of the Toolbox. It appears in the Component Tray.

2. **Drag a** `Label` **control from the Toolbox onto the form. Change the** `Text` **value to be blank, and name it** `FileName`. **Set the** `AutoSize` **to** `False`, **and change the** `BackColor` **to** `ActiveCaption`.

3. **Drag a** `TextBox` **control onto the form. Change the** `Multiline` **property to** `True`. **Change the name to** `FileContents`.

4. **Drag a new button to the form, and set the** `Text` **value to** `Open a File`. **Name the button** `OpenFile`.

   Your environment should look something like Figure 16-1.

5. **Double-click the button to enter the code editor. Visual Studio then makes the** `OpenFile Click` **event handler.**

6. **Add the following code into** `OpenFile_Click` **to get the contents of the file into a** `String` **variable:**

```
Imports System.IO
Public Class Form1
    'This is for the contents of the file.
    Dim myFileContents As String
    Private Sub OpenFile_Click(ByVal sender As System.Object, ByVal e As _
        System.EventArgs) Handles OpenFile.Click
        'Open the dialog and make sure it was successful
        If OpenFileDialog1.ShowDialog() = DialogResult.OK Then
            'Open a streamreader with the file name from the dialog
            Dim myStreamReader As New _
            StreamReader(OpenFileDialog1.FileName)
            'Read the file with the streamreader
            Dim myFileContents As String = myStreamReader.ReadToEnd()
            'Close the streamreader - it uses resources
            myStreamReader.Close()
            'Set the output fields
            FileName.Text = OpenFileDialog1.FileName.ToString
            FileContents.Text = myFileContents
        End If
    End Sub
End Class
```

7. **Run the application, and click the button.**

   If all is well, when you click the button, you will be able to select a file and see its contents. If you put the `inputFile.txt` file in the `C:\` directory, you can see the results in Figure 16-2.

You can choose from a lot of options for the `OpenFileDialog` control. You can set the default file type that is to be opened, the title of the dialog box, and the starting directory, just for starters. Check out the Properties window for the control to see what I mean.

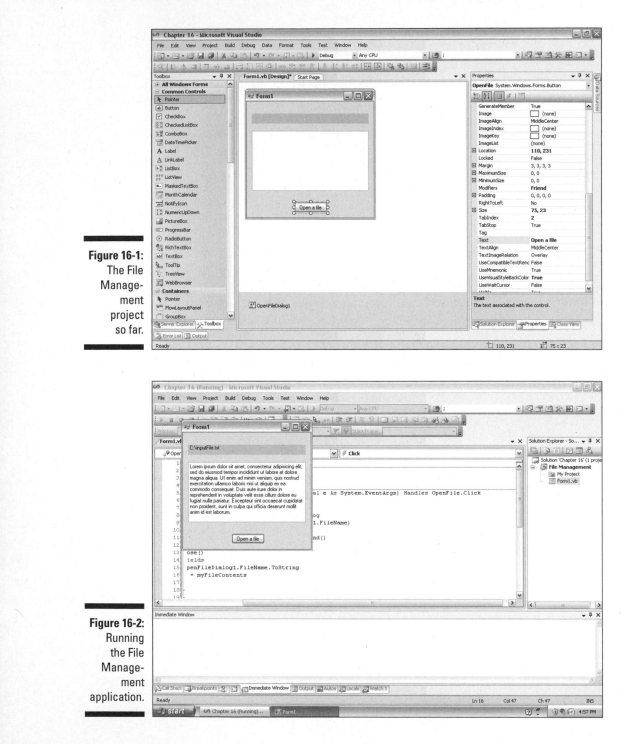

Figure 16-1:
The File
Manage-
ment
project
so far.

Figure 16-1:
The File
Manage-
ment
project
so far.

Figure 16-2:
Running
the File
Manage-
ment
application.

Changing the contents of a file

If you followed the steps in the previous section, you have a string with a file's contents, and you need to get something else into the file. You use the StreamReader to get the information out of a file, and, not surprisingly, you use the StreamWriter to get the information back into the file.

Though the examples in this chapter use text files, you should be aware of two caveats. First, any file that is formatted as text can be managed this way. (Open the file in Notepad first to make sure that you do indeed have a text file.) Second, binary files such as images can be handled with streams, too, but the output will be something other than a string (a bitmap, for instance).

For this example, the contents of the file are in a string called myFile Contents. To get the filename, you use the SaveFileDialog, which is discussed in the next section. To use the same filename, you can follow these steps:

1. **Add a button to the form and name it** SaveFile.

2. **In the code, make a new** StreamWriter **and give it the filename and contents:**

```
Private Sub SaveFile_Click(ByVal sender As System.Object, ByVal e As
        System.EventArgs) Handles SaveFile.Click
    'You can get the filename from the label
    Dim myStreamWriter As StreamWriter = New StreamWriter(FileName.Text)
    'Then use the TextBox to get the contents.
    myStreamWriter.Write(FileContents.Text)
    myStreamWriter.Close()
End Sub
```

3. **Run the application. Change the content in the text box, and click the Save File button to save the contents.**

Saving a file

If you want the user to be able to save the file with a different filename, you can use the SaveFileDialog. This is just like the OpenFileDialog, except it allows the user to make a new filename and to save the renamed file in a different directory.

To use it, just drag a `SaveFileDialog` to the form and then change the code in the `SaveFile_Click` subroutine to the following:

```
Private Sub SaveFile_Click(ByVal sender As System.Object, ByVal e As
        System.EventArgs) Handles SaveFile.Click
    If SaveFileDialog1.ShowDialog() = DialogResult.OK Then
        Dim myStreamWriter As New StreamWriter(SaveFileDialog1.FileName)
        If Not (myStreamWriter Is Nothing) Then
            'Then use the TextBox to get the contents.
            myStreamWriter.Write(FileContents.Text)
            'Close the StreamWriter - it uses resources
            myStreamWriter.Close()
        End If
    End If
End Sub
```

When you run the application, you have a chance to give the file a new name. Note that the `SaveFileDialog`, like the `OpenFileDialog`, has a lot of yummy options to define what the user can and can't do. You can see some of them in Figure 16-3.

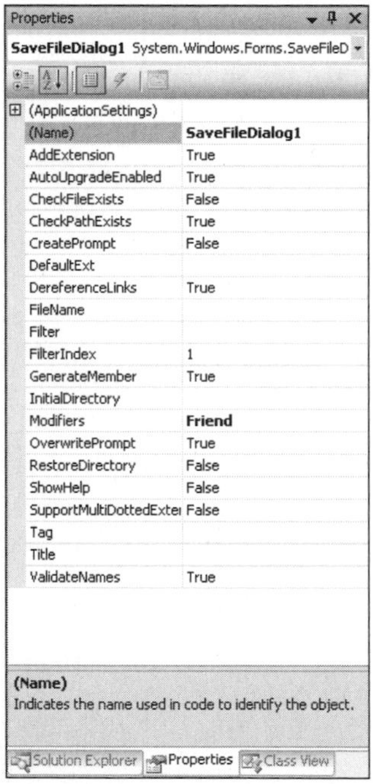

Figure 16-3:
Properties
for the
SaveFile
Dialog
control.

Properties	▾ ┃ ✕
SaveFileDialog1 System.Windows.Forms.SaveFileD ▾	

⊞ (ApplicationSettings)	
(Name)	**SaveFileDialog1**
AddExtension	True
AutoUpgradeEnabled	True
CheckFileExists	False
CheckPathExists	True
CreatePrompt	False
DefaultExt	
DereferenceLinks	True
FileName	
Filter	
FilterIndex	1
GenerateMember	True
InitialDirectory	
Modifiers	**Friend**
OverwritePrompt	True
RestoreDirectory	False
ShowHelp	False
SupportMultiDottedExter	False
Tag	
Title	
ValidateNames	True

(Name)
Indicates the name used in code to identify the object.

Solution Explorer   Properties   Class View

Listing directories and files

Directories and files are in collections as part of the `System.IO.File` and `System.IO.Directory` objects. When you call one of those methods, you get an array of strings that are the subdirectories in the directory you specify.

So, for instance, if you write a little code like this . . .

```
Dim subDirectory As String
For Each subDirectory In Directory.GetDirectories("C:\")
    Console.Write(subDirectory)
Next
```

. . . you get something like this:

```
C:\Documents and Settings
C:\Program Files
C:\WINDOWS
```

The same thing works for files. Notice, though, that I didn't have to dimension a copy of the `Directory` class — I just got to use it. That's because the `Directory` class is shared, which allows you to use it without instantiating it. This cuts down on clutter in your code — and on memory use as well.

On the other hand, the shared classes in `System.IO` check their security access every time they are called, while the instantiated classes check only once, when they are instantiated. If you are going to use the classes repeatedly, you should use the `DirectoryInfo` and `FileInfo` classes, described in the next section.

Viewing file information

If, for instance, you need more information about a directory than the other directories in it, you might want to use the `DirectoryInfo` (or `FileInfo`, for files) class. This class is similar to the related class without the `Info` tag, but it requires a `New` statement, as shown in the following code:

```
Dim subDirectory As String
For Each subDirectory In Directory.GetDirectories("C:\")
    Console.Write(subDirectory)
    Dim myDirectory As DirectoryInfo = New
            DirectoryInfo(subDirectory)
    Console.Write(myDirectory.CreationTime)
    Console.Write(myDirectory.LastAccessTime)
    Console.Write(myDirectory.Parent)
    myDirectory = Nothing
Next
```

The purpose of using `DirectoryInfo` in line 4 is to clarify the use of the file system and set up an object, however briefly, that has a base directory. If you are going to use the `Directory` object (here, `myDirectory`) more than once, it is worth using the `DirectoryInfo` and `FileInfo` classes.

Keeping an eye on files

`FileSystemWatcher` is a great little tool that keeps an eye on files for you. If something happens, such as a rename or file content change, it lets you know by throwing an event that you can catch with code.

To see how `FileSystemWatcher` can be used, you can add a little feature to the file editor you build in the preceding sections. The addition of a `File SystemWatcher` informs you when something about the files change. Follow these steps to add a `FileSystemWatcher`:

1. **Add a `FileSystemWatcher` to the File Management application.**

2. **Add a `Label` under the label you added previously.**

   You may need to widen the form.

3. **Change the `BorderStyle` of the `Label` to `Fixed3D`, and set the `AutoSize` value to `False`.**

4. **Stretch the `Label` out to an appropriate size. Set the `TextAlign` value to `MiddleCenter`.**

   Your application should look something like Figure 16-4.

5. **Add the following two lines of code to the `OpenFile_Click` event handler:**

   ```
   FileSystemWatcher1.Path = "C:\"
   FileSystemWatcher1.EnableRaisingEvents = True
   ```

6. **Click the Object drop-down list in the Code View and select the `FileSystemWatcher`; then, in the Event drop-down list, select the `Changed` event.**

   Visual Studio creates an event handler subroutine.

7. **Add the following bold line of code that writes the details of the file change to the `Label` object into the `FileSystemWatcher1_Changed` handler that was generated for you:**

   ```
   Private Sub FileSystemWatcher1_Changed(ByVal sender As
           Object, ByVal e As
           System.IO.FileSystemEventArgs) Handles
           FileSystemWatcher1.Changed
      Label1.Text = String.Format("{0} was written to at
           {1}", e.Name, DateTime.Now.ToString)
   End Sub
   ```

The event arguments provide the filename and other details. Other events, such as `Renamed`, even provide the `OldName`. This would be exceptionally useful for logging file access or changes to files in your system. It's a powerful object for system management.

Chapter 17

Accessing the Internet

· ·

· ·

*I*n my honest opinion, the reason that Microsoft had to create the .NET Framework in the first place was the lack of Internet interoperability within the existing infrastructure. Visual Basic 6 just couldn't handle the Internet. The Internet works differently than most platforms, such as PCs. The Internet is based on *protocols* — carefully defined and agreed upon ways to get things like mail and file transfers working. Microsoft's environment before 2002 distinctly didn't handle those as well.

As you can see throughout this book, the .NET Framework is designed from the ground up to take the Internet and networking in general into consideration. Not surprisingly, that is nowhere more clear than it is in the System. Net namespace. The Internet takes first chair here, with Web tools taking up nine of the classes in the namespace.

In this second version of the framework, even more Internet functionality is baked in. While in version 1, the focus was on tools used to build other tools (low-level functions), now it contains features that are useful to you, such as Web, mail, and FTP. Secure Sockets Layer — the Internet's transport security — is much easier to use in this version, as is FTP and mail, which previously required other harder-to-use classes.

System.Net is a big, meaty namespace, and finding your way around it can be difficult. My goal for this chapter is to take things that you do often and show the basics, and then give you the tools to research the more complex features of the classes.

Networking is a big part of the .NET Framework, and all the functionality is in this namespace — a whole book can be (and has been) written on the subject. For the purposes of this introduction to networking with VB, I show you these features:

- ✔ Getting a file from the network
- ✔ Sending e-mail
- ✔ Logging the transfers
- ✔ Checking into the status of the network around your running application

Keep in mind that I am not denying the importance of sockets, IPv6, and other advanced Internet protocols. I am just suggesting those parts of the namespace that you will be using every day. As always, there is more to find out about System.Net.

Getting to Know System.Net

The System.Net namespace is full of classes that are very confusing if viewed in the documentation, but make a lot of sense when used in an application. The namespace removes all the complexity of dealing with the various protocols used on the Internet.

Over 2,000 RFCs exist for Internet protocols (an *RFC* is a Request For Comments, a document that is sent to a standards body to get reviewed by peers before it becomes a standard), and if you have to learn all of them separately, you will never get your project done. The System.Net namespace is about making that less painful.

System.Net is not just for Web projects. As with everything else in the base class library, you can use System.Net with all kinds of projects. You can do the following:

- ✔ Get information out of Web pages on the Internet and use it in your programs
- ✔ Move files via the Internet using FTP (File Transfer Protocol)
- ✔ Send e-mail easily
- ✔ Use more advanced network structures
- ✔ Secure communications over the Internet using the SSL protocol

If you need to check on the connectivity of a computer from a Windows application, you can use System.Net. If you need to build a class that will download a file from a Web site, System.Net is the namespace you need. Just because most of the classes relate to the Internet doesn't mean that only Web applications can use it. That's the magic of System.Net. Any application can be a connected application. While some parts of the namespace function do make the development of Web applications easier, the namespace in general is designed to make any application work with the Web.

How the Net Classes Fit into the Framework

The System.Net namespace contains 62 classes and six smaller namespaces. Even as I write this, I am overwhelmed. However, if you look closely, you can see patterns.

If you need help using classes, you can find more information in Chapters 1 and 3.

The classes are very well named, and you will note that a few protocols get a number of classes each. After you translate, you can narrow down what you need based on the way the protocol is named:

- ✔ Authentication and Authorization: These classes provide security.
- ✔ Cookie: This class manages cookies from Web browsers and is typically used in ASP.NET pages.
- ✔ DNS (Domain Name Services): These classes help to resolve domain names into IP addresses.
- ✔ Download: This class is used to get files from servers.
- ✔ EndPoint: This class helps to define a network node.
- ✔ FileWeb: This brilliant set of classes describes network file servers as local classes.
- ✔ FtpWeb: This class is a simple File Transfer Protocol implementation.
- ✔ Http (HyperText Transfer Protocol): This class is the Web protocol.
- ✔ IP (Internet Protocol): This class helps to define network endpoints that are specifically Internet related.
- ✔ IrDA: This class is an infrared endpoint. Infrared ports are networks, too!
- ✔ NetworkCredential: This class is another security implementation.
- ✔ Service: This class helps manage network connections.
- ✔ Socket: This class deals with the most primitive of network connections.

✔ `Upload`: This set of classes helps you to upload information to the Internet.

✔ `Web`: These classes help with the World Wide Web — largely implementations of the `http` classes that are more task-oriented.

This list is so extensive because the classes build on each other. The `End Point` classes are used by the `socket` classes to define certain network specifics, and the `IP` classes make them specific to the Internet. The `Web` classes are specific to the World Wide Web. You will rarely use highest-level classes, but it is often tough to see what is needed when.

Most of the functions that you use every day, though, are encapsulated within seven mostly new namespaces under the `System.Net` namespace:

✔ `Cache`: This function has a lot of enumerators that manage the browser and network-caching functions built into the namespace.

✔ `Configuration`: This function grants access to the properties that you need to set to make many of the other `System.Net` classes work.

✔ `Mail`: This function takes over for `System.Web.Mail` to facilitate the sending of Internet e-mail.

✔ `Mime`: This function bundles file attachments with the `Mail` namespace.

✔ `NetworkInformation`: This function gets details about the network around your application.

✔ `Security`: This function implements the network security managed by many classes of `System.Net`.

✔ `Sockets`: This function utilizes the most basic of network connections available to Windows.

Using the System.Net Namespace

The `System.Net` namespace is very *code-oriented,* which means that few implementations are specifically for user interfaces. Almost everything you do with these classes is behind the scenes. You have few drag-and-drop user controls — the `System.Net` namespace is used in the Code View.

To demonstrate this, in the rest of this chapter, I go over building a Windows Forms application that has the following requirements:

✔ Check the network status.

✔ Get a specific file from the Internet.

✔ E-mail it to a specific e-mail address.

✔ Log the whole transaction.

This is not an insignificant set of requirements. In fact, even in the 1.0 and 1.1 versions of VB.NET, this would be very difficult. One of the main goals of the `System.Net` namespace in this version is to make these kinds of tasks — very common tasks — much easier. You can get started by loading the sample code or by starting a new project and following the steps in the following sections.

Checking the network status

First, you need to inform the user about network connectivity by following these steps:

1. **Create a new Windows Application project in Visual Studio.**

   I called mine `NetworkTools`.

2. **Reference the** `System.Net` **namespace by adding the line** `Imports System.NET` **to the top of the code.**

3. **Add a** `StatusStrip` **control to the form by dragging it from the Toolbox.**

4. **Select the** `SmartTag` **that appears and add a** `StatusLabel`.

5. **Back in Design View, double-click the form to get the** `Form_Load` **event handler and move to Code View.**

6. **Add the code in bold from the following listing to see whether the network is available and display it in the status bar:**

```
Imports System.Net
Public Class Form1
    Private Sub Form1_Load(ByVal sender As System.Object, ByVal e As
            System.EventArgs) Handles MyBase.Load
        If NetworkInformation.NetworkInterface.GetIsNetworkAvailable Then
            ToolStripStatusLabel1.Text = "Connected"
        Else
            ToolStripStatusLabel1.Text = "Disconnected"
        End If
    End Sub
End Class
```

That's all there is to it. The `NetworkInformation` class contains a bunch of information about the status of the network, current IP addresses, the gateway being used by the current machine, and more.

Keep in mind that the `NetworkInformation` class will only work on a local machine. If you use this class in an ASP.NET Web Forms application, you will be getting information about the server.

Downloading a file from the Internet

So, next, you need to get a file from the Internet. This can be accomplished a number of ways, but one of the most common is by using FTP. FTP is a light-weight protocol that is favored because it is secure and supported on many systems.

To build an application that uses FTP, follow these steps:

1. **Drag a button onto the form from the Toolbox.**

2. **Double-click the button to get the** `Click` **event handler.**

3. **Add the required imports —** `System.Net`, `System.Net.Mail`, **and** `System.IO` **— to the top of the code.**

4. **Create a new subroutine called** `Download File` **that accepts a remote filename and a local filename as strings.**

5. **In the new subroutine, dimension a new** `FileStream` **(called** `local FileStream`**) and** `FTPWebRequest` **(called** `myRequest`**), as shown in Listing 17-1.**

    The `FileStream` references a local file and accepts the local file that is passed into the subroutine. The `FtpWebRequest` is the same thing for the remote file.

6. **Set the** `Method` **parameter of the** `FtpWebRequest` **to** `WebRequestMethods.Ftp.Downloadfile`.

7. **Set the** `Credentials` **property of the** `FtpWebRequest` **to a new** `NetworkCredential` **with anonymous information, as I did in Listing 17-1.**

8. **Create a new** `WebResponse` **object from the** `myRequest` **method.**

    This gets the statement back from the FTP server regarding how your request will be handled.

9. **Get the** `Stream` **from the** `response` **object.**

10. **Read the file into a 1,024-byte buffer, one block at a time, using a While loop, as shown at the end of Listing 17-1.**

Listing 17-1: The DownloadFile Method

```
Protected Sub DownloadFile(ByVal remoteFile As String, _
ByVal localFile As String)

    Dim localFileStream As New FileStream(localFile, FileMode.OpenOrCreate)
    Dim myRequest As FtpWebRequest = WebRequest.Create(remoteFile)
    myRequest.Method = WebRequestMethods.Ftp.DownloadFile
```

```
    myRequest.Credentials = New NetworkCredential("Anonymous", _
            "bill@sempf.net")
    Dim myResponse As WebResponse = myRequest.GetResponse
    Dim myResponseStream As Stream = myResponse.GetResponseStream
    Dim buffer(1024) As Byte
    Dim bytesRead As Integer = myResponseStream.Read(buffer, 0, 1024)
    While bytesRead > 0
        localFileStream.Write(buffer, 0, bytesRead)
        bytesRead = myResponseStream.Read(buffer, 0, 1024)
    End While
    localFileStream.Close()
    myResponseStream.Close()

End Sub
```

11. Call the `DownloadFile` **method from the** `Button1_Click` **event handler, as I show in the following code:**

```
Private Sub Button1_Click(ByVal sender As System.Object, _
ByVal e As System.EventArgs) Handles Button1.Click
    DownloadFile("ftp://ftp.vbfordummies.com/sampleFile.bmp", _
            "c:\sampleFile.bmp")
End Sub
```

This is a very watered-down FTP example, but it gets the point across. The `WebRequest` and `WebResponse` classes in the `System.Net` namespace are fully utilized to create the more complete `FtpWebRequest`, for instance. Properties such as the `Method` of download and `Credentials` make it an easy call.

In fact, the toughest part of this process is dealing with a `FileStream` object, which is still the best way to move files and is not specific to the `System.Net` namespace. Streams are discussed in Chapter 16, which covers the `System.IO` namespace, but they have significance to the network classes, too. Streams represent a flow of data of some kind, and a flow of information from the Internet qualifies.

That's what you are doing when you get a Web page or a file from the Internet — gathering a flow of data. If you take a second to think about it, it makes sense that this is a flow, because the status bar in an application shows a percentage of completion. It's just like pouring water into a glass; the flow of data is a stream, so the concept is named `Stream`.

This concept holds true for getting a file from the World Wide Web, as well. HTTP, the protocol of the Web, is just another protocol that defines how a document is moved from a server on the Internet to your local machine. In fact, the code even looks strikingly similar to the FTP example, as you can see in the following example. The same stream is recovered; just the formatting is different.

```
Protected Sub DownloadWebFile(ByVal remoteFile As String, _
ByVal localFile As String)
    Dim localFileStream As New FileStream(localFile, FileMode.OpenOrCreate)
    Dim myRequest As WebRequest = WebRequest.Create(remoteFile)
    myRequest.Method = WebRequestMethods.Http.Get
    Dim myResponse As WebResponse = myRequest.GetResponse
    Dim myResponseStream As Stream = myResponse.GetResponseStream
    Dim buffer(1024) As Byte
    Dim bytesRead As Integer = myResponseStream.Read(buffer, 0, 1024)
    While bytesRead > 0
        localFileStream.Write(buffer, 0, bytesRead)
        bytesRead = myResponseStream.Read(buffer, 0, 1024)
    End While
    localFileStream.Close()
    myResponseStream.Close()
End Sub
```

You will need to pass in a Web address, so your subroutine call would look
like this:

```
DownloadWebFile("http://www.vbfordummies.com/sampleFile.bmp",
                "c:\sampleFile.bmp")
```

Note the changes, which are marked as bold. `myRequest` is now a `Web
Request` rather than an `FtpWebRequest`. Also, the `Method` property of
`myRequest` has been changed to `WebRequestMethods.Http.Get`. Finally,
the `Credentials` property has been removed because the credentials are
no longer required.

E-mailing a status report

E-mail is a common requirement of networked systems. If you are working in
an enterprise environment, you are going to write a larger-scale application
to handle all e-mail requirements, rather than make each individual application e-mail-aware.

However, if you are writing a stand-alone product, it might require e-mail support. Because I happen to be writing a stand-alone application, that is exactly
what I'm going to do.

E-mail is a server-based operation, so if you do not have an e-mail server that
you can use to send from, this might be hard. Many ISPs no longer allow *relaying,* which is sending an outgoing message without first having an account and
logging on. Therefore, you might have trouble running this part of the sample.

If you are in a corporate environment, however, you can usually talk to your e-mail administrator and get permission to use the e-mail server. Because outgoing requests are usually only harnessed inside the firewall, relaying is often available. To build your e-mail function, try these steps:

1. **Add a text box to the default form in Design View, and then change to Code View.**

2. **At the top of the Code View, make sure that you have referenced the** `System.Net.Mail` **namespace.**

3. **Create a new subroutine called** `SendEmail`.

   It should accept the From e-mail address, the To e-mail address, the subject of the e-mail, and the body of the e-mail.

4. **Dimension a new** `MailMessage` **and pass in the** `fromAddress`, `toAddress`, `subject`, **and** `body` **parameters, as follows:**

   ```
   Dim message As New MailMessage(fromAddress, toAddress, _
   subject, body)
   ```

5. **Dimension a new** `SmtpClient`, **and pass in the address of your mail server.**

   This can be an IP address, machine name, or URL.

6. **Use the** `Send` **method of the** `SmtpClient` **object you created to send the** `MailMessage`, **which is passed in as a parameter.**

   When you're finished, make sure that you set the values of the `Mail Message` and `SmtpClient` to Nothing, because they do take up resources.

Listing 17-2 shows the completed subroutine.

Listing 17-2: The SendEmail Subroutine

```
Sub SendEmail(ByVal fromAddress As String, ByVal toAddress As String, _
            ByVal subject As String, ByVal body As String)
    Dim message As New MailMessage(fromAddress, toAddress, _
                                   subject, body)
    Dim mailClient As New SmtpClient("localhost")
    mailClient.Send(message)
    message = Nothing
    mailClient = Nothing
End Sub
```

Notice that I used `localhost` as the e-mail server name. If you have e-mail server software installed locally, even just IIS 6.0 with SMTP, this will work. Most of the time, you will have to put another e-mail server name in the `SmtpClient` constructor. The e-mail server name can often be found in your Outlook preferences.

After you have written your method, you need to call it after the file is downloaded in the `Button1_Click` event handler. Change the code of that subroutine to the following to call that method:

```
Private Sub Button1_Click(ByVal sender As System.Object, _
     ByVal e As System.EventArgs) Handles Button1.Click

        DownloadFile("ftp://ftp.vbfordummies.com/sample
        File.bmp", _
     "c:\sampleFile.bmp")
  SendEmail(TextBox1.Text, TextBox1.Text, "FTP
        Successful", _
     "FTP Successfully downloaded")
End Sub
```

Notice that I sent in the value of the text box twice: once for the To address and once for the From address. This isn't always necessary, because you may have a situation where you want the e-mail to come only from a Webmaster address or to go only to your address.

You should have enough code in place to run the application now. Press F5 to launch the application in Debug mode and give it a try.

When you click the button, the application should download the file to the local drive and then e-mail you to inform you that the download is complete. A whole host of things can go wrong with network applications though, and you should be aware of them. Here are just a few:

- ✔ For most network activity, the machine running the software must be connected to a network. This isn't a problem for you as the developer, but you need to be conscious of the end users, who may need connectivity to have access to the features they want to use. Use of the network status code can help inform users as to the availability of those features.

- ✔ Firewalls and other network appliances sometimes block network traffic from legitimate applications. Some examples of this include:

    - FTP is often blocked from corporate networks.

    - Network analysis features of .NET are often blocked on corporate servers. If the server is available to the public, these openings can cause holes for hackers to crawl through.

- Speaking of hackers, make sure that if you do use incoming network features in your application, you have adequately secured your application. More on this can be found in the excellent book *Writing Secure Code,* Second Edition, by Michael Howard and David C. LeBlanc (published by Microsoft Press).

- E-mail is especially fragile. Often, Internet service providers will block e-mail from an address that is not registered on a mail server. This means that if you are using your `localhost` server (as in the example in Listing 17-2), your ISP might block the e-mail.

✔ Network traffic is notoriously hard to debug. For instance, if the sample application works, but you never receive an e-mail from the `SmtpServer` you coded, what went wrong? You may just never know. XML Web services (covered in Chapter 7) have a similar problem — it is spectacularly tough to see the actual code in the SOAP envelope to tell what went wrong.

Logging network activity

This brings me to the next topic, which is network logging. Because network activity problems are so hard to debug and reproduce, Microsoft has built in several tools for the management of tracing network activity.

What's more, as with the available ASP.NET tracing, `System.Net` namespace tracing is managed completely by using the configuration files. This means you don't need to change and recompile your code when you want to use the functions. In fact, with a little management, you can even show debug information to the user by managing the `config` files your application uses.

Each kind of application has a different kind of configuration file. For Windows Forms applications, which you are using here, the file is called `app.config` and is stored in the development project directory. When you compile, the name of the file is changed to the name of the application, and it is copied into the `bin` directory for running.

If you open your `app.config` file now, you see that some diagnostic information is already in there, as shown in Listing 17-3. You are going to add some information to that.

Listing 17-3: The Default app.config File

```
<?xml version="1.0" encoding="utf-8" ?>
<configuration>
    <system.diagnostics>
        <sources>
            <!-- This section defines the logging configuration for
                My.Application.Log in Windows Forms projects.-->
```

(continued)

Listing 17-3: *(continued)*

```
              <source name="Microsoft.VisualBasic.Logging.Log.WindowsFormsSource"
                switchName="DefaultSwitch">
                 <listeners>
                     <add name="FileLog"/>
                     <!-- Uncomment the below section to write to the Application
              Event Log -->
                     <!--<add name="EventLog"/>-->
                 </listeners>
              </source>
         </sources>
         <switches>
             <add name="DefaultSwitch" value="Information" />
         </switches>
         <sharedListeners>
             <add name="FileLog"
                 type="Microsoft.VisualBasic.Logging.FileLogTraceListener,
                Microsoft.VisualBasic, Version=8.0.0.0, Culture=neutral,
                PublicKeyToken=b03f5f7f11d50a3a, processorArchitecture=MSIL"
                 initializeData="FileLogWriter"/>
             <!-- Uncomment the below section and replace APPLICATION_NAME with
                 the name of your application to write to the Application Event Log
                 -->
             <!--<add name="EventLog"
                 type="System.Diagnostics.EventLogTraceListener"
                 initializeData="APPLICATION_NAME"/> -->
         </sharedListeners>
     </system.diagnostics>
 </configuration>
```

First, you need to add a new source for the `System.Net` namespace. You see that a source is already in place for the `My` object (introduced in Chapter 3); you add one for the `System.Net` namespace as well.

Next, you add a switch to the `Switches` section for the source you added. Finally, you add a `SharedListener` to that section and set the file to flush the tracing information automatically.

The finished `app.config` file, with the adds in bold, is shown in Listing 17-4. It is also in the sample code on this book's companion Web site.

Listing 17-4: The Finished app.config File

```
<?xml version="1.0" encoding="utf-8" ?>
<configuration>
    <system.diagnostics>
        <sources>
            <source name="Microsoft.VisualBasic.Logging.Log.WindowsFormsSource"
                switchName="DefaultSwitch">
                <listeners>
                    <add name="FileLog"/>
```

```
            </listeners>
        </source>
        <source name="System.Net">
            <listeners>
                <add name="System.Net"/>
            </listeners>
        </source>
    </sources>
    <switches>
        <add name="DefaultSwitch" value="Information" />
        <add name="System.Net" value="Verbose" />
    </switches>
    <sharedListeners>
        <add name="FileLog"
            type="Microsoft.VisualBasic.Logging.FileLogTraceListener,
            Microsoft.VisualBasic, Version=8.0.0.0, Culture=neutral,
            PublicKeyToken=b03f5f7f11d50a3a, processorArchitecture=MSIL"
            initializeData="FileLogWriter"/>
        <add name="System.Net"
            type="System.Diagnostics.TextWriterTraceListener"
            initializeData="my.log"/>
    </sharedListeners>
    <trace autoflush="true" />
    </system.diagnostics>
</configuration>
```

Run the application again and watch the Output window. Advanced logging information is shown there because of your changes to the configuration file. Additionally, a log file was written. In the development environment, this is in the bin/debug folder of your project. You might have to click the Show All Files button at the top of the Solution Explorer to see it.

In that folder, you should see a file called my.log. This is where the Shared Listener that you added to the app.config file directed the logging information. My copy of that file is shown in Listing 17-5 — your mileage may vary.

Listing 17-5: The Log Information

```
System.Net Information: 0 :
            WebRequest::Create(ftp://ftp.vbfordummies.net/sample.bmp)
System.Net Information: 0 : Exiting WebRequest::Create() ->
        FtpWebRequest#37460558
System.Net Information: 0 : FtpWebRequest#37460558::GetResponse()
System.Net Information: 0 : Exiting FtpWebRequest#37460558::GetResponse()
System.Net Information: 0 : Associating Message#59487907 with
            HeaderCollection#23085090
System.Net Information: 0 : HeaderCollection#23085090::Set(mime-version=1.0)
System.Net Information: 0 : Associating MailMessage#6964596 with
            Message#59487907
System.Net Information: 0 : SmtpClient::.ctor(host=24.123.157.3)
```

(continued)

Listing 17-5: *(continued)*

```
System.Net Information: 0 : Associating SmtpClient#17113003 with
          SmtpTransport#30544512
System.Net Information: 0 : Exiting SmtpClient::.ctor()    -> SmtpClient#17113003
System.Net Information: 0 : SmtpClient#17113003::Send(MailMessage#6964596)
System.Net Information: 0 : SmtpClient#17113003::Send(DeliveryMethod=Network)
System.Net Information: 0 : Associating SmtpClient#17113003 with
          MailMessage#6964596
System.Net Information: 0 : Associating SmtpTransport#30544512 with
          SmtpConnection#44365459
System.Net Information: 0 : Associating SmtpConnection#44365459 with
          ServicePoint#7044526
System.Net Information: 0 : Associating SmtpConnection#44365459 with
          SmtpPooledStream#20390146
System.Net Information: 0 : HeaderCollection#30689639::Set(content-transfer-
          encoding=base64)
System.Net Information: 0 : HeaderCollection#30689639::Set(content-transfer-
          encoding=quoted-printable)
System.Net Information: 0 : HeaderCollection#23085090::Remove(x-receiver)
System.Net Information: 0 : HeaderCollection#23085090::Set(from=bill@sempf.net)
System.Net Information: 0 : HeaderCollection#23085090::Set(to=bill@sempf.net)
System.Net Information: 0 : HeaderCollection#23085090::Set(date=1 Apr 2008
          16:32:32 -0500)
System.Net Information: 0 : HeaderCollection#23085090::Set(subject=FTP
          Successful)
System.Net Information: 0 : HeaderCollection#23085090::Get(mime-version)
System.Net Information: 0 : HeaderCollection#23085090::Get(from)
System.Net Information: 0 : HeaderCollection#23085090::Get(to)
System.Net Information: 0 : HeaderCollection#23085090::Get(date)
System.Net Information: 0 : HeaderCollection#23085090::Get(subject)
System.Net Information: 0 : HeaderCollection#30689639::Get(content-type)
System.Net Information: 0 : HeaderCollection#30689639::Get(content-transfer-
          encoding)
System.Net Information: 0 : Exiting SmtpClient#17113003::Send()
```

Reading this file, you can see that the reference numbers that match the requests on the server all appear, dramatically improving the ease of debugging. Also, because everything is in order of action, finding out exactly where the error occurred in the process is much easier.

Chapter 18

Creating Images

● ●

In This Chapter

▶ Understanding the `System.Drawing` namespace

▶ Finding out how the drawing classes fit into the .NET Framework

▶ Using `System.Drawing` to create a simple game application

● ●

*N*o one is going to write the next edition of *Bioshock* using Visual Basic. It just isn't the kind of language that you use to write graphics-intensive applications such as shoot-'em-up games.

That said, Visual Basic packs a fair amount of power into the `System.Drawing` classes. While these classes are somewhat primitive in some areas, and using them might cause you to have to write a few more lines of code than you should, there isn't much that these classes can't do with sufficient work.

The drawing capability provided by the .NET Framework is divided into four logical areas by the namespace design provided by Microsoft. All the general drawing capability is right in the `System.Drawing` namespace. Then you find several specialized namespaces:

> ✔ `System.Drawing.2D` has advanced vector drawing functionality.
>
> ✔ `System.Drawing.Imaging` is mostly about using bitmap graphic formats, such as `.bmp` and `.jpg` files.
>
> ✔ `System.Drawing.Text` deals with advanced typography.

In this chapter, I focus on the base namespace and cover just the basics of drawing in Visual Basic. (Discussing every aspect of drawing could easily fill an entire book.)

Getting to Know System.Drawing

Even at the highest level, graphics programming consists of drawing polygons, filling them with color, and labeling them with text — all on a canvas of some sort. Unsurprisingly, this leaves you with four objects that you find are the core of the graphics code you write: graphics, pens, brushes, and text.

Graphics

Generally speaking, the Graphics class creates an object that is your palette. It is the canvas. All the methods and properties of the Graphics object are designed to make the area you draw upon more appropriate for your needs.

Also, most of the graphics- and image-related methods of other classes in the framework provide the Graphics object as output. For instance, you can call the System.Web.Forms.Control.CreateGraphics method from a Windows Forms application and get a Graphics object back that enables you to draw in a form control in your project. You can also handle the Paint event of a form, and check out the Graphics property of the event.

Graphics objects use pens and brushes — discussed later in this chapter in the "Pens" and "Brushes" sections — to draw and fill. Graphics objects have methods such as the following:

- DrawRectangle
- FillRectangle
- DrawCircle
- FillCircle
- DrawBezier
- DrawLine

These methods accept pens and brushes as parameters. You might think "How is a circle going to help me?" but you must remember that even complex graphic objects such as the Covenant in *Halo 2* are just made up of circles and rectangles — just thousands and thousands of them. The trick to useful art is using math to put together lots of circles and squares until you have a complete image. The sample application described later in this chapter is a very simple example of just that.

Pens

You use pens to draw lines and curves. Complex graphics are made up of polygons, those polygons are made up of lines, and those lines are generated by pens. Pens have properties such as

- ✔ Color
- ✔ DashStyle
- ✔ EndCap
- ✔ Width

You get the idea: You use pens to draw things. These properties are used by the pens to determine how things are drawn.

Brushes

Brushes paint the insides of polygons. While you use the pens to draw the shapes, you use brushes to fill in the shapes with color, patterns, or gradients. Usually, brushes are passed in a parameter to a *DrawWhatever* method of the pen objects. When the pen draws the shape it was asked to draw, it uses the brush to fill in the shape — just the way you did in kindergarten with crayons and coloring books (the brush object always stays inside the lines though).

Don't look for the Brush class, however. It is a holding area for the real brushes, which have kind of strange names. Brushes are made to be customized, but you can do a lot with the brushes that come with the framework as is. Some of the brushes include

- ✔ SolidBrush
- ✔ TextureBrush
- ✔ HatchBrush
- ✔ PathGradientBrush

While the pens are used to pass into the Draw methods of the Graphics object, brushes are used to pass into the Fill methods that form polygons.

Text

Text is painted with a combination of fonts and brushes. Brushes work just like pens; the Font class uses brushes to fill in the lines of a text operation.

System.Drawing.Text has collections of all the fonts installed in the system running your program, or installed as part of your application. System. Drawing.Font has all the properties of the typography, such as the following:

- ✔ Bold
- ✔ Size
- ✔ Style
- ✔ Underline

The Graphics object, again, provides the actual writing of the text on the palette.

How the Drawing Classes Fit into the Framework

The System.Drawing namespace breaks drawing into two steps:

- ✔ Create a System.Drawing.Graphics object.
- ✔ Use the tools in the System.Drawing namespace to draw on it.

It seems straightforward, and it is. The first step is to get a Graphics object. Graphics objects come from two main places — existing images and Windows Forms.

To get a Graphics object from an existing image, look at the Bitmap object. The Bitmap object is a great tool that allows you to create an object using an existing image file. This gives you a new palette that is based on a bitmap image (a JPEG file, for example) that is already on your hard drive. It's a very convenient tool, especially for Web images. Here is how you load a bitmap:

```
Dim myBitmap As New Bitmap("c:\images\myImage.jpg")
Dim myPalette As Graphics = Graphics.FromImage(myBitmap)
```

Printing a form

In VB6 and earlier, one of the most common ways to get information to paper was to just print a form. This functionality was lacking in VB 2002, 2003, and 2005 but came back in a Power Pack and is now built into Visual Studio 2008. It is available to all languages, but should be most useful to VB programmers.

If you need to build a report, you should use Microsoft Report Viewer, which I don't cover in this book. If you just want to get some text and images to the user's printer, though, the PrintForm component should do the trick.

To use the PrintForm component, drag it from the Toolbox onto your form in Design View. It will appear in the component tray. In the event handler for your print function (the MenuItem.Click function, for instance), set up the Form property of the component, the Print Action, and then call the Print command. It looks like this:

```
With PrintForm1
    .Form = TheFormIWantPrinted 'use Me
        for current form
    .PrintAction = PrintToPrinter
        'other options are File or
        Preview
    .Print()
End With
```

The form will be sent to the windows Print function, just as if you had used the Print dialog box to print a file.

Now the object myPalette is a Graphics object whose height and width are based on the image in myBitmap. What's more, the base of the my Palette image looks exactly like the image referenced in the myBitmap object.

You can use the pens, brushes, and fonts in the Graphics class to draw right on that image, as if it were a blank canvas. I use it to put text on images before I show them on Web pages and to modify the format of images on the fly, too.

The second way to get a Graphics object is to get it from Windows Forms. The method that you are looking for is

```
System.Windows.Forms.Control.CreateGraphics
```

This method gives you a new palette that is based on the drawing surface of the control being referenced. If it is a form, it inherits the height and width of the form and has the form background color. You can use pens and brushes to draw right on the form.

When you have a `Graphics` object, the options are pretty much endless. Sophisticated drawing is not out of the question, though you would have to do a ton work to create graphics like those you see in *Halo 3* using Visual Basic. (There isn't a Master Chief class that you can just generate automatically.)

Nonetheless, even the most complex 3D graphics are just colored polygons, and you can make those with the `System.Drawing` class. In the following sections, I build a cribbage board with a `Graphics` object, pens, brushes, and fonts.

Using the System.Drawing Namespace

Good applications come from strange places. Gabrielle (my wife) and I enjoy games, and one of our favorites is the card game cribbage. We were on vacation in Disney World when she had the urge to play, but we didn't have a cribbage board. We had cards, but not the board.

However, I did have my laptop, Visual Studio, and the `System.Drawing` namespace. After just an hour or two of work, I built an application that serves as a working cribbage board!

This is a fairly complete application, and I don't have enough pages to walk you through it step by step. Load the application from the Web site at `www.vbfordummies.net`, and follow along with the rest of this chapter. This isn't a complex application, but it is long.

Getting started

Cribbage is a card game where hands are counted up into points, and the first player to score 121 points wins. It's up to the players to count up the points, and the score is kept on a board.

Cribbage boards are made up of two lines of holes for pegs, usually totaling 120, but sometimes 60 holes are used and you play through twice. Figure 18-1 shows a typical cribbage board. Cribbage boards come in a bunch of different styles — check out `www.cribbage.org` if you are really curious; it has a great gallery of almost 100 boards, from basic to whimsical.

For this example, I just create the board image for an application that keeps score of a cribbage game — but it wouldn't be beyond Visual Basic to write the cards into the game, too!

So the board for this application has 40 holes on each of three pairs of lines, which is the standard board setup for two players playing to 120, as shown in Figure 18-2. The first task is to draw the board, and then to draw the pegs as the players' scores — entered in text boxes — change.

The premise is this: A player plays a hand and enters the resulting scores in the text box below his or her name (refer to Figure 18-2). When the score for each hand is entered, the score next to the player's name is updated, and the peg is moved on the board. The next time that same player scores a hand, the peg is moved forward and the back peg is moved into its place. Didn't I mention the back peg? Oh, yes, the inventor of cribbage was paranoid of cheating — if you're unfamiliar with cribbage, you may want to check out the rules at www.cribbage.org.

Figure 18-1:
A traditional cribbage board; photo by AJ Turtle.

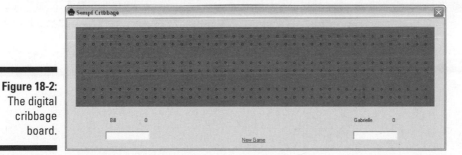

Figure 18-2:
The digital cribbage board.

Setting up the project

To begin, create a playing surface. I actually set up the board shown in Figure 18-2 without drawing the board itself — I paint that on later with `System.Drawing`. My board looked a lot like Figure 18-3 when I was ready to start with the business rules.

I used a little subroutine to handle score changes by calling the subroutine from the two text boxes' `OnChange` events. The code that calls the subroutine follows:

```
Private Sub HandleScore(ByVal scoreBox As TextBox, ByVal points As Label, _
    ByVal otherPlayer As Label)
    Try
        If 0 > CInt(scoreBox.Text) Or CInt(scoreBox.Text) > 27 Then
            ScoreCheck.SetError(scoreBox, "Score must be between 0 and 27")
            scoreBox.Focus()
        Else
            ScoreCheck.SetError(scoreBox, "")
            'Add the score written to the points
            points.Text = CInt(points.Text) + CInt(scoreBox.Text)
        End If
    Catch ext As System.InvalidCastException
        'Something other than a number
        If scoreBox.Text.Length > 0 Then
            ScoreCheck.SetError(scoreBox, "Score must be a number")
        End If
    Catch ex As Exception
        'Eek!
        MessageBox.Show("Something went wrong!  " + ex.Message)
    End Try
    'Check the score
    If CInt(points.Text) > 120 Then
        If CInt(points.Text) / CInt(otherPlayer.Text) > 1.5 Then
            WinMessage.Text = scoreBox.Name.Substring(0, _
            scoreBox.Name.Length - 6) & " Skunked 'em!!!"
        Else
            WinMessage.Text = scoreBox.Name.Substring(0, _
            scoreBox.Name.Length - 6) & " Won!!"
        End If
        WinMessage.Visible = True
    End If
End Sub
```

All of this changing of screen values causes the `Paint` event of the form to fire — every time VB needs to change the look of a form for any reason, this event fires — so I just tossed a little code in that event handler that would draw my board for me:

```
Private Sub CribbageBoard_Paint(ByVal sender As Object, ByVal e As
        System.Windows.Forms.PaintEventArgs) Handles MyBase.Paint
    PaintBoard(BillsPoints, GabriellesPoints)
End Sub
```

From that point on, my largest concern is drawing the board itself.

Drawing the board

I need to paint right on a form to create the image of the board for my cribbage application, so I use the `CreateGraphics` method of the form control. From there, I need to do the following:

- ✔ Paint the board brown using a brush.
- ✔ Draw six rows of little circles using a pen.
- ✔ Fill in the hole if that is the right score.
- ✔ Clean up my supplies.

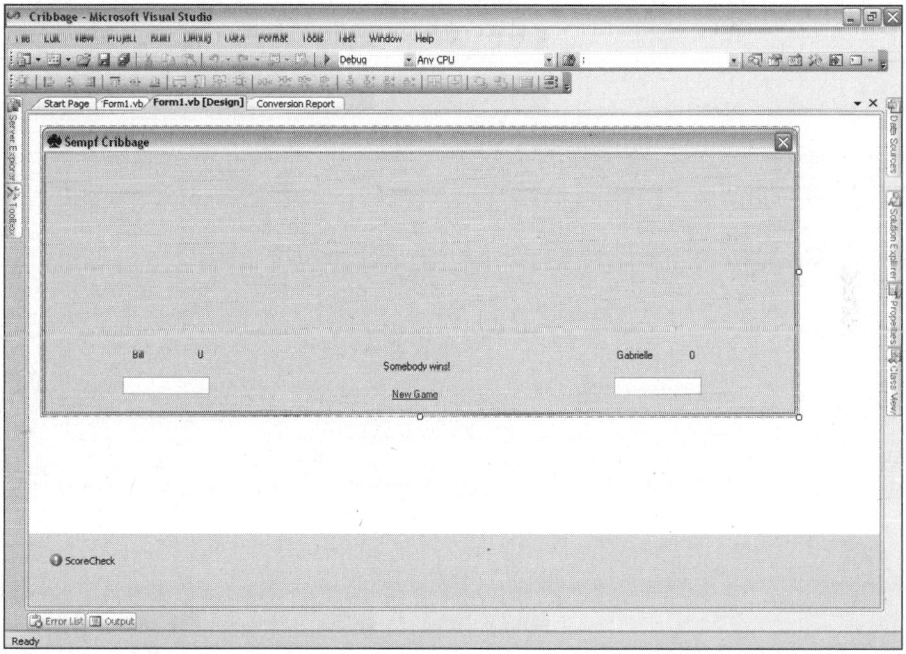

Figure 18-3: The basic board.

To that end, I came up with the `PaintBoard` method, which accepts the labels that contain the standing scores for both players. It is shown in Listing 18-1.

Listing 18-1: The PaintBoard Method

```
Private Sub PaintBoard(ByRef Bill As Label, ByRef Gabrielle As Label)
    Dim palette As Graphics = Me.CreateGraphics
    Dim brownBrush As New SolidBrush(Color.Brown)
    palette.FillRectangle(brownBrush, New Rectangle(20, 20, 820, 180))
    'OK, now I need to paint the little holes.
    'There are 244 little holes in the board.
    'Three rows of 40 times two, with the little starts and stops on either end.
    'Let's start with the 240.
    Dim rows As Integer
    Dim columns As Integer
    Dim scoreBeingDrawn As Integer
    Dim blackPen As New Pen(System.Drawing.Color.Black, 1)
    Dim blackBrush As New SolidBrush(Color.Black)
    Dim redBrush As New SolidBrush(Color.Red)

    'There are 6 rows, then, at 24 and 40, 80 and 100, then 140 and 160.
    For rows = 40 To 160 Step 60
        'There are 40 columns. They are every 20
        For columns = 40 To 820 Step 20
            'Calculate score being drawn
            scoreBeingDrawn = ((columns - 20) / 20) + (((( rows + 20) / 60) - 1)
              * 40)
            'Draw Bill
            'If score being drawn = bill fill, otherwise draw
            If scoreBeingDrawn = CInt(Bill.Text) Then
                palette.FillEllipse(blackBrush, columns - 2, rows - 2, 6, 6)
            ElseIf scoreBeingDrawn = BillsLastTotal Then
                palette.FillEllipse(redBrush, columns - 2, rows - 2, 6, 6)
            Else
                palette.DrawEllipse(blackPen, columns - 2, rows - 2, 4, 4)
            End If
            'Draw Gabrielle
            'If score being drawn = Gabrielle fill, otherwise draw
            If scoreBeingDrawn = CInt(Gabrielle.Text) Then
                palette.FillEllipse(blackBrush, columns - 2, rows + 16, 6, 6)
            ElseIf scoreBeingDrawn = GabriellesLastTotal Then
                palette.FillEllipse(redBrush, columns - 2, rows + 16, 6, 6)
            Else
                palette.DrawEllipse(blackPen, columns - 2, rows + 16, 4, 4)
            End If
        Next
    Next
    palette.Dispose()
    brownBrush.Dispose()
    blackPen.Dispose()
End Sub
```

Aside from the math, note the decision making. If the score being drawn is the score in the label, fill in the hole with a red peg. If it is the last score drawn, fill in the hole with a black peg. Otherwise, well, just draw a circle.

It is tough to fathom, but this is exactly how large-scale games are written. Admittedly, big graphics engines make many more If-Then decisions, but the premise is the same.

Also, large games use bitmap images sometimes, rather than drawing all the time. For the cribbage scoring application, for example, you could use a bitmap image of a peg instead of just filling an ellipse with a black or red brush!

Part V
The Part of Tens

The 5th Wave   By Rich Tennant

"It's a horse racing software program. It analyzes my betting history and makes suggestions. Right now it's suggesting I try betting on football."

In this part . . .

In this part, you find tips on everything from moving on after reading this book to finding resources online. There is even more information on the Web site: `www.vbfordummies.com`. I hope you will find it to be a useful reference!

Chapter 19

Ten Tips for Using the VB User Interface

In This Chapter

▶ Finding multiple ways to generate event handler code

▶ Copying text the way you really want it

▶ Making good use of the toolbars

▶ Extending VB with your own creations

▶ Using the same cool tricks as the pros

*V*isual Studio is a great tool for writing Visual Basic code, but so much goes into using this tool that you might not find the really neat features until the next version is out! To help you find cool features for writing VB code, I compiled this list of (almost) ten tips for working with the Visual Studio interface. I hope that these tips make your coding more enjoyable!

Generating Event Handlers from the Properties Window

When you're working in the Design View for Web or Windows Forms and you double-click a control, Visual Studio treats you to the code for the default event handler. But what if you don't want the default event handler? Any given object often has several events that you might want to access, and Visual Studio can just as easily (and automagically) generate code for any one of those events.

Follow these few steps to give it a try:

1. **Create a new Visual Basic 2008 Windows Application project. (It works in Web Forms, too.)**

2. **Drag a control to the default form.**

   I use a text box in this example.

3. **Select your control and then press F4 to expand the Properties window.**

4. **In the Properties window, click the Event button (which looks like a little lightning bolt).**

   You see a list of associated events, something like the list shown in Figure 19-1.

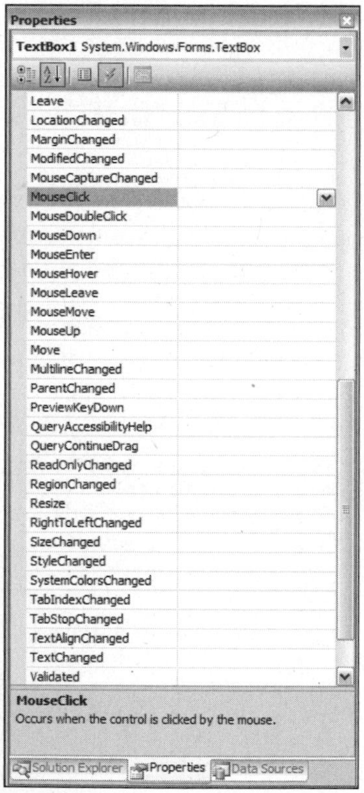

Figure 19-1: The listing of events for a text box control.

5. **Double-click an event from the list to generate the event handler code.**

The events listed in Figure 19-1 are all the events exposed by the `TextBox` object. I selected the `MouseClick` event. This means that anytime the user clicks in the text box, my code will run.

When you double-click an event in the events window, the generated code looks something like the following:

```
Private Sub TextBox1_MouseClick(ByVal sender As System.Object, _
         ByVal e As System.Windows.Forms.MouseEventArgs) _
         Handles TextBox1.MouseClick


End Sub
```

Check the `Handles` statement at the end of the declaration; it should match the event you selected.

Generating Event Handlers from the Code View

The preceding section shows you how to create event handlers from the Design View — but the Design View isn't the only part of the Visual Basic interface with automatic features. The Code View has a few tricks, too. Specifically, the events are handily listed along the top of the Code View, for both navigation among events and creation of new ones. I show this placement in Figure 19-2.

Figure 19-2 also shows the new default handler I created by double-clicking a button and then clicking the drop-down list above and to the right of the code window. You can see that `MouseClick` is bold, which means that the `MouseClick` method exists. All other events exposed by the `Button` object are shown as well.

The drop-down list just to the left shows the objects instantiated in the form. In this example, the list would show just the `Button` and the `Form` objects. The following steps outline the process for creating a new event in this view:

1. **Right-click the form you want to edit, and choose View Code to go to Code View.**

2. **Select the object you need to handle an event for from the leftmost drop-down list.**

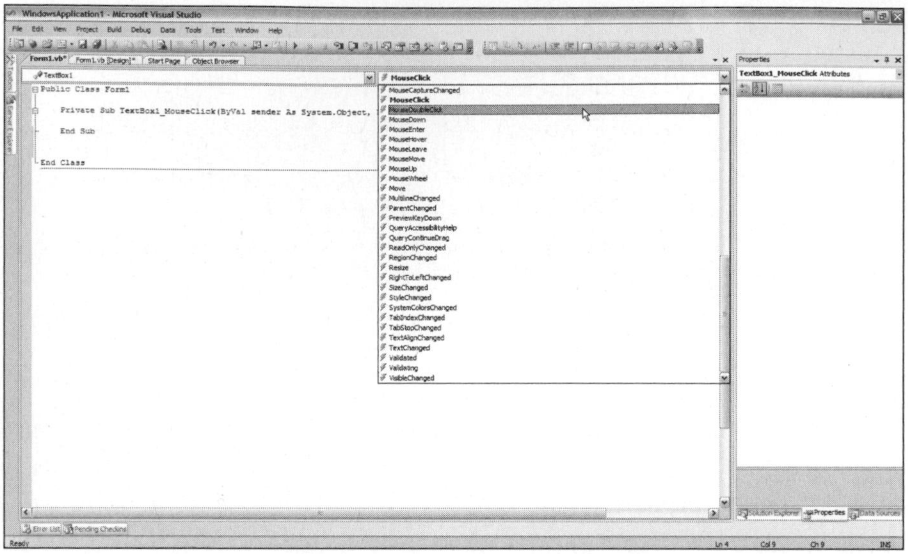

Figure 19-2:
The event
selector in
Code View.

3. **Select the event you would like to handle from the rightmost drop-down list.**

   At this point, Visual Studio creates the stub of the subroutine for you, and you can add the code you need right to it.

   Later, if the code in the form gets long, you can navigate back to the event handler the same way and make changes.

Pasting Text as HTML

When making Web pages in Web Forms, you may often find yourself pulling content from other Web pages open in Internet Explorer or from Office documents. For example, when you're creating static Web sites, the content may come to you in the form of a Word document.

The problem with getting content this way comes from the interactivity between Microsoft programs. Did you ever notice that, when you cut from Excel and paste to Word, the table structure remains? Microsoft products try to maintain formatting whenever possible. Take a look at this example:

1. **Open any Word document that contains formatted text.**

   For this example, I just use the Word document for this chapter.

2. **Open Visual Studio and start a new Web site.**

3. **In the default page, click the Design tab to change to Design View (if you're not already in Design View).**

4. **Highlight text from the Word document and choose Edit⇨Copy.**

5. **Back in Visual Studio, position the cursor in the default Web page and choose Edit⇨Paste.**

6. **Click the Code tab to change to Code View, and look at the text your cut-and-paste job left behind.**

   My example leaves the text shown in Listing 19-1.

Listing 19-1: Messy HTML from the Paste Command

```
<h1>
 Paste as HTML</h1>
<p class="MsoNormal">
 When making Web pages in Web Forms, you may often find yourself pulling content
              from other
 Web pages open in Internet Explorer or from Office documents
.<span style="mso-spacerun: yes">  </span> For example, when you're
                creating static Web
 sites, the content may
 <?xml namespace="" prefix="st1" ?>
 <st1:state w:st="on"><st1:place w:st="on">come</st1:place></st1:state>
 to you in the form of a Word Document.</p>
```

Most of the time, you don't want to retain the formatting from other programs when dealing with a Web application. You want to copy content from the other program (Word document, Excel spreadsheet, and so on) and paste just the text so that you can apply styles suitable for a Web page. If that's the case, choose the Edit⇨Paste Alternate command instead of the Edit⇨Paste command in the preceding Step 5.

Customizing Your Toolbars for Every File Type

While in the Web Forms builder of Visual Studio, you may notice something else that is cool. When you switch between the Design View and Code View, your toolbars — the buttons under the menus — change. In fact, your working area might even change size because toolbars are added or removed.

This changing-of-the-toolbars happens because Visual Studio supports a different toolbar setup for each file type and view. HTML and ASPX pages can have totally different toolbars, and the Design View and Code View can have different toolbars for each file type.

You can customize your workspace by specifying the toolbars you want to see for any given file type or view. Simply open a file of the desired type and right-click in the ribbon bar (the gray area under the menus). When you do, you get a long list of the toolbars available, and you can just click the ones you want. I list some toolbars and their contents in Table 19-1.

Table 19-1	Toolbars for Different File Types and Views
Toolbar Name	*What It's Good For*
Build	Has buttons that match the Build menu and enable you to compile your project with various options.
Class Designer	Holds design tools that are appropriate for making DLL files.
Debug	Has buttons that function similarly to the Debug menu and enable you to enter Debug mode or debug other running programs.
Device	Contains tools to help you work with Smart Devices (such as mobile phones) and give you access to the emulators for Pocket PCs.
Layout	Holds tools (such as the Alignment feature mentioned in Chapter 4) that are useful for structuring forms.
Query Designer	Has tools to help create SQL and XML data queries.
Style Sheet	Contains buttons for applying CSS styles to HTML.

Adding Extender Providers

Extender providers could really use their own chapter, but because of everything else about Visual Basic I need to tell you, I give you a brief look at them here. An *extender provider* provides an extension — specifically new properties — to an existing object or group of objects. Try this:

1. **Open Visual Studio and start a new VB Windows Application project.**

2. **Drag a `Button` object onto the form.**

   Suppose that you want to enhance your button with a *ToolTip* — the little floating window that appears in some applications when you mouse over an object on the screen. In a VB Windows Application project, you can't add a ToolTip directly to the `Button` object.

3. **To add a ToolTip property to the button, add a `ToolTip` object to the form.**

   You can find the `ToolTip` object in the Toolbox. The ToolTip will appear in the Component Tray.

4. **Return to the Properties window for the button.**

   Notice that, at the bottom of the window in the Misc category, a ToolTip now exists!

Because the ToolTip is an extender provider, it is designed to give all objects that populate an interface a new property, in this case, a ToolTip. Although adding a property to an object might seem a little odd, it is actually a great way to extend the functionality of a set of controls. And I think that Microsoft's doing so was quite brilliant.

You can actually create your own extender providers to do everything from adding textual strings for reference all the way to making new functional and graphical elements. These properties give you a powerful way to extend the user interface controls provided by Microsoft.

Using Visual Components That Are Not So Visual

I would be remiss if I didn't tell you about the Component Tray and, especially, the visual components that are not so visual. Though Visual Basic is set up as a rapid, point-and-click development tool, lots of objects (that aren't all that visible) still should be and are managed by the visual development tools.

The *Component Tray* is a special section of the form designer that shows up when you are using a nonvisual component such as the timer or dataset. Figure 19-3 shows the Component Tray, which displays only a few actual features, because the majority of the point-and-click development involves moving visual components around on the screen.

Other parts of the book refer to nonvisual components a number of times. In Part II, you find out about the `Menu` object. In Part III, I show you the `Timer` object. Part IV has information about `Data` objects. In this chapter's previous section, I show you the `ToolTip` object. Not all of these have usable parts that you see on-screen, but they do show up in the Component Tray.

And, although you can't reposition these components on-screen, you can do the following:

- Right-click the component to get a context-sensitive menu, just like you do for a button or other window component.

- Open the Properties window and click the component in the tray to select it for editing purposes. In the Properties window, you can change the component name and other common properties.

Here's one caveat to keep in mind: Declaring the object in Code View doesn't immediately make it a Component Tray object. Generally speaking, if you want to edit a component in Design View, you need to create it in Design View. Most developers are primarily either Code View developers or Design View developers. As you find your personal style, you'll get to know how often you'll use the Component Tray.

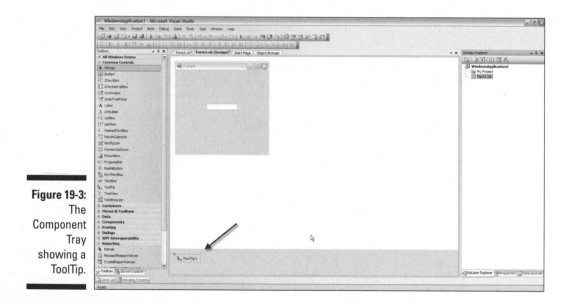

Figure 19-3:
The Component Tray showing a ToolTip.

Recording Macros

Macros are so cool that they get their own user interface, which I show in Figure 19-4. And macros are so powerful and flexible, they have the potential to totally change your development patterns. Here, I present a small part of their power. (I leave the experimenting up to you.)

One of the neatest things you can do is record a keystroke-saving macro for later playback. If you have a task (such as formatting text) that you expect to do more than once, record it as a macro.

One of my favorite ways to use a macro is to record HTML formatting. I have a whole host of macros I recorded to format strings for paragraphs and lists. Formatting with prerecorded macros makes site management with Visual Studio a breeze.

To get to the macros, you can do a few things:

- ✔ Press Alt+F8 to open the Macro Explorer in Visual Studio.
- ✔ Select Tools➪Macros➪Macros IDE from the menu bar.
- ✔ Right-click in the ribbon bar and select Macros.

Figure 19-4:
The Macro
IDE.

Fire up the Macro Explorer (press Alt+F8) and follow these steps to see how it's done:

1. **Start with a new Web project in Visual Studio. Right-click the HTML Designer and select View Code to change to Code View.**

2. **Open the default Web page and paste a few lines of text into the Code View.**

   For example, copy some text from Notepad, just as if you received it from a client, and paste the text in the Code View. Each paragraph will be one long line of text in the Code View screen.

3. **Click to the left of the first line of text to leave the cursor at the beginning of the first line that you want to format.**

4. **Choose Tools⇨Macro⇨Record Temporary Macro.**

   The Record panel appears and starts capturing every significant command you give Visual Studio.

5. **Type the following to record formatting for an HTML paragraph:**

   • Type the HTML paragraph tag, **<p>**, at the start of the text you want to format. If Visual Studio adds the rest of the paragraph tag, just delete it by pressing Delete.

   • Press End to move the cursor to the end of the line of text.

   • Type the HTML close paragraph tag, **</p>**.

   • Press the right-arrow key, which moves the cursor to the start of the next line.

6. **Click the Stop Recording button on the Record panel.**

The macro is now recorded and, what's more, it is actually code that resides in the temporary macro spot in the Macro Explorer. Listing 19-2 shows this code.

Listing 19-2: The Paragraph Macro

```
Imports EnvDTE
Imports EnvDTE80
Imports System.Diagnostics

Public Module RecordingModule
 Sub TemporaryMacro()
 DTE.ActiveDocument.Selection.Text = "<P>"
 DTE.ActiveDocument.Selection.Delete(4)
```

```
DTE.ActiveDocument.Selection.EndOfLine()
DTE.ActiveDocument.Selection.Text = "</P>"
DTE.ActiveDocument.Selection.CharRight()
End Sub
End Module
```

If you right-click `TemporaryMacro` and select Edit, you can see the code in the Macro IDE, where you can do the following:

- Make changes to the macro.

- Delete unnecessary code lines (such as the line created when I deleted the automatically generated paragraph close tag in my example) to save a cleaner macro.

- Make the macro permanent by copying the code into another module in the macro recorder and saving it.

- Right-click and choose Save As to save the file with a different name in the Macro Explorer.

- Run the macro from the Macro Explorer by double-clicking it, or use the context menu in Code View, as shown in Figure 19-5.

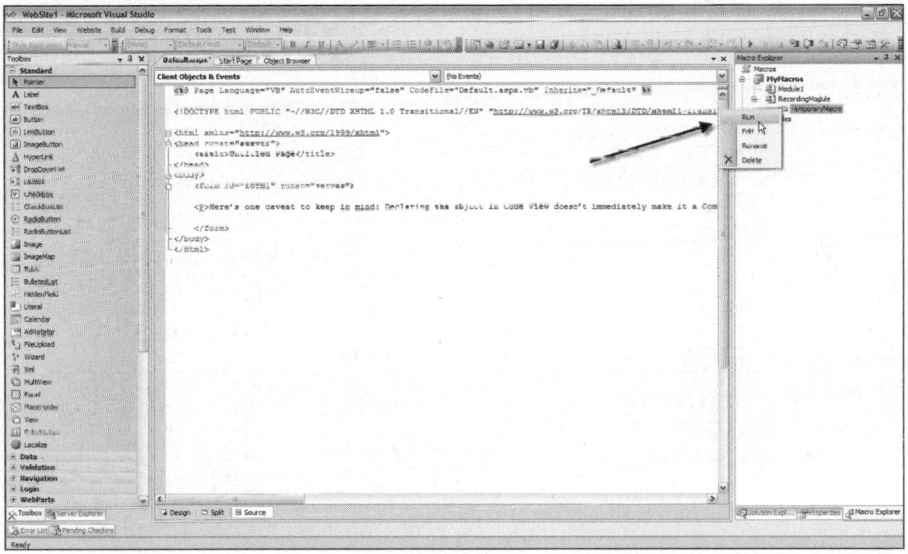

Figure 19-5:
Running a
macro.

Using the Task List

The Task List is a very cool personal project management feature of the Visual Studio IDE. To show it, choose View➪Other Windows➪Task List or press Ctrl+Alt+K. To use it, just click the Create New User Task button and then start typing. When you've completed the task in your Task List, you can just check it off.

You can do a lot more with this tool than just make to-do lists. It is fully integrated with source control, too, so pending check-ins and so on show up in the list. Also, you can add tokens into the code that show up in the Task List.

To add a token, open any project and add a comment that starts with TODO. You'll notice that after you add a TODO comment, a Comment shows up with Comments in the Task List drop-down list, as shown in Figure 19-6. Double-clicking a Comment Task brings you to the file and line where the comment was inserted. You can use this to keep track of things you need to remember as you do them.

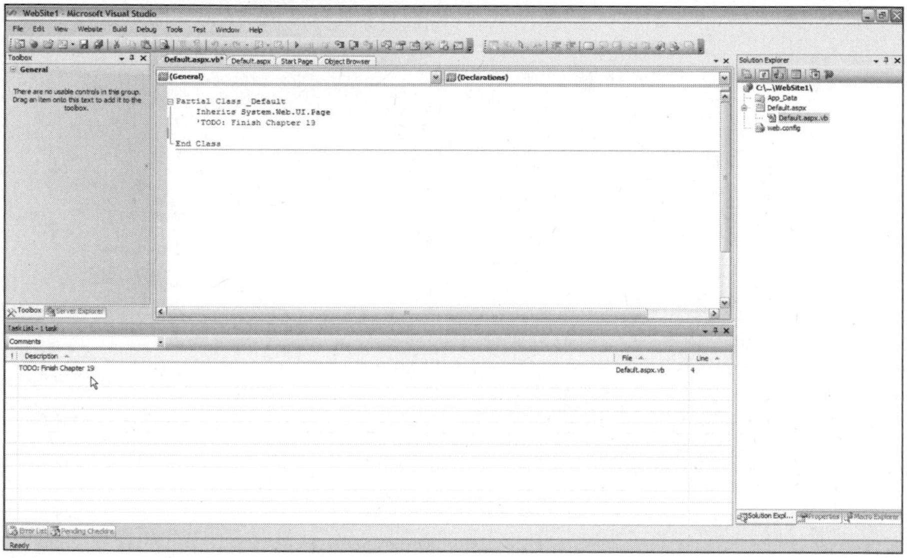

Figure 19-6: The Task list.

The other tokens include HACK and UNDONE. These don't usually get their own Task List filter, but you can use them for marking questionable code that you might need to revisit, or work that needs to be completed. You can add new tokens in the Environment section of the Options panel.

Inserting Snippets in Your Code

A really cool Visual Studio feature, like CodeSwap, is the Insert Snippet feature. This organizational tool has several easy-to-use but hard-to-remember bits of code in various categories, including those shown in Figure 19-7.

To use the Insert Snippet feature, just right-click your VB code in the Code View and select Insert Snippet. The code is well-factored and includes a lot of template-type things, too, such as array looping and complex algorithms. All the new stuff in VB 2008 is in there, too, like Linq and Windows Presentation Foundation. If you have a tough problem to solve, take a look at the Insert Snippet feature.

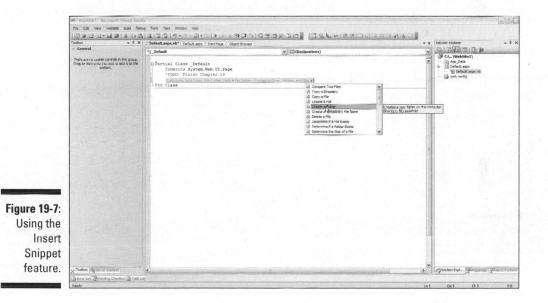

Figure 19-7:
Using the Insert Snippet feature.

Chapter 20

Ten Ideas for Taking Your Next Programming Step

....

....

*W*ithout a doubt, by the time you've worked through the examples in this book, you'll be an expert. Experts shine by going out on their own and trying new things. This chapter is all about the things that you can go and try in the real world after you've gotten down the basics of Visual Basic and you're ready to find some programming challenges.

Get Visual Basic 2008 for Home Use

If you primarily use Visual Basic for work, you may want to get a copy of Visual Basic 2008 Express Edition for home use so that you can have fun with after-hours projects. While you can download the .NET SDK and use the command line, I recommend using the Express Edition.

The Express Edition is a copy of Visual Studio 2008 for hobbyists. It is missing a few of the features of the Professional version that I discuss elsewhere in this book, but nothing significant is left out. The Express Edition is perfect for the odd open-source project.

Express editions are — at the time of this writing — free. Note that the Professional edition contains a lot of stuff that you can't do in Express, which is why I chose Professional for this book. Nonetheless, it is a great learning tool.

Update Code to Use New Tools

This used to be a section on writing your own tools, and it had some sample code from my Data Object Generator. Honestly, I don't use that tool anymore, because I think DataSets and the Visual DataSet Designer are so much better. In fact, I have gone back to a number of old projects and updated them to use the DataSet designer.

In and of itself, that is a great tip. Update your applications to use the new tools. If you are working on a heavily object-driven application, use Linq in your business layer code to get the right data out at the right time. If you have a program that you have maintained for years that notifies managers that they need to approve documents, update it to use Windows Workflow Foundation.

The new tools that Microsoft provides are just a reflection of what we, the community, have shown that we need on a regular basis. Don't overlook them. Table 20-1 shows a list of the new things that I have updated projects with recently, and what I replaced. As always, your mileage may vary, but do pick a project and give it a try.

Table 20-1	Things to Update
Update This	**With This**
Hand-coded data objects	DataSets
Logic for moving information around among interested groups	Windows Workflow Foundation
Old, tired Windows Forms code	Windows Presentation Foundation
COM+	Windows Communication Foundation
INI files	Config files
Complex object-mapping code	Linq

Join an Online Competition at TopCoder

Another great thing to do to stretch your coding legs is to participate in an online competition. TopCoder (www.topcoder.com) is the best you'll find — a free competition in which you can answer problems using VB and compete for fame, fortune, and projects. For example, one of the easier problems to solve involves taking data about students and figuring out a way to extract the oldest student by using a specified class and method.

The Single Round Match user interface is one of the best Java UIs I have seen, as shown in Figure 20-1. You are in a virtual room with other coders, which gives you some level of insight on how others are tackling the problems. It's pretty exciting.

Figure 20-1:
The
TopCoder
arena.

Another popular use of TopCoder is its Component Development Contests. These aren't times, but have due dates, and if you are judged the best by your peers, you could garner a little cash. It's a good test of abilities.

The problems you find on TopCoder sound a lot like quizzes in a programming class, and that's a fair comparison. The goal is to write the best code you can that solves the problem and to have your code compared to that of other programmers.

Participate in an Open Source Project

Open source software is software governed by one of a myriad of free licenses, which state rules such as "This software is free for use, but any adjustments made to it must also be provided for free to the community." Open source's most famous output, Linux, might get all the press, but a ton of open source .NET projects are available, too.

Before you just jump in, though, take a look around. Two of the best places to find projects are SourceForge.net (`http://sourceforge.net`) and CodeZone (`www.codezone.com/MyCodezone.CodezoneCom`). Log on and look at the projects. Find one that interests you, get the code, and play around with it. See whether you can make improvements.

Then log on to the message board and talk to the designers. These should be people you could go have a drink with, you know? Talk about the project. See whether it is something that you would want to donate a handful of hours a month to.

You can garner a ton of benefits from working on open source projects. First, it might be the only chance you get, depending on your situation, to work with expert .NET programmers. Second, you get a genuine chance to practice coding on a peer-reviewed project. Third, you may end up being able to point to a public application that you participated in building. This is a great resume builder.

Above all that, though, open source projects are fun. As I write this, a quick look at the applications available on a few project sites include the following:

- A Web portal project
- XML documentation tools
- An object relational framework
- IIS Web managers
- Line-counting utilities
- An HTTP proxy

This points out another benefit — some really cool software is available, free for the downloading. All you are morally obligated to do to pay for it is to help out a little. It's a fair price; that's for sure!

Use Third-Party Tools in Your Projects

When you are looking to do more sophisticated things with VB, look at some third-party tools to integrate into your projects. Great examples of third-party tools are user controls for Web Forms projects and form controls for Windows Forms applications.

Software created by third-party individuals is a great way to inexpensively expand your horizons without spending hundreds of hours programming and testing. Don't be put out by "Not-built-here syndrome" — third-party software has its benefits.

For starters, third-party software is often peer reviewed. Take a look at www.windowsforms.net. The top-ten user-ranked controls are right there on the home page. Search for a form that you might need. All the controls have a download and view rating, and many of them are reviewed by users.

For Web Forms, check out www.asp.net. As with the Windows Forms .NET Web site, the code samples in the Control Gallery of the ASP.NET site are rated and counted by other users.

Programmers use third-party software, and when you know your way around the language, you should, too. If you still aren't sure, look for a Microsoft-certified vendor — called an ISV (Independent Software Vendor). My company is one — many others are, too. It's Microsoft's mark for a company that knows what it is building.

To look for certified vendors, check out the resource directory at http://directory.microsoft.com/mprd. This page allows you to find a partner by specialty (you would want an ISV) and location (which might not matter for just finding control builders).

Also in the arena of third-party software for programmers are add-ins for Visual Studio. The Visual Studio Integration Program (available at http://msdn.microsoft.com/vstudio/extend) provides vendors with a ton of great tools for integrating their products into Visual Studio, and it just helps you to move right along.

Dotfuscator, which I mention in Part I, is an example of an add-in. It is a Windows Forms application that seamlessly integrates into Visual Studio to assist you with programming chores — in this case, to protect your source code. You can find out more about Dotfuscator in the Visual Studio help files.

Trying add-ins from vendors is a lot like trying a control — research, check the reviews, and test, test, test. And have fun! Half of the reason to try out new things is for the thrill.

Integrate a Public Web Service

Chapter 7 describes how to build and integrate a Web service, but integrating a public service is a special treat. Many people and companies with special information have provided said information in public XML Web services for you to try out. You have to pay to use some of these services, while others are free. Even if it is just for a fun side project, you should certainly try to integrate a public service once or twice.

Public Web services are going through something of a shift in power as of this writing, with the small startups gradually being replaced with the Net Internet Monsters like Amazon and Google. The principles are still the same, though.

As you look at these, keep in mind that you are stepping out of the .NET world in many instances. XML Web services are cross platform, so as many Perl and Java services as ASMX services are out there. Some of them might return something unexpected and, as such, mess up a perfectly good program. Be prepared, and trap errors often.

One of the small free startup service hosters that is still around that doesn't require a bunch of registration (like Google and Amazon do) is WebServicesX. It has a number of good sample services that are easy to consume. I'll start with the Zip Code Info service, to get a city name from the zip code.

To use a service you find on a public service host site, first make sure that you are connected to the Internet, and then download and use the service by following these steps:

1. **Open Visual Studio and start a new Windows Application project.**

2. **On the form, add a label object and keep the default name.**

3. **Right-click the project and select Add Service Reference.**

   The Add Service Reference dialog box appears, as shown in Figure 20-2.

4. **Enter the URL for the service in the URL text box and click the Go button.**

   For example, the WSDL file for the service I use for this example is at `www.webservicex.net/uszip.asmx?WSDL`.

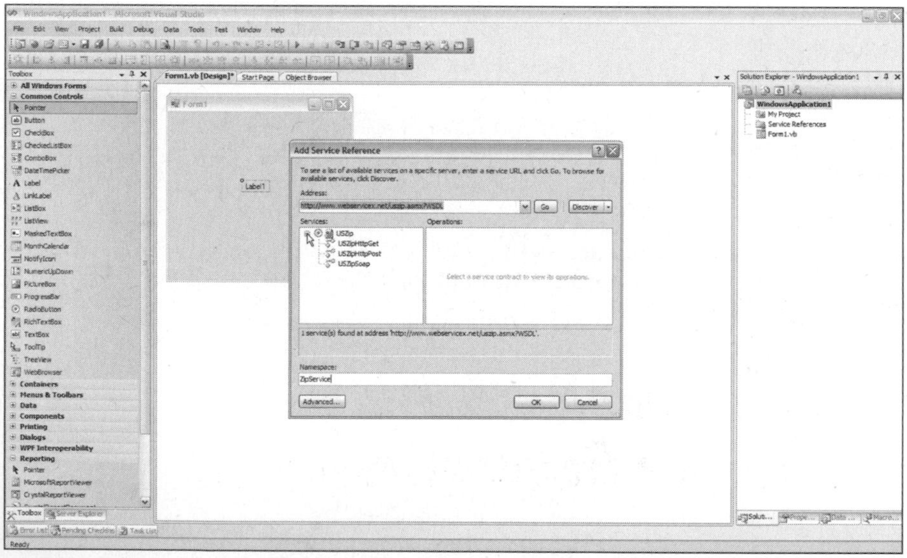

Figure 20-2:
Adding a reference to the `USZip` Code.

5. **Enter a name for the service in the Web Reference Name text box and click the Add Reference button.**

   For example, I entered the name **ZipService**.

6. **Double-click the form to get the** Form1_Load **event handler.**

7. **Add the code to enable the service.**

   I entered the following code to enable USZipCode:

```
Private Sub Form1_Load(ByVal sender As System.Object, ByVal e As
        System.EventArgs) Handles MyBase.Load
    Dim myZipService As ZipService.USZipSoapClient = New
        ZipService.USZipSoapClient()
    Dim myCity As Xml.XmlNode =
        myZipService.GetInfoByZIP("43123").FirstChild
    Label1.Text = myCity.FirstChild.InnerText.ToString
End Sub
```

8. **Run the code by pressing F5.**

   The service returns the current temperature, based on the zip code you supply in the myTempService.getTemp method, as shown in Figure 20-3.

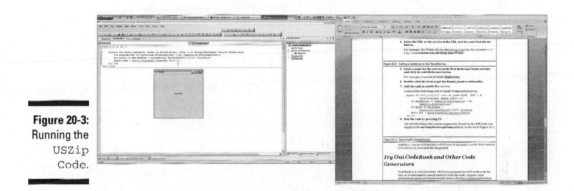

Figure 20-3: Running the USZip Code.

And there you are — that's all it takes to integrate a public Web service! Give it a try in your next for-fun project.

Try Out CodeRush and Other Code Generators

CodeRush is a *code generator,* which is a program that writes the code for you, or at least makes it much easier to write the code. Largely, code generator programs are based around taking a database schema and writing the access code. Some code generators, though, do oh so much more.

The goal is to write better code more quickly, and enjoy it. CodeRush — and other code generator programs like it — are a great way to start. They are not a substitute for knowing how to do it yourself, but they are a great tool when you are in the production world. You can find out more about CodeRush at `www.coderush.com`.

To be fair, CodeRush is more than a simple code generator. For instance, CodeRush has the following neat features:

- ✔ It allows you to see the code you have built in a visual tool, even if the code is a class library!
- ✔ It intelligently selects code for you, rather than just selecting a line.
- ✔ It has a very sophisticated copy feature that makes sure that you get the entire block of code. For example, if you select a Try-Catch block, it copies to the `End Try` statement.
- ✔ It, of course, generates code with a set of great code templates.

When you're setting up a project, and you're at the point where you really know what you're up against, you should look into using a productivity tool such as CodeRush to help you code faster and more accurately. Using a code generator can improve the whole experience of writing a program!

Write a Web Part

SharePoint is a portal server by Microsoft for the corporate set. By *portal server,* I mean a predesigned intranet page that includes space to store documents, schedules, and so on. Don't cringe — it is actually a pretty good product, unlike a lot of similar efforts.

Web Parts are the little holes in which the documents and schedules are placed. Basically, instead of writing a custom page or user control every time you need a new page or control on your intranet, you can invoke a standard Web Part and configure it slightly to fit your needs.

SharePoint comes with 15 or so Web Parts, which include the following:

- ✔ Discussion board
- ✔ Fax control

> ✔ Document storage
>
> ✔ Link list
>
> ✔ Help Desk

What should interest you, though, as a VB programmer, is the ability to write a new Web Part. In total, the process for writing a Web Part from scratch is actually very complicated. Microsoft makes it much easier by providing a new project type for Web Parts — just like a Windows Application project or a Web Service project.

The output of a Web Part is a DLL, just like a class library project (in fact, it is a class library). The trick to getting rolling with a new Web Part, though, is to download the SDK from the SharePoint site at `http://msdn.microsoft.com/sharepoint` and install it. Then you will have access to a new project type when you open Visual Studio and choose File➪New➪Project.

A new product, called SharePoint Designer, is also out there; it makes it easy for even end users to develop SharePoint Web Parts. It is part of the MSDN Library, and is downloadable from `http://office.microsoft.com/en-us/sharepointdesigner/default.aspx`. SharePoint Designer, shown in Figure 20-4, is a high-powered HTML designer that has all the piping for SharePoint built in.

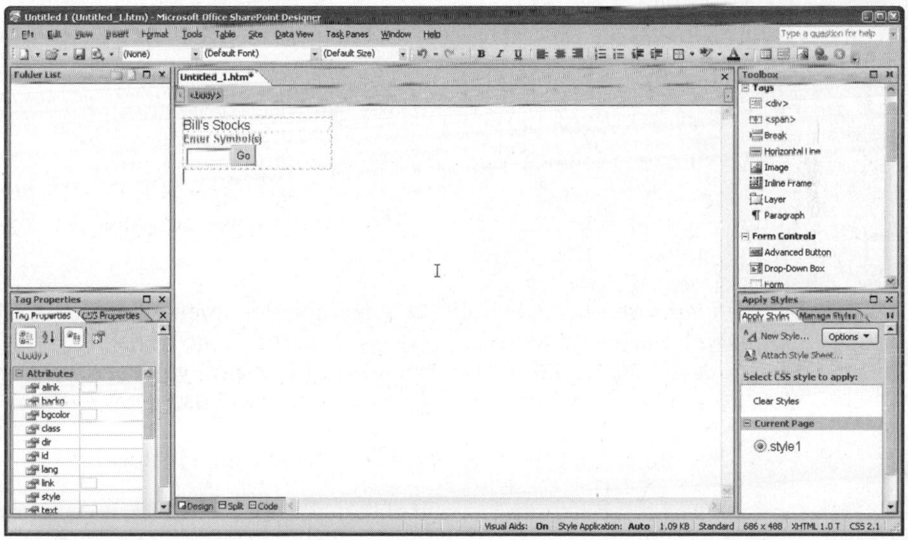

Figure 20-4: SharePoint Designer.

Outside of Web Parts are Workflows, which is more the direction in which SharePoint is going. These define the process around the distribution of information, and can be developed using Windows Workflow Foundation. To take a look at a starter Workflow, look at the Windows Workflow Foundation project type in Create Project in Visual Studio.

Use the DTE

The *DTE (Design Time Environment)* is the automation object model — the class library that you use to create new add-ins and wizards for Visual Studio itself. Yes, that's right; I am recommending that you further your understanding of Visual Basic by creating an add-in for Visual Studio itself.

I could get into the philosophical implications of this, but I'll leave it at this: The more you work in depth with something, the better you get at it.

To use the DTE, you again need to start a new project type by choosing File➪New➪Project. In the New Project dialog box, look in the Project Types list on the left, click the plus sign next to Other Project Types, and then select Extensibility. In the Templates box on the right, select the Visual Studio Add-in (shown in Figure 20-5) and then click the OK button.

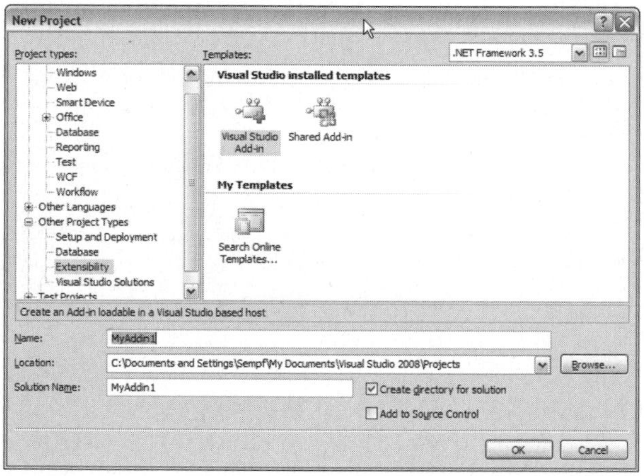

Figure 20-5: Selecting an add-in in the New Project dialog box.

What is great about this is that like the SharePoint Web Part, Microsoft has done all the plumbing for you. A lot of code is involved in making an add-in work, but much of the code is automatically supplied by the project type.

When you've loaded the Visual Studio Add-in project, you have access to almost every part of a Visual Studio project. Need to loop through the files in a project? No problem. Want to check out a selected piece of code? Done. Want to change a line of text into an HTML paragraph? Check this out:

```
Sub MakeParagraph()
    DTE.ActiveDocument.Selection.Text = "<P>"
    DTE.ActiveDocument.Selection.EndOfLine()
    DTE.ActiveDocument.Selection.Text = "</P>"
    DTE.ActiveDocument.Selection.CharRight()
End Sub
```

Like the data object generator, the DTE can be a powerful ally. It's worth giving it a shot!

Write an Article about What You Have Discovered

Say you've become pretty knowledgeable about Visual Basic, or perhaps you've figured out a clever way to fix a problem you encountered while creating a program. Especially when you figure out something on your own by creating a unique block of code to solve a problem, you may want to share your knowledge by writing an article.

A bunch of great, popular sites accept short articles from new authors. Don't expect money, but you do get two important things if your article is accepted and published: the acknowledgment of your peers and the firm education that comes with researching something solidly enough to write about it. To get started, check out these sites:

www.dotnetjunkies.com/community.aspx

www.asptoday.com/Info.aspx?view=WriteForUs

www.4guysfromrolla.com/authors.shtml

www.asp101.com/resources/submit.asp

If you're interested in writing an article, write it! Don't make up excuses like you're too shy or unknown to publish an article. In 2001, I wrote an article for Intranet Journal that is still up (www.intranetjournal.com/articles/200107/ia_07_25_01a.html), and I couldn't believe the furor it started. Now look where I am!

Chapter 21

Ten Resources on the Internet

In This Chapter

▶ Researching with Web sites

▶ Sharing ideas with online communities

▶ Finding sample code

What would we do without the Internet to turn to? In this chapter, I show you my favorite online sites for getting information about Visual Basic. You can find a lot of junk out there on the Internet, but you can also find a lot of good stuff, too. The trick lies in telling the two apart.

MSDN Library

```
http://msdn.microsoft.com/library
```

The MSDN Library is without a question the number one resource for .NET research. MSDN stands for Microsoft Developer Network, and the name *MSDN Library* suits the site just fine; it is effectively a big online document storage location.

The site's search feature works great (type your sought-after term in the Search For text box and click the Go button), but don't overlook just browsing through the site. The tree to the left has a very intelligently designed table of contents built in, and you can find a ton of sample code and resources just by digging through. Be careful, though, the content includes some older stuff, and you want to focus on VB 2008 documents.

VBForDummies.net

```
www.vbfordummies.net
```

VBForDummies.net is my site. My goal for using this type of site is to post bits of the book, as well as other documents and code. I'm using Graffiti, the

ASP.NET content management system, to build the site. It allows for a log of community involvement that you're probably used to by now, such as comments to my blog posts and forums to ask questions.

Channel 9

```
http://channel9.msdn.com
```

A discussion platform extraordinaire, Channel 9 answers all the tough questions about the internals at Microsoft. All the programming geeks in the company hang out there, and the discussions are frank and enlightening.

Additionally, you find a lot of features that replace the now-defunct GotDotNet, such as the SandBox, where you can find user samples of code both simple and impossibly complex.

My favorite part of the site, though, is the blue card interviews. The site was originally manned by blogger-extraordinaire Robert Scoble, and the feeling on the site is as though he had never left. The interviews are relaxed and natural, and they have tons of great information.

ASP.NET Web

```
www.asp.net
```

As with GotDotNet, the ASP.NET community was started by a Microsoft team — but this time it was the ASP.NET team. ASP.NET Web is the place to go for any download, control, or question about Web Forms development.

```
http://quickstarts.asp.net/QuickStartv20/default.aspx
```

Also — don't miss this — the ASP.NET site is the hosting location for the QuickStart Tutorials. You may find that these tutorials are similar to this book, with to-the-point explanations and lots of examples. The QuickStart Tutorials are solution driven, too, so they answer real rather than theoretical questions. The code samples are based on the inline scripting model, which I didn't use in this book. This model offers another way to build ASP.NET Web Forms projects. You can catch on to this model pretty quickly by looking at the examples in the QuickStart.

The Microsoft Public Newsgroups

`http://msdn.microsoft.com/newsgroups/managed`

I used to be a huge fan of the Usenet, but with the proliferation of spammers, it has really gone downhill. Microsoft has made a major effort, though, to get the Usenet started up again for Microsoft developers using the Managed Newsgroup model. If you have an MSDN subscription and have signed up with the Managed Newsgroup service, you get an answer to any posted question within 48 hours (or two business days) from a Microsoft employee or MVP. It's a great plan, and it's free with the MSDN subscription.

.NET 247

`www.dotnet247.com/247reference/default.aspx`

I'll admit it — I am going to promote another author here. Matt Reynolds is a fantastic writer and coder, and he has put up a fantastic resource in .NET 247. This site looks through the Usenet for posts that actually have something interesting in them, and then indexes these posts to make the information useful. I highly recommend that you take advantage of the content on .NET 247.

Google CodeSearch

`www.google.com/codesearch`

While much of the Google Code Repository is not Microsoft code, it is still a tremendously valuable resource. Aside from searching for off-color phrases (which is tremendously amusing), you can find algorithms that can easily be translated to VB with a little know-how.

Regular expressions out of Perl are very useful, for instance. Perl is a language that makes heavy use of Regular Expressions, and our .NET Regular Expressions are similar. With good search criteria, it is easy to find Perl regular expressions that match things you might need — search "Regex Email," for example.

kbAlertz

```
www.kbalertz.com
```

What is kbAlertz.com? The kbAlertz site says it best:

> "kbAlertz.com is an e-mail notification system that scans the entire Microsoft Knowledge Base every night, and e-mails you when updates or additions are made to the technologies you subscribe to. Since we scan the entire knowledge base, we also have a pretty good search system for you to use on the left menu."

Using kbAlertz isn't about VB 2008 as much as it's about having access to information that's handy for anyone in a Windows environment. I subscribe to the alerts and get information on changes to the security best practices, among other things.

CodePlex

```
www.codeplex.com
```

Speaking of open source code (weren't we?), don't overlook CodePlex — Microsoft's new Open Source Management System. This is an all-.NET library of open source projects that you can join, use, or browse.

I use open source projects as my own personal education medium. Throughout my career, I have looked at how other people have done things, both good and bad, and formulated my own plans. CodePlex is a great place to do that.

It's also a lot of fun. Right now, the most popular project is a .NET driver for the nunchucks from the Wii. Cool stuff.

<Microsoft> Google for Searching

```
www.google.com/microsoft
```

With all of these specialty sites for finding and sharing code, don't forget about good old Google. The trick for using Google to find useful bits of code is to refine your search technique. I search for the exact class I need code for and add the term *VB.NET*, and I usually find what I need. For instance, I needed to connect to an Excel spreadsheet as a data source recently. I could have pieced together the needed code from the MSDN documentation, but instead I turned to Google. I searched with the phrase "vb.net OleDbConnection Excel" and got four examples as the first four hits.

Now to do a proper search, you need to know a little about what you are searching for. So don't go off half-cocked, or your results will be too broad. To narrow your search and get good results on Google, use one very specific term (like *OleDbConnection*) with one or more broad terms (like *vb.net* and *Excel*).

Index

• *Symbols* •

... (ellipsis) button, in a
    property, 28
/ (division) operator, 170
− (subtraction) operator, 170
+ (addition) operator, 170,
    227–228
* (asterisk), next to a filename
    in Design View, 24
% (modulo) operator, 170
* (multiplication) operator, 170
_ (underscore character),
    starting private variables,
    114–115

• *A* •

abstract concepts, comparing
    with real world, 48–49
abstract environment, handling
    errors in, 205–206
abstraction, contained by
    reusable code, 198
access to a resource,
    implementing threading
    for, 233
AccessControl namespace,
    251
accessibility keywords, 119
AccessRule class, 251
Adapter classes, 257
adapters
    creating and using, 256
    database-specific, 254
Add a New Data Source
    button, 33
Add Connection dialog box, 32,
    259–260
add function, 226
add-ins
    described, 41
    included with Visual Studio
        2008, 41–42
    for Microsoft Office
        applications, 21
Add method, with DateTime,
    171–172
Add New Data Source link,
    258–259

Add Reference dialog box,
    116–117, 207–208, 212
Add Reference panel, 269, 270
Add Service Reference dialog
    box, 132–133, 330
Add Tab option, in the Toolbox,
    27
Add Watch, selecting in Code
    View, 144
addition (+) operator, 170,
    227–228
ADO.NET
    collecting searches, 55
    compared to LINQ, 270
    described, 47
    implementation of, 254
Affected users, in DREAD, 242
Align All Controls Center
    option, 71
Align feature, on the Format
    menu, 71
Alphabetical List of Products
    view, 34
Alt+F8, 319–320
Anchor tab, in Source View, 103
AppActivate function,
    217–218
app.config file, 293–295
Append function, in the
    StringBuilder class,
    168
Application State, in Trace,
    151
ApplicationException
    throwing, 206
    using, 184
applications
    adequately securing, 293
    building for Windows, 65–68
    compiling into Windows
        programs, 19
    connecting to a data
        source, 32
    creating in Visual Studio 2008,
        12
    designing
        screens for, 54–56
        in Visual Basic 2008, 43–58
    developing in .NET, 11
    gathering requirements for,
        51–52
    layers of, 44

running, 19–20, 70
state of, 85–86
storing data for, 53–54
writing test plans for, 57–58
AppWinStyle parameter, of
    the Shell command, 217
architecture-neutrality, of Web
    services, 125
Array class, methods in, 228
articles, writing, 335
ASCX file, 209–210
Ask a Question button, on
    the Document Explorer
    toolbar, 39
ASMX-based service, getting
    WSDL from, 136
ASP.NET
    accompanying Web
        applications, 90
    applications, publishing, 91
    code samples, 329
    compared to Windows Forms,
        84
    constraints, 84
    described, 83–84, 93
    enabling interaction with the
        user, 48
    encapsulating CGI
        functionality, 97–102
    saving the application
        State, 86
    server controls, 89
    user controls. *See* user
        controls
    as user-interface oriented, 47
    Web Forms namespaces,
        88–89
ASP.NET 2.0 For Dummies
    (Hatfield), 39, 93, 106
ASP.NET Trace, in the MSDN
    Library, 152
ASP.NET Web
    overview, 338
    Service template, 128
    Site template, 90–91
aspnet_wp.exe file, 154
aspx.vb file, 90
.aspx.vb file, 90
assemblies, controlling access
    within, 203
assumptions, killing software
    projects, 57

BUSINESS, CAREERS & PERSONAL FINANCE

0-7645-9847-3

0-7645-2431-3

Also available:
- Business Plans Kit For Dummies
  0-7645-9794-9
- Economics For Dummies
  0-7645-5726-2
- Grant Writing For Dummies
  0-7645-8416-2
- Home Buying For Dummies
  0-7645-5331-3
- Managing For Dummies
  0-7645-1771-6
- Marketing For Dummies
  0-7645-5600-2

- Personal Finance For Dummies
  0-7645-2590-5*
- Resumes For Dummies
  0-7645-5471-9
- Selling For Dummies
  0-7645-5363-1
- Six Sigma For Dummies
  0-7645-6798-5
- Small Business Kit For Dummies
  0-7645-5984-2
- Starting an eBay Business For Dummies
  0-7645-6924-4
- Your Dream Career For Dummies
  0-7645-9795-7

HOME & BUSINESS COMPUTER BASICS

0-470-05432-8

0-471-75421-8

Also available:
- Cleaning Windows Vista For Dummies
  0-471-78293-9
- Excel 2007 For Dummies
  0-470-03737-7
- Mac OS X Tiger For Dummies
  0-7645-7675-5
- MacBook For Dummies
  0-470-04859-X
- Macs For Dummies
  0-470-04849-2
- Office 2007 For Dummies
  0-470-00923-3

- Outlook 2007 For Dummies
  0-470-03830-6
- PCs For Dummies
  0-7645-8958-X
- Salesforce.com For Dummies
  0-470-04893-X
- Upgrading & Fixing Laptops For Dummies
  0-7645-8959-8
- Word 2007 For Dummies
  0-470-03658-3
- Quicken 2007 For Dummies
  0-470-04600-7

FOOD, HOME, GARDEN, HOBBIES, MUSIC & PETS

0 7645-8404-9

0-7645-9904-6

Also available:
- Candy Making For Dummies
  0-7645-9734-5
- Card Games For Dummies
  0-7645-9910-0
- Crocheting For Dummies
  0-7645-4151-X
- Dog Training For Dummies
  0-7645-8418-9
- Healthy Carb Cookbook For Dummies
  0-7645-8476-6
- Home Maintenance For Dummies
  0-7645-5215-5

- Horses For Dummies
  0-7645-9797-3
- Jewelry Making & Beading For Dummies
  0-7645-2571-9
- Orchids For Dummies
  0-7645-6759-4
- Puppies For Dummies
  0-7645-5255-4
- Rock Guitar For Dummies
  0-7645-5356-9
- Sewing For Dummies
  0-7645-6847-7
- Singing For Dummies
  0-7645-2475-5

INTERNET & DIGITAL MEDIA

0-470-04529-9

0-470-04894-8

Also available:
- Blogging For Dummies
  0-471-77084-1
- Digital Photography For Dummies
  0-7645-9802-3
- Digital Photography All-in-One Desk Reference For Dummies
  0-470-03743-1
- Digital SLR Cameras and Photography For Dummies
  0-7645-9803-1
- eBay Business All-in-One Desk Reference For Dummies
  0-7645-8438-3
- HDTV For Dummies
  0-470-09673-X

- Home Entertainment PCs For Dummies
  0-470-05523-5
- MySpace For Dummies
  0-470-09529-6
- Search Engine Optimization For Dummies
  0-471-97998-8
- Skype For Dummies
  0-470-04891-3
- The Internet For Dummies
  0-7645-8996-2
- Wiring Your Digital Home For Dummies
  0-471-91830-X

* Separate Canadian edition also available
† Separate U.K. edition also available

Available wherever books are sold. For more information or to order direct: U.S. customers visit www.dummies.com or call 1-877-762-2974.
U.K. customers visit www.wileyeurope.com or call 0800 243407. Canadian customers visit www.wiley.ca or call 1-800-567-4797.

SPORTS, FITNESS, PARENTING, RELIGION & SPIRITUALITY

0-471-76871-5

0-7645-7841-3

Also available:

- Catholicism For Dummies
  0-7645-5391-7
- Exercise Balls For Dummies
  0-7645-5623-1
- Fitness For Dummies
  0-7645-7851-0
- Football For Dummies
  0-7645-3936-1
- Judaism For Dummies
  0-7645-5299-6
- Potty Training For Dummies
  0-7645-5417-4
- Buddhism For Dummies
  0-7645-5359-3

- Pregnancy For Dummies
  0-7645-4483-7 †
- Ten Minute Tone-Ups For Dummies
  0-7645-7207-5
- NASCAR For Dummies
  0-7645-7681-X
- Religion For Dummies
  0-7645-5264-3
- Soccer For Dummies
  0-7645-5229-5
- Women in the Bible For Dummies
  0-7645-8475-8

TRAVEL

0-7645-7749-2

0-7645-6945-7

Also available:

- Alaska For Dummies
  0-7645-7746-8
- Cruise Vacations For Dummies
  0-7645-6941-4
- England For Dummies
  0-7645-4276-1
- Europe For Dummies
  0-7645-7529-5
- Germany For Dummies
  0-7645-7823-5
- Hawaii For Dummies
  0-7645-7402-7

- Italy For Dummies
  0-7645-7386-1
- Las Vegas For Dummies
  0-7645-7382-9
- London For Dummies
  0-7645-4277-X
- Paris For Dummies
  0-7645-7630-5
- RV Vacations For Dummies
  0-7645-4442-X
- Walt Disney World & Orlando
  For Dummies
  0-7645-9660-8

GRAPHICS, DESIGN & WEB DEVELOPMENT

0-7645-8815-X

0-7645-9571-7

Also available:

- 3D Game Animation For Dummies
  0-7645-8789-7
- AutoCAD 2006 For Dummies
  0-7645-8925-3
- Building a Web Site For Dummies
  0-7645-7144-3
- Creating Web Pages For Dummies
  0-470-08030-2
- Creating Web Pages All-in-One Desk
  Reference For Dummies
  0-7645-4345-8
- Dreamweaver 8 For Dummies
  0-7645-9649-7

- InDesign CS2 For Dummies
  0-7645-9572-5
- Macromedia Flash 8 For Dummies
  0-7645-9691-8
- Photoshop CS2 and Digital
  Photography For Dummies
  0-7645-9580-6
- Photoshop Elements 4 For Dummies
  0-471-77483-9
- Syndicating Web Sites with RSS Feeds
  For Dummies
  0-7645-8848-6
- Yahoo! SiteBuilder For Dummies
  0-7645-9800-7

NETWORKING, SECURITY, PROGRAMMING & DATABASES

0-7645-7728-X

0-471-74940-0

Also available:

- Access 2007 For Dummies
  0-470-04612-0
- ASP.NET 2 For Dummies
  0-7645-7907-X
- C# 2005 For Dummies
  0-7645-9704-3
- Hacking For Dummies
  0-470-05235-X
- Hacking Wireless Networks
  For Dummies
  0-7645-9730-2
- Java For Dummies
  0-470-08716-1

- Microsoft SQL Server 2005 For Dummies
  0-7645-7755-7
- Networking All-in-One Desk Reference
  For Dummies
  0-7645-9939-9
- Preventing Identity Theft For Dummies
  0-7645-7336-5
- Telecom For Dummies
  0-471-77085-X
- Visual Studio 2005 All-in-One Desk
  Reference For Dummies
  0-7645-9775-2
- XML For Dummies
  0-7645-8845-1